Representations of Islam in United States Comics, 1880–1922

Representations of Islam in United States Comics, 1880–1922

Maryanne A. Rhett

BLOOMSBURY ACADEMIC
LONDON • NEW YORK • OXFORD • NEW DELHI • SYDNEY

BLOOMSBURY ACADEMIC
Bloomsbury Publishing Plc
50 Bedford Square, London, WC1B 3DP, UK
1385 Broadway, New York, NY 10018, USA

BLOOMSBURY, BLOOMSBURY ACADEMIC and the Diana logo are trademarks of
Bloomsbury Publishing Plc

First published in Great Britain 2020
Reprinted 2020

ISBN: HB: 978-1-3500-7324-1
ePDF: 978-1-3500-7325-8
eBook: 978-1-3500-7326-5

Typeset by Deanta Global Publishing Services, Chennai, India
Printed and bound in Great Britain

To find out more about our authors and books visit www.bloomsbury.com and
sign up for our newsletters.

To Mom and Dad.
Always teaching me to see beyond what is right in front of me.

Contents

Illustrations

Figures

Table

Acknowledgments

I was lucky, for a variety of reasons, in writing this book, a second text which has allowed me to pursue my deepest interests. The work herein reflects the research I was able to undertake during a post-tenure sabbatical in 2016–17. Sabbatical is a magical thing, and for me, even now that I have returned to the classroom (thankfully) and the meetings (less thankfully) I still feel the spell of it when I sift through all I found. It is because of where I work, Monmouth University, that I was able to take my sabbatical and I was encouraged to follow my interests. No one looked at me askance when I said, "I'm going to go study comics from the turn of the twentieth century and how they dealt with Islam." Monmouth University is a wonderfully nurturing environment for me, even more so because I am in a department that takes seriously its desire to see everyone grow as scholars and teachers. I have received nothing but support and help since joining the department in 2008, and that is truer still when I reflect on how we engage with each other. I have, on more than one occasion, come to the office to find a note in my mailbox letting me know that I should check out this or that newspaper or magazine because there might be something in there that could help me in my research. Melissa Ziobro has been particularly diligent in tagging me on social media posts and mentioning interesting tidbits along the way. Hettie Williams's "Works in Progress" luncheon series, at which we have all taken turns presenting, are the informal gatherings necessary for scholarly growth. Williams's foresight into arranging these luncheons has helped many of us and made us a stronger community in turn. Along the way I have been fortunate in the mentorship I have received. For this book, two women in particular stand out in this regard: Katherine Parkin and Candice Goucher. They have helped guide my direction and foster my thoughts. An additional group of women, Heidi Bludau, Hillary DelPrete, Maureen Dorment, and Brooke Nappi, have been tremendous not only in helping me navigate the academic world but also as friends who let me bounce ideas around and keep me focused when I want to go off down a rabbit hole.

In much the same way as my research is enriched by my colleagues, there are hosts of friends and family who, especially on social media, have helped and guided this process. My sister Sarah, who for a second time, is my beleaguered editor and has yet another book in her head that is not her own. My parents, Jane and Jim Rhett, are really central to this book's existence. It was Dad who first introduced me to comics via Hulk, Spiderman, and Super Girl. It took years, if not decades, for me to understand what this introduction meant, but I am eternally grateful. It was Mom who saw, in the artifacts I use in this book, so much more than I did when first she looked at them. I would have never known what a chatelaine was without her, and the connections she made across stories and genres were invaluable to helping me weave together my thoughts. There was a distinct moment when she pointed out to Sarah and me the connections between Bluebeard and 1001 Arabian Nights, at which Sarah and I both slapped our foreheads. It still amazes us that we did not see it sooner!

If my sister and parents have been inundated with my thoughts and questions about the book, my husband Colin Meckel and our two boys Alfred and Henry have had to endure it night and day. (I'm not sure who inspired whom, but Alfred and Henry have taken up writing their own books, which has occasionally, pushed me to get moving on this one.) I would not have made it to this point without them! Online and off, the conversations I had with so many of my friends helped me delve deeper into what I was seeing and to find new and exciting avenues to pursue. To Lawrence Abrams, Bridget Keown, and Kaleb Knoblauch, my presentation and writing partners, your work has inspired me and pushed me to deep digger and be more thoughtful in my analysis. Thank you so very much as well: Jeremy Neill, Rachel Gillett, Andrew Ciraulo, Dylan Maynard, Thanasis Kinias, Mary Pinckney, Shawna Herzog, and Ginger Geissinger for checking in, helping me work through ideas, and just being there for my off-the-wall thoughts.

Lastly, but perhaps most importantly, I owe heartfelt thanks to the unnamed thousands who have sat in archives digitizing newspapers over the decades. You are the real heroes of academia. So much of my work here was made distinctly easier (and more effective) because of this miracle of the modern age. In particular those who work(ed) with the Library of Congress are some real champions. That the digitized works I was able to look through could be searched by keyword is still even more astounding. My work, and the work of thousands of others around the world, is made easier and more efficient by you.

Introduction and Definitions

On November 6, 1898, readers of the *New York Journal and Advertiser*'s "humorous weekly" were regaled with illustrated vignettes of Kaiser Wilhelm II's tour "Around the Orient Circle."[1] The full-page spread offered imagined depictions of Wilhelm's journeys through the Near East, situating him firmly inside a series of tropes used to depict a tourist's experiences and expectations of travels in the Levant and Egypt. The cartoons equally mocked the emperors' gullibility and the Orient as being defined by "honest shell games" and harem peep shows (Figure 1.1). The *Journal and Advertiser*'s spread was typical in scope and content for the era, in establishing or reestablishing tropes about the Islamic world for popular consumption in the United States. The sniggering Turkish escorts who led Wilhelm to the historic find of "Nero's fiddle" fill one set of archetypes as fez wearing, scimitar carrying companions. The Kaiser himself is depicted as participating in his own Orientalization, having a photograph taken at various stops on the tour, each allowing him to dress in local attire and "play Eastern." The "Arab colonel," "Bulgarian Dervish," "Turkish pasha," "Bashi-Bazzok Admiral," and "Armenian Patriarch," all offer the *Journal and Advertiser*'s readers a neatly packaged set of archetypes from which they may draw future assumptions about the Near East and its peoples. Similarly, the bazaar scene at the bottom of the page reinforces assumptions with which US comic readers were already familiar. Presented with a series of stalls and options from the "Only Straight 3 Card Monte on Earth" to "Omar's Circassian Beauty Show" the Kaiser, his entourage, and the locals following along establish further popular assumptions about race, class, and gender, all of which are useful for understanding how Islam and Muslims came to be codified in the popular imaginations of the United States between 1880 and 1922.

This book explores the interconnectedness of political and social constructions in comics and cartoons at the turn of the twentieth century by situating their production inside the cultural context of the era. The years

Figure 1.1 "The Kaiser's Swing around the Oriental Circle." *New York Journal and Advertiser*. November 6, 1898.

1880–1922 witnessed the United States emerge on the world stage as not only a global political, imperial, and economic power but also a desirable destination for millions seeking relief from a variety of oppressions. Wars, shifting sovereign boundaries, increased immigration, rapidly changing technology, and cultural mores coupled up with the tropes and formulas of art and literature to bring forth in newspapers, magazines, and journals tangible interpretations grappling with the changing world. This narrative is no more static than the culture it reflects. In the board sweeping generalizations and sociopolitical tumult of turn of twentieth century, the twenty-first century is foreshadowed.

More specifically, this book takes into account this historical context while examining the place of Islam and Muslims within the narrative. Building on a rich history of literary and artistic formulas vis-à-vis expectations of the Islamic Orient, US populations, whether well-read or barely literate, had a collective understanding about that romanticized space that captivated the imagination. Comic artists and creators of the time knew this and used the wealth of Orientalist backstory to add depth to their character and storylines, but in so doing, of course, they manipulated knowledge production as well, and what was *known* of the Orient was reinterpreted through the lens of the comic and the cartoon.

It is, perhaps, surprising that this nexus of elements is the means by which we may develop a deeper understanding of US-Islamic history and simultaneously further break down the myth of American exceptionalism. This era, from 1880 to 1922, culminated in the Great War and the subsequent global rearrangements brought on by treaties, and mandates was marked by a myriad of near hysterical tirades against foreign aliens,[2] highly misunderstood discussions of religious groups,[3] and sensational depictions of wars and battles raging between domineering Western powers and shaky Eastern states.[4] The war that came before the First World War, the one waged to sell newspapers and magazines, was fought in words and images. The images, in particular, had far-reaching implications beyond the eventual "hot war" of the 1910s, implications that resonate with us still today.

Part of the rationale for focusing on the time frame 1880–1922 is the fact that the era encompasses a moment when Islam becomes a real point of discussion in US journalism. Despite this fact, as will be discussed below, there remains a significant void in US-Islamic history about this time period, and yet a surprisingly large swath of news media actively engaged in discussing Islam and Muslims. Newspapers from New York to Hawaii and from Michigan to Texas featured stories about local Islamic connections, global Islamic news, and illustrations, comics, and cartoons that reinforced or problematized assumptions about the nature of Muslims and the Islamic world. Magazines and journals circulated across the United States and its territories, echoing the narratives of their newspaper counterparts and deeply embedded Ameri-centric narratives in the context of global events. This moment of growing interest in news about the Islamic world was furthered by the nature of worldwide events. The revolts in the Sudan (1881–85), the Boxer rebellion in China (1900), the rise of the Senussi brotherhood in North Africa (late 1800s), the Spanish-American War (1898), the Balkan Wars (1912–13), Armenian and other Christian massacres in Ottoman territory (at various points from the 1890s through the 1910s), the First World War (1914–18), and the series of treaties that closed the Great War and created the nation-state structures and mandate system which followed (1919–24), all contributed to a narrative that demanded explanation of Islam and recognition that Muslims were active participants in the modern world. This last realization in particular came to be at odds with the cozier notion that Muslims existed as characters in fairy tales and as quaint exotic "Others" discounted from the modernity of New York City or San Francisco. This education, not necessarily part of some concerted propagandistic campaign to lead Americans into believing one thing or another, informed US audiences about their place in the world and the nature of their global neighbors.

The period between 1880 and 1922 is additionally important as it roughly coincides with an era known to some comics' scholars as the "Platinum Age," while others refer to it as the "Victorian Age." Using Gemstone Publishing's periodization, the Platinum Age ran between the 1880s and the 1930s.[5] The most distinguishing feature of this era from those that came after it is the "modern" comic book format, first introduced by Max Gaines in 1933. The era most familiar to the average person with a passing knowledge of comics is likely the Golden Age (1937 to about 1955), during which time the "superhero" and the costumed crime fighter became the paramount characters in comic books. In 1938, *Superman* first debuted, adorned with superhuman abilities, decidedly shifting from the nature of comics' characters in previous years. The foundations of Golden Age storylines and tropes were set down in the Platinum Age by the romantic heroes, bumbling slapstick-prone protagonists and the scheming archvillains. The cultural tropes and gendered assumptions that became stock in trade for Gold, Silver, Bronze, and Modern Age comics (1930s–present) are embedded in Platinum Age works, so much so, that their echoes live on with us today. Deconstructing all of the images, symbols, and tropes which defined the Platinum Age would require several volumes. This work purposefully chooses to look at only the intersection of Islam, gender, and fin de siècle US sociopolitical issues.

The artifacts of sequential and nonsequential art—comics, political and editorial cartoons, "funnies" or other cartoons, illustrations, and illustrated (and sometimes serialized) advertisements—are the tools this work uses for unraveling the story of US-Islamic history at the turn of the twentieth century. There is no one term which works well for encapsulating the whole of this field, though "comic" and "cartoon" will be used most often. These artifacts are reflective of a mainstream American society and are illustrative of how comics became a staple of that society, but they are encumbered by the class and racial divides that also dominated that society. Consciously this work recognizes that the artifacts around which it builds a narrative are hampered by the access restrictions inherent in the era's media. "Mainstream," therefore, refers to that selection of the US populous which reaches the widest possible sample. The artifacts with which this work is concerned are pulled from US newspapers, journals, and magazines, representing a swath of American popular culture and discourse, united in their depiction of "Oriental" portrayals, uses, and treatments in an era that is largely assumed, today, to have been marked by American uninterest in the region, peoples, or religion.

Comics and sequential art at the fin de siècle

Since 1993, anyone looking to understand what a comic is has probably turned first, or at least eventually, to Scott McCloud's *Understanding Comics*. McCloud's work is a useful primer on what a comic is, how one can be read, and what tools are gained in being able to deconstruct the pieces of a comic. For McCloud, comics are "juxtaposed pictorial and other images in deliberate sequence, intended to convey information and/or produce an aesthetic response in the viewer."[6] This technical definition helps us understand what materials this book is working with, but it does leave out one component which should not be overlooked: the single-panel cartoon/comic and its variants, for example, editorial or political cartoons. McCloud addresses this omission, noting that "for all the doors that our definition opens, there is one which it closes. Single panels . . . are lumped in with comics yet there's no such thing as a sequence of one!"[7] McCloud acknowledges that such single panels are "cartoons" but maintains that the single-panel cartoon

> might be classified as "comic art" in the sense that they derive part of their visual vocabulary from comics . . . [and they] might also be labelled comics for [their] juxtaposition of words and pictures. . . . A great majority of modern comics do feature words and pictures in combination and it's a subject worthy of study, but when used as a definition for comics, I've found it to be a little too restrictive for my taste.[8]

There is, this book contends, utility in being more inclusive in defining "comic." This work is specifically interested in the notion of "[conveying] information and/or [producing] an aesthetic response in the viewer" vis-à-vis the materials being examined. Moreover, as Sarah Rhett noted in a private discussion about this very point, "one can argue, and perhaps a bit too philosophically, a single panel *is* a deliberate [sequence]. One is meant to see a single frame with contents and take it in whole. The sequence is, 0+1+0. Zero is merely a place holder for nothing. A comic strip of four panels is simply 1+1+1+1."[9] For our purposes then, the word "comic" or "cartoon," as they are used herein, includes juxtaposed images in deliberate sequence and those of the single panel.

As a means of understanding historical narratives, McCloud's work is doubly useful in its broad defense of a more immense time line of the history of comics than is generally acknowledged in modern classrooms and scholarship. McCloud points to both the Bayeux Tapestry and the Mexican Codex as being within the same category of "comics" as they both offer "deliberate chronological order" and "clear divisions of scene by subject matter."[10] Despite McCloud's defense of far earlier examples of "comics," many scholars still tend to dismiss pre-superhero comics as somehow less significant. Marc Singer's 2002 article about race in comics is a good place to witness this dynamic. Singer notes that

> comic books, and particularly the dominant genre of superhero comic books, have proven fertile ground for stereotyped depictions of race. Comics rely upon codified representations in which characters are continually reduced to their appearances, and this reductionism is especially prevalent in superhero comics, whose characters are wholly externalized into their heroic costumes and aliases.[11]

As will become clearer over the course of this book, the reductionism which Singer points to is not limited to the superhero comic and is, in fact, an essential part of understanding the basic research questions of this book in terms of Platinum Age cartoons and comics.

The serial cartoons examined herein have many of the same qualities that modern readers associate with comic books but were printed in weekly newspaper cartoon or "funnies" sections. Unlike comic strips typical in modern newspapers (think of "Calvin and Hobbes" or "Peanuts"), these comics frequently ran a half of or all of a full page. Their length, and typically their serial nature, means that they look more like proto-comic books than the "Sunday funnies" American audiences associate with newspapers today. Unlike the superhero comics that came after them, Platinum Age comics were not usually centered on the superhuman qualities of one or two protagonists, but rather about every day and the (highly outlandish) adventures they have. In this regard they are more reflective of the adventure and travel literature of their day than perhaps the modern (post-1933) comic book. Such adventure stories of the late 1800s and early 1900s were often serialized themselves and ran in newspapers and literary journals. Works, like those of Edgar Rice Burrows and Sax Rohmer, were accompanied by rich illustrations; some even became comic books themselves later in time (e.g., *Tarzan*) and are thus just as much a part of the Platinum Age panoply of graphic narrative as their comic strip allies.

Comics: Not just brain candy

Comics and cartoons at the turn of the twentieth century were fairly serious stuff. Not only did their foci depict heavy, adult themes and content but their content was also so important that analysts regularly dissected their themes and characters in periodicals around the world. This is not to say that children's cartoons did not exist as well. There were plenty of cartoons dedicated to the children's sections of newspapers; however, the vast majority of comics and cartoons at the turn of the nineteenth century were intended either for adults or for both adults and children. The latter category may bring to mind the 1990s television cartoons like *The Animaniacs*, which were marketed to kids but written with a great deal of adult humor and reference. In 1883 Henry James said of *Punch* that it is "for the family—*Punch* may be sent up to the nursery. This surely may be admitted; and it is the fact that *Punch* is for the family that constitutes its high value. The family is, after all, the people; and a satirical sheet which holds up the mirror to this institution can hardly fail to be instructive."[12] How much enjoyment or understanding those in the nursery received from *Punch* cartoons lamenting the state of Parliamentary politics, the plight of Anglo-Indians, or the colonial wars of East Asia and Africa remains to be seen.

On some level the idea that cartoons and comics were essential to the education of the masses and not just juvenile fluff is antithetical to the way many think today. It can be argued that this is because in the United States, there is a tendency to see cartoons through the lens of the Comics Code Authority (CCA) and the vision of society created by Fredric Wertham's *Seduction of the Innocent*.[13] It is not uncommon today to hear comics and cartoons derided as "material for children" and not serious. Moreover, the myth which compounds this vision of comics is that the readership was almost exclusively white and male. Scholars like Qiana Whitted, in her *EC Comics: Race, Shock, and Social Protest*, explore and debunk these narratives of all-white readerships, and yet the child-centric, all-male, all-white discourse remains prevalent.

It is widely understood that the creation of the CCA resulted in an infantilization of comics, as a laundry list of things that comics could and could not depict pushed storylines into conventional and mundane directions. The list included prohibitions against sexual innuendo and aggression, graphic violence and gore, vampirism, werewolfism, and a myriad of other repressive or prudish constraints.[14] Additionally, the Code actively promoted civil and national loyalty in prohibiting the presentation of "policemen, judges, government officials, and respected institutions . . . in such a way as to create disrespect for established authority."[15] In the end, after the Comic Code's development (1954), superheroes were increasingly paired off with sidekicks or spent more time with heteronormative love interests, and audiences became younger. This change helped to solidify the notion that comics are for kids, but the CCA did more than this. It created a form of cultural amnesia to the significance, even seriousness, of comics and cartoons.

Of course, comics had their detractors well before the CCA. Anti-comics crusaders existed right alongside the Platinum Age materials. As a result there is an interesting parallel which exists between the efforts of anti-comics activists, in both the early 1900s and the 1950s, *and* efforts to create global political salvation through American democracy. In the 1950s, when Congress discussed the threat to US culture and youth brought on by comics, it was in the shadow of the more sinister McCarthyism and the Second Red Scare. Fifty or so years previously, fear over the demise of American "civilization" thanks to comics was set in a similarly pro-Western democracy-imperialist framework. In 1906, *The Atlantic* published a set of protests against the Sunday funnies, claiming that the "average editor of the weekly comic supplement should be given a course in art, literature, and common sense, and Christianity."[16] The *Boston Herald* went so far as to drop its comics supplement in 1908, even though support for the cartoon remained strong across the country. According to Albert Payson Terhune of *The World*, "You hear it said that the comics often teach lessons of immorality or disobedience, I do not think so."[17] Rudolph Block, editor of the comic supplement for the Hearst Newspapers, declared, "A person devoid of a sense of humor sees no difference between one comic supplement and another, any more than a person without an ear for music can distinguish between good and bad music. . . . The quality of comic supplements varies as much as the quality of editorial comment of news selection and typographical display."[18] There is an adage that Americans learn their geography from the wars the government engages in.[19] One could argue, and with more certainty, that Americans learn their politics from the comics and cartoons they read.

Even when cartoons under discussion actually were intended for younger readers, American newspapers recognized their universal appeal. In a November 1905 article about the evolution of the comic and comic artist, the author notes that the children of today are lucky to have the Sunday funnies, and perhaps they should not be so quick with their "surreptitious snort of scorn when papa explains to the callers that he takes so many Sunday papers because the youngsters want to see the comic supplements."[20] Moreover, comics themselves were self-reflective of their place in the wider world. "Hoist, the friend of the comic people" by L. M. Glackens appeared in *Puck* in 1906, depicting William Randolph Hearst's run in the New York gubernatorial race and his support from the cartoons (and cartoon industry).[21]

Beyond this, newspapers across the United States actively discussed, even if the visuals were not actually reproduced, cartoons and comics. One example of this kind of analysis comes from the August 2, 1899, *Hawaiian Star* about a cartoon which appeared in a recent edition of the *St. Louis Republic*. The *Hawaiian Star* claimed that the cartoon "sizes up the world's situation rather correctly."[22] The image depicted a group of nations personified—the United States, France, England, China, Spain, Russia, Germany, and Turkey—with an associated issue—for example, France with the Dreyfus affair, Spain with the Carlists, the United States with the Philippines, and so on. What is more, such ekphrasis of cartoons were not limited to the more "highbrow" forms of political satire. The adventures of Happy Hooligan and Hairbreadth Harry, superstars of their day, both received detailed accounts in papers either in drumming up interest for upcoming issues or as a way of not reproducing the actual strips.[23] Such discussions of cartoons and comics were common and telling of their power as a medium for communicating pertinent and significant information.

Power to the people

Despite the tendency to view the history of comics as one largely male and largely white, turn of the century evidence suggests that this is a superficial reading of the history. The June 13, 1914, *Maryland Suffrage News* reprinted a brief yet significant piece from *The Woman Voter*, which avowed *Puck*'s pro-suffrage sentiment while drawing general attention to the significance of humor and humor magazines in the cause of women's suffrage. The article stated that "*The Judge* has long been a friend of woman suffrage and has for more than two years published a department called 'The Modern Woman.'"[24] *The Voter* went on to indicate that not only was *Judge* an ally to the cause but that a number of cartoons published first therein had since been printed in *The Voter*, namely, the work of Lou Rogers. Rogers was central not only to suffrage narrative but also to all of comics history. Her work, it has been posited, may have even been the inspiration for Wonder Woman's likeness, particularly her "Tearing off the Bonds," which ran in an October 1912 issue of *Judge*.[25] Not only was Roger's a dedicated *Judge* contributor, but when Margaret Sanger "published *Birth Control Review* in violation of the [Comstock Act] . . . Rogers contributed spot art, full-page cartoons, and spreads to the publication."[26] *The Voter* closed by observing that while "*Puck* [too] has announced its advocacy of votes for women . . . *Life* is against us. The moral is obvious."[27]

Among African American publications the power of the cartoon and the comic was front and center in discussion as well. In 1902, *The Colored American* ran a brief article arguing for the power of cartoons, citing an earlier article from *The Baptist Vanguard*:

> Cartoons in journalism are far more powerful than many of our journalists seem to think. We wish the Negro press of the country could form a cartoon syndicate and thus be easily able for all Negro papers to furnish an apt cartoon once or twice a month—or once a week—on live questions. These cartoons would serve as eye openers not only to the race, but they would attract the reading public in spite of prejudice.[28]

The Colored American and its arguments about the significance of the cartoon in setting "the whole American people to thinking more deeply than Puck or Judge or Truth"[29] focused, in April 1901, on its recent hiring of a dedicated cartoonist in a short piece, "The Cartoon Feature." The importance of the cartoon (or comics) in informing popular consciousness on the question of race is not only critical to African American history (as is reinforced in Qiana Whitted's work) but also informative on the narrative of many marginalized groups.

Reflecting further on these connections among race, gender, and cartoons/comics, while comics scholars do not tend to view many of Fredric Wertham's conclusions favorably, his insights into the depictions of race in comics were not off base and indeed resonate still. In 1950, a *New York Times* piece covering the New York state Joint Legislative Committee to Study the Publication of

Comics (which later fed into the national conversation on comics) reflected on Wertham's assertion that

> the hero is nearly always "regular-featured and 'an athletic, pure American white man.'... The villains, on the other hand, are foreign-born, Jews, Orientals, Slavs, Italians and dark-skinned races."[30]

Scholars have rightly pointed out that Wertham's contentions lacked critical nuance; *Superman*, for example, although couched in pro-American rhetoric, particularly during the Second World War was, after all, an alien from another planet, not even of the *human* race.

Even earlier, Frederick Burr Opper wrote, "Caricature Country and Its Inhabitants," about how the US comics consuming audience "has gradually become familiar with the topography and the natives of ... Caricature Country." In this land, Opper notes,

> Colored people and Germans form no small part of the population. . . . The negroes spend much of their time getting kicked by mules, while the Germans, all of whom have large spectacles and big pipes, fall down a good deal. . . . There is a sprinkling of Chinamen, who are always having their pigtails tied to things; and a few Italians, mostly women, who have wonderful adventures while carrying enormous bundles on their heads. The Hebrew residents of Caricature Country, formally numerous and amusing, have thinned out of late years, it is hard to say why. This is also true of the Irish dwellers, who at one time formed a large percentage of the population.[31]

That racial diversity and thoughtful depictions were lacking, as evidenced in both Opper and Wertham's testimonies, is spot on. The 2010 *Encyclopedia of Comic Books and Graphic Novels* further notes that

> though more recent artists have sought to undermine ... exaggerated portraits of Italian, Jewish, and Irish citizens ... [or] the swollen lips, enlarged eyes, simply drawn faces, and predisposition to slapstick [that distinguished African-American portrayals] ... through complex characterization and socially conscious storylines, several mainstream publications continue to include few or no non-white characters.[32]

In 2018, the National Council of Teachers of English released a list of graphic novels which highlight themes of diversity, underscoring the staggering lack of inclusion prior.

Early cartoons, more often than not, focused on stories about white, youngish males. Depictions of women and girls, like characters of color (both male and female), were often flat. Like so many of their modern counterparts, women and people of color were plot devices there to drive the narrative, not to *be* the narrative. This trajectory, as demonstrated in the closing chapter, appears to be changing as comics' publishers are increasingly incorporating more diversity (gender, ethnicity, and abilities) into their title lists. The evolution of more thoughtful and inclusive storylines is nevertheless relatively recent. For the vast majority of comics and cartoon history, the white male hero/protagonist has been the norm. Serial comics, such as those listed below, on which some of this project focuses, offer a look into these complicated questions of race and gender, especially as they relate to the Islamic world.

1. *Hairbreadth Harry*, published between 1919 and 1933.
2. *Happy Hooligan*, produced between 1900 and 1932.[33]
3. *Jerry MacJunk*, first produced between 1910 and 1914; reprinted between 1915 and 1918.[34]
4. *Mutt and Jeff*, first published in 1907, remained in syndication until the 1980s.
5. *Old Opie Dilldock's Stories*, 1907–08 by F. M. Howarth, 1908–14 by W. L. Wells.[35]
6. *Sambo (and His Funny Noises)*, syndicated between 1905 and 1913.[36]

Of these serialized comics the multidimensional *Old Opie Dilldock* plays with aspects of racial fluidity the most and *Sambo* is the only one not centered on a white male character. Even still, in both of these cases there are concerns. *Sambo* is reliant on and strongly identified with highly problematic minstrel tropes common to the era and *Dilldock's* openness is dependent on the active creator of the series.

Beyond the weekly comics of the newspapers, magazines of the era also offer a rich graphic discussion of the themes with which this work is interested, as the holders of editorial and other single-panel cartoons and as the platform for ornate advertisements that were themselves often serialized. *Puck, Judge, Life, Cartoons Magazine,* and *Harper's Weekly* are some of the most prominent in the US context.[37] While this project is specifically attuned to the story being depicted in US popular culture, British, French, Japanese, and other non-US cartoons[38] make their way into the US market and as such become a part of that story. This especially goes a long way to underscore the argument that the United States was not a political island at the fin de siècle. *Punch* cartoons, both the London publication and the subsequent Punches from Cairo, Tokyo, and so on, for example, appear frequently in works like *Cartoons Magazine* and larger circulation newspapers.[39] Thus, non-US comics take their place alongside indigenous pieces and therefore, despite modern perceptions of the United States at the turn of the twentieth century being focused on isolationist and "American exceptionalist" policy, in terms of cartoons and comics the United States was deeply embedded in a global discourse.

Because this book is largely interested in *popular* culture, an awareness of class comes into what is and is not read, seen, and discussed. There is a great deal of history suggesting that *Punch* and other global comics were common in upper socioeconomic echelons of US society, but access at lower socioeconomic echelons was rare, especially whole publications. Some global artifacts found their way into broader socioeconomic strata discussions piecemeal, through the reproduction of discreet, individual comics in US media.

A word on Islam in the United States and the United States in Islam

Part of the motivation behind this book is a desire to better understand just how the US populous was embedded in global discussions about religion and political policy and how it understood those relationships and specifically what Islam looked like to that populous. Unconsciously or not, how the image of Islam was being developed in the United States happened in conjunction with a sense of American identity. These two things intertwined, the former worked to create the latter.

It is not uncommon to find scholarship on the role of Islam in America jumping over the period between 1880 and 1922. Sarah Howell observes this phenomenon well, noting,

> Scholars have tended to skim briefly over the surface details of the arrival and settlement of Muslim immigrants in the first half of the 20th century, or the first conversions of blacks to Sunni Islam . . . in the race to provide the more accessible history of the post-1965 immigration and dramatic mass conversion of the National of Islam (NOI) to Sunni Islam.[40]

Howell's point that 1965 is the lynchpin moment in US-Islamic history is at the heart of Susan Nance's *How the Arabian Nights Inspired the American Dream, 1790–1935* in which she contends that "before the 1965 Immigration Reform Act brought large numbers of Africans and Asians to the United States, many people welcomed Easterners to the country as exotic visitors."[41] It is not clear why Nance is effectively discounting the millions of Africans forcibly brought to the United States (and before) as part of the Atlantic slave trade, because surely they constituted "large numbers of Africans," nor is it clear what constitutes "large numbers" in general, as there had certainly been Asians coming to the United States (and its territories in the Pacific) for some time, in what could be an equally vague "sizable numbers." Nance's broad sweep "Africans and Asians" as being welcomed as exotic visitors, moreover, is seriously problematic when we take into account not only the history of slavery but also the (im)migration of peoples who came to work the mines and build the railroads. These (im) migrants were welcomed with anti-immigrant laws and racial discrimination, not as quaint "exotic visitors." Nance further narrows argument in noting that "nor were there obvious plans for the U.S. government to engage in war or diplomacy so as to incorporate any part of North Africa, West Asia, or South Asia into American imperial domains."[42] This second point elucidates some of what we learn in the first, namely, that by "Easterners" Nance is indicating "Islamic" but is leaving it sufficiently broad to incorporate non-Islamic artifacts and peoples, such as from pre-Islamic eras or the Hindu world.

Sally Howell, utilizing Yvonne Haddad's work, presents a third possibility, which reorients the narratives' history as being born from larger geo-religious trends. Haddad writes that pre–Second World War Muslims in the United States "tried to both fit into the new culture and interpret it in new ways [tending to] emphasis the respect Islam had for Jesus and his mother Mary. . . . [But] to the immigrants who have come since 1960, however, this kind of accommodation seems too high a price to pay. They are critical of their coreligionists."[43] As Howell notes, the post-1965 Islamic immigrant community sought "to bring about an international Islamic revival. . . . Living and working in cities and on college campuses that generally did not have Muslims communities with deep historical roots, they were not concerned with Islam's past in the United States and were quick to simplify the experiences of their predecessors."[44] Howell's *Old Islam in Detroit* re-centers the narrative by taking into account the myriad reasons that early-twentieth-century US Islam was ignored, forgotten, or subsumed. A similar pattern emerges when we look at the history of Islam in US comics. A. David Lewis and Martin Lund's *Muslim Superheroes: Comics, Islam, and Representation* presents the first fully developed analysis of Islam in superhero comics. While effectively doing the same thing as scholars of US-Islamic history, who focus on post-1965, in narrowing the scope of their work to the superhero era, leeway needs to be given to Lewis and Lund as their volume is carving a path in a field with very little backstory.

Returning to Nance's contentions, then, her work suggests that she is laboring within the confines of Oriental imagery, in a Saidian sense; yet despite this, Nance attempts to distance her work from that of Edward Said, and her dislike of relying too heavily on his suppositions is not without merit. Nance points to Said's own distinction between European and American Orientalism, noting that the imperial experience of European states, which created the vast majority of Orientalist artifacts Said focused on, was not the same in the American context. Arguably Nance and Said go too far in advocating for an American exceptionalist vision of this story, one of the things which is so appealing about the Howell-Haddad approach. In her own introduction, Nance states,

> My research has shown me that the most numerous attempts by people in the United States, native-born or foreign-born, to take on Eastern personae occurred before the American moment in the Middle East began in the 1930s. In this earlier period, the U.S. political and territorial expansion was focused on the American West, Canada, the Pacific, Central America by way of Panama, and the territories of the Spanish Empire: Cuba, Puerto Rico, and the Philippines. That is, playing Oriental was most ubiquitous *before* Eastern nations or natural resources became practically or politically relevant to the bulk of the population of the U.S. government.[45]

Because "Eastern" means "Islamic" in Nance's work, it becomes problematic that she includes the Philippines in what the United States focused on. The Philippines, as discussed in the next chapter, brought nearly 300,000 Muslims under the United States' jurisdiction. Islam was very much something the United States was thinking about, politically and socially; at precisely the same time Nance argues "playing Oriental was most ubiquitous." The imperial legacy which so concerned Said may have *looked* different than the one the United States was engaged in, but the Orientalist artifacts are all very much of a piece. According to Edward Said's 1978 work *Orientalism*,

> To speak of Orientalism, therefore, is to speak mainly, although not exclusively, of a British and French cultural enterprise, a project whose dimensions take in such disparate realms as the imagination itself, the whole of India and the Levant, the Biblical texts and the Biblical lands, the spice trade, colonial armies and a long tradition of colonial administrators, a formidable scholarly corpus, innumerable Oriental "experts" . . . , a complex array of "Oriental" ideas (Oriental despotism, Oriental splendor, cruelty, sensuality), many Eastern sects, philosophies, and wisdoms domesticated for local European use.[46]

It is confusing that Nance relies on Said's own definition of the Orient while making an American exceptionalist case. The term "Oriental" was in common usage at the fin de siècle and was broadly applied to almost anyone from outside North America and (Western) Europe. While in the twenty-first-century United States the term may be more typically associated with the Far East (China, Japan, Korea, etc.), it would have, at the turn of the twentieth century, included peoples of Asia and North Africa. Often inclusion or exclusion of East Asia in the definition of Oriental assumes an Islamic or non-Islamic connection to the word. A problem in defining Oriental in exclusively Islamic terms, however, as both Said and Nance are largely doing, is that it simultaneously excludes large numbers of Muslims and ignores the conflated nature of Oriental in Western cultural creations.[47] The Oriental in a turn-of-the-twentieth-century comic or cartoon was often a representative of Islam, Hinduism, East Asia, Pharaonic Egypt, and the Biblical Levant, among many other things, rolled into one.

In 1909, the *San Francisco Call* ran a snippet article entitled "Hindu, Thought to be an Anarchist, is Jailed." The article, out of Vancouver, British Columbia, reported that "the person of H. Rahim, an East Indian Mohammedan [was] arrested by the federal immigration authorities."[48] Thus, we are left wondering, Is Mr. Rahim Hindu or Muslim? Was he of subcontinent extraction and thus "Hindu" as being equated with India and at the same time a practicing Muslim? Possibly. It is this effect of conflation which has such a profound impact on the general understanding of Oriental, and countless other associated words, at the time. In a parallel way, when war broke out in 1914, one thread common in the United States' press, and apparently eagerly followed by readers, discussed and developed the idea that the German government was acquiring a "call for Jihad" from the leaders of the Ottoman state. The fear of "holy war" was so significant that it was frequently reported on and speculated about in various media outlets and by a large number of adventure novels and serial fiction. The fear engendered by the unknown potential of jihad was reflective of earlier eras, in particular the Crusades and foreshadows of postmillennial/Y2K discussions. The questions circulating in the US press about jihad did not remain focused on what is today termed the Middle East but included extensive examinations of how, among others, Chinese Muslims would take to the news of a global jihad and what that might mean for American missionaries in China.[49] The fact that all Muslims are the same and that they will blindly follow any "Islamic" leader was reinforced and troubled as popular culture grappled with Oriental and Eastern characters.[50]

Chapter overview

Following on this introductory chapter, Chapter 2 "What Muslims?" examines regional demographics and unravels the narrative that comics offer us in teaching/reinforcing who and what a Muslim was for US audiences at the turn of the twentieth century. In scholarship on US-Islamic history, works like *The Muslim Community in North America*, by Earle H. Waugh, Baha Abu-Laban, and Regula B. Qureshi, and Yvonne Yazbeck Haddad and Jane Idleman Smith's coedited volume *Muslim Communities in North America* are extremely useful foundational works but spend the clear majority of their energies on Muslim-American history from the 1930s to the present. Edward E. Curtis's *Muslim in America*, Sarah Howell's *Old Islam in Detroit*, and Stacy Fahrenthold's *Between the Ottomans and the Entente*, all grapple with aspects of Muslim-American populations in the United States, and to some degree or other, in this "missing period." Curtis's work upholds the traditional assumptions about Muslim demographics in the United States stating, "Most of the Ottoman emigrants who arrived in the United States from the 1880s through World War I were Christian: One early historian of the Arab American community estimated that less than 10 percent of the total population was Muslim."[51] However, Fahrenthold observes that "a general lack of empirical data elsewhere makes even preliminary guesses about the mahjar's confessional makeup difficult," and the often repeated 90 to 95 percent Christian Arab numbers (as in Curtis' work) "relies on Lebanese and US census data that have been shown to bolster Christian immigrant numbers while underreporting Muslim ones."[52] The question of demographics, then, is clearly one of the difficulties that scholars of the turn of the twentieth century have yet to fully untangle.

Similarly, Muslims before the fin de siècle largely remain a part of a larger discussion of slavery in the United States, such as in Sylviane A. Diouf's *Servants of Allah: African Muslims Enslaved in the Americas*. All of this is not to say Muslims disappear from the record in total during this time. Works like Kemal H. Karpat's "The Ottoman Emigration to America, 1860–1914" and Stacy Fahrenthold's "What Can We Learn from America's Other Muslim Ban (Back in 1918)" help establish a clearer picture of the space inhabited by Muslims and Middle Easterners in US society at turn of the twentieth-century , but do so by focusing on only one portion of the larger Islamic community (specifically immigrants from Ottoman territories).

In 2015, the *U.S. News and World Report* article "Islam in America: The United States' Historical Openness towards Muslims Must Be Upheld" highlighted the long, but undeveloped history of Muslims and the United States. This popular account of the history of Muslims in the United States mentions that the first country to recognize the United States' independence, in 1777, was Morocco, and that John Adams, Thomas Jefferson, and Benjamin Franklin were all interested in and scholars of (to some extent) Islam and Islamic history. Still, and despite Nance's assertion to the contrary, works like Geysar Gurbanov and Karine V. Walther's *Sacred Interests* help underscore that the United States was diplomatically and militarily involved with Islamic states well before the Cold War, as in the case of the Barbary Wars.

While there is a sense of connectedness between the Islamic world and the United States in an "outside" way prior to the 1960s, the idea that Muslims were a part of the "inside" construction of the United States comes as a more general surprise. Edward Curtis asserts that approximately one-third of "Syrian and Lebanese North Dakotans during this time [1880s to 1910s] was [*sic*] Muslim, and more than one hundred Muslims lived in Ross alone."[53] In Cedar Rapids, Iowa, Curtis later says, a "group that eventually called itself the 'Mother Mosque of America' rented space for prayers in 1925."[54] There is more evidence than this of mosque construction, in the period between 1880 and 1922, and this gives us important clues to the small, but not inconsequential number of Muslims living in the United States at the turn of the twentieth century.

Chapter 3 "Our Muhammaden Wards" develops the "are they us?" narrative established in Chapter 2 a bit further by looking at how the acquisition of the Philippines and the subsequent increase of over 300,000 Muslims into American jurisdiction impacted the United States' understanding of itself vis-à-vis the Islamic world. It should be noted here that several terms were used, seemingly interchangeably and randomly in Anglophone media when talking about practitioners of Islam. "Mohammedan" or "Muhammedan," "Mahometan," and "Mussulman" were the most common. The term "Moslem" came to be used with increasing frequency in the early 1900s, but "Muslim" did not become common until the second half of the century, around the time of the Second World War.[55] In the Philippines, the term "Moro" was commonly used in discussing Muslims, a term generally believed to be a corrupted version of "Moor," brought to the Philippines by the Spanish in the sixteenth century.[56]

The awareness and the subsequent difficulties the US government faced with their new "Muslim Wards," particularly in relation to issues of paternalism (e.g., imperialism and education), slavery, and polygamy, were played out across the country's newspapers, magazines, and journals. The consternation caused by questions of polygamy and slavery in the Philippines reasserted sentiments of

Americans as set forth by the Republican Party Platform of 1856. The Platform, in denouncing expansionist slave-holding agendas and the advent of the Church of Jesus Christ of Latter-day Saints and its practice of plural marriage, decried both as the "twin relics of barbarism." The Platform's resurrection at the turn of the twentieth century fueled self-reflection as both polygamy and slavery in the Philippines were testing the meaning of "being American." G. M. Lamsa's 1921 book *Life in the Harem* underscored the "us v. them" dynamic in its opening line: "The life of the women in the Harems is one of the most barbarous conditions still existing in the East. Democracy and civilization have not had any effect upon the slavery of womanhood."[57] With such sentiments it was hardly surprising to find Muslim harems making national headlines before and during the Spanish-American War, particularly in scandalous or overwrought ways. In 1897, the Los Angeles *Herald* asked the provocative question, "Are Moslem Harems Possible in the U.S.?"[58] Polygamy became a bellwether for freedom of religion tests, but it also opened the door further for questions about women's rights. Although policymakers debated whether a Muslim's rights to practice polygamy were protected by the First Amendment when Latter-day Saints' plural marriages were not, the "harem" became a symbol of both oppression and, ironically, freedom.

Chapter 4 "Harem Peeping" looks specifically at the ways women, and images of them, functioned as conduits of the culture which shaped American understandings of Muslims and Islamic societies. Physical space(s) is central to this chapter, in looking at how popular culture used the harem as a means for discussing needed cultural changes and for codifying male and female. Moreover, by the 1910s, "harem trousers" filled US fashion pages, which noted that the "trend of taste is distinctly toward harem apparel," and despite the secluded nature of the real harem, "harem pants" were favored for the "double reasons of their grace and utility"[59] by an ever-increasing number of American women seeking a public life. Oriental style including "'slave' bracelets and 'barbaric jewelry'"[60]dominated US consumption interests even while, and indeed alongside, US women's suffrage movements became increasingly active.

The United States developed a highly tangled relationship with the Ottoman Empire in the years leading up to the First World War. When the extent to which Islam was to play a role in the Philippines became fully known, some US officials looked to the Ottoman sultan for moral support,[61] but at the same time American newspapers were riddled with articles and cartoons denouncing the Ottoman state for atrocities against Christian populations across the region. When the United States entered the First World War then, it was surprising to many that it did not declare war on the Ottomans while nevertheless engaging against Germany and Austria-Hungary. For the United States, between 1914 and 1918, Ottoman and Middle Eastern cultural accouterment remained "acceptable" outlets of cultural expression and appropriation, even if its people were not welcomed.[62] Although German measles became "Liberty Measles," after the United States declared war, the "harem trouser" or "Turkish trouser" was wholly a part of modern US society.

While US consumers, predominantly white, upper, and upper-middle class consumers, devoured "Oriental" goods and looks, the political place of actual Muslims in the eyes of US policy and media was far less open. Chapter 5 "Conspiracy at Scimitar Point" explores the tenuous relationship between the United States and the Ottoman Empire between 1880 and 1922. Perhaps more than all other Islamic peoples, the "Turk" appears with the most frequency in US comics. This persona, as is discussed in Chapter 2, became a stand-in for a variety of concepts, notably Muslims.

Even though the United States did not openly go to war with the Ottomans, cartoonists waged their own campaign against Ottoman policies and practices. Increasingly, after the massacres of Armenians and other Christians in the late 1800s (and then again in the 1910s), American popular consciousness understood Turks and, by extension, Muslims as despotic Sultans or scimitar-wielding villains. This image, of course, was accentuated by its masculinity. Conflicting with the feminine Islam discussed in Chapter 4, the "bloody scimitar" came to be the ubiquitous marker of masculine Islamic imagery.

Massacres, like that of the Armenians, were also perpetual fodder for anti-Turkish sentiment in American newspapers and comics. When the United States entered the First World War, however, the nastiness of the Turk was transposed onto the German Hun, and the Turkish caricature took on a more Smeed-like nature to the German Captain Hook. Oriental imagery was foisted on the embodiment of the German, often Kaiser Wilhelm himself, and the male Turk was consequently denuded of it. This evolution both aided a narrative of German depravity and emasculated Turkish worth.

Even as the Turkish character took second place to the German Hun in the First World War, other fears stoked the fires of paranoia around the Islamic community more broadly. One of the rationales for not going to war with the Ottoman state was as a means of protecting American missionaries therein. Missionaries, often when they returned to the United States, carried with them manic visions of the rapid spread of Islam across the world. These reports, coupled with the history with which the US news consuming audience was already familiar, heighten the sense of impending doom. Reporters and illustrators filled

US newspapers, almost as much as their British counterparts, with narratives of General Gordon and the Battle of Khartoum.[63] When American forces joined the Eight Nation Alliance, newspapers across the country tried to explain who the Boxers were and what was going on in China.[64] As the Boxer Rebellion's narrative unfolded, so too did the United States' involvement in the Philippines, and in both scenarios the unexpected role of Muslims added to what the US populous "knew" about Islam. As the twentieth century rolled on, so too did other stories of Muslim agitation, like the new and, supposedly, rapidly spreading formation of the Senussi movement in North Africa.[65]

Seeing conspiracies among religious groups was hardly new in the twentieth century, but as warfare changed and the speed and ease of transportation and communication evolved, fear of religious conspiracies increased and became valuable for creating "knowledge" of "Others." As in the case of the infamous *Protocols of the Elders of Zion*, most of these "vast conspiracies" were fabricated to help governments and empires consolidate power through the scapegoating of others. Even in cases where there was reality underlying the narrative (i.e., the Senussi) it was embellished to such a hysterical degree as it rarely looked like the story on the ground. In the late nineteenth and early twentieth centuries those conspiracies thought to be Islamic in nature found audiences in several outlets, both fictional and not. John Buchan's 1916 work *Greenmantle* is perhaps one of the best fictional examples of these perceived threats.

Playing with classic Orientalist tropes and formulas, Chapter 6 "Disguise or Acculturation" analyzes how Islam is depicted in dress and costume. This examination not only speaks in large part to archetypes as they were constructed and perpetuated but also offers insights into how US identity was created simultaneously, in tandem and a part from. On the one hand, when presumably Muslim characters appear in their "native" surroundings depictions of long flowing robes, veils, and turbans are intended to lend an air of authenticity to the narrative/visual rhetoric. Yet, when an Anglo-American character dons a robe or veil he (typically) is in disguise. He is playing out an act of deception, intended to both fool those who cannot see through his act and elude his nemeses (also frequently in disguise). However, as with so much in the field of Orientalism, it is not always a black-and-white issue. There are a number of cases in the comics we have before us when we see Anglo-Americans portrayed in Oriental dress, but not as a means of deception or even necessarily as one of appropriation. Similarly, in a handful of places we have Muslims depicted in Western settings not necessarily seen riding camels and beturbened but navigating a path between assimilation and cultural observance. The US West's cultural creation as a tandem project with Oriental themes is well examined in Susan Kollin's *Captivating Westerns*, where she notes that "the Western has frequently helped extend this tale of progress, borrowing the logics of orientalism in justifying contemporary US foreign policy, especially in the Middle East."[66] In the West, popular culture navigates these lines between acculturation and appropriation in the formation of new mores.

Chapter 7 "Echoes of the Past, Shadows of the Future" considers how the ripples of past constructions of the Orient are felt in modern popular culture. Looking back on how Muslims and Islam were visually depicted in the early years of the twentieth century, it becomes clear that remnants remain evident in their modern-day counterparts. While the overtly racialized physical descriptions may be gone, the role of women, the place of Islam vis-à-vis Christianity, and the fears of hegemonic Islamic empires still dominate US comics and media.

What Muslims?

On April 11, 1909, the Los Angeles *Herald* reprinted the New York *Herald's* full-page article, "Miniature Foreign Lands in New York City." Focusing on "Little Syria," the article vacillates between quaint vignettes about booksellers and fruit vendors and the inherently foreign nature of the community. Little is said in the article about the community's demographics, except that it varies in population between 5,000 and 10,000 depending on the season. Hints are given that the population of Little Syria is entirely Christian. Children in the school room are seen learning a Bible passage, and a little discussion of good-natured ribbing between Armenian and Syrian populations suggest it is between coreligionists. Nowhere, in the article, is the reader led to believe that among the 5,000 to 10,000 living in Little Syria are Muslims, adapting just as readily to their lives in New York as the identifiable Christians.

At the fin de siècle the number of Muslims who were either living under American jurisdiction or holding American citizenship was low. That population remained low into the first decades of the twenty-first century, though certainly higher today than then. In 2010, according to the Pew Research Center, the population of Muslims in the United States was estimated to be 2,595,000, about 0.8 percent of the total population.[1] Pew reports indicate that today there are "fewer Muslims of all ages in the U.S. than there are Jews by religion (5.7 million) but more than there are Hindus (2.1 million) and many more than there are Sikhs."[2] Similar data from the turn of the twentieth century does not exist. As will be discussed below, what data from the era that does exist tends to focus almost exclusively on Judeo-Christian denominations and communities. As acknowledged by Fahrenthold, in terms of immigration data the records are even less sincere and certain.

In 1850, census takers in the United States began asking a few questions about religious organizations, although the permanent government agency, the US Census Bureau, was not officially established until 1902. The subsequent Census of Religious Bodies was not itself established until 1906.[3] Like the population census the Religious Bodies census was conducted every ten years, starting in 1906. The 1906, 1916, 1926, and 1936 publications were printed, but funding was restricted for 1946, and by 1956 funding was discontinued. Part of the reason Congress decided to end funding of the survey was due to "growing public debate over the propriety, merit and feasibility of the Census Bureau asking questions about religion."[4] In October 1976 "Congress enacted a law . . . including the prohibition against any mandatory question concerning a person's 'religious beliefs or to membership in a religious body.'"[5] Using data from the four published Religious Bodies censuses, we find that even though they had the permission and apparatus to gather data on religious constituencies in the United States, their scope was narrow. The studies were "limited to [the] continental United States, and [did] not include statistics of organizations in outlying possessions or in foreign lands."[6] The substantive focus of these censuses was less concerned with membership numbers, than with real estate and the financial health of institutions. A significant number of the questions asked of the pastors or clerks on the census schedule focused on location, number of buildings and their value, property value beyond structures, educational expenditures, and debt. Still, the schedule did afford space for the total number of members for each organization.

The Religious Bodies census data from 1906 through 1936 are revealing, partly in how ambiguous they are. In addition to a wide variety of Christian sects, data on Baha'is, Japanese Buddhists (sometimes), the Vedanta Society, and even in 1936 the Mayan Temple were recorded. Chinese Buddhists were mentioned in earlier census tables, but no statistical data was given. In 1926 no Buddhist groups were listed, and in 1936 the Buddhists were back, under the auspices of the Buddhist Mission to North America. Judaism was surveyed, sometimes by heads of household, sometimes as individual members, but not demarcated beyond "Jewish Congregations." Unlike the Jewish example, however, the Church of Latter-day Saints, commonly referred to as Mormons, were surveyed in two categories: the Church of Latter-day Saints and the Church of the Reorganized Latter-day Saints. The more common term "Mormon" was in use at the turn of the twentieth century, just as it is today, and it is worth giving special attention in their numbers because they take part in a surprising number of the narratives this work covers. A word must be mentioned too about the present call by Church of Jesus Christ of Latter-day Saints leadership to end the use of the term "Mormon" except in proper names (e.g., the Book of Mormon).[7] In 2018, the leadership issued a revised stylebook which advocated for referring to practitioners of the faith as "members of The Church of Jesus Christ of Latter-day Saints" or "Latter-day Saints." The full title of the faith is cumbersome for works like this, and the style guide eschews abbreviations, like "the Mormon Church" and "LDS." The guide states, "When a shortened reference is needed, the terms 'the Church' or the 'Church of Jesus Christ' are encouraged. The 'restored Church of Jesus Christ' is also accurate and encouraged."[8] Since Latter-day Saints' faith is not the only Christian faith discussed in this work nor the only institution to refer to itself as "the Church" or even "the Church of Jesus Christ," a shortened "the Church" is clearly impractical. In the terminology question we see yet another parallel to Islamic history in the West. "Mormon" was a term first used by the faith's detractors. Similarly, outdated terms like "Mohammadan," "Mahometan," and "Mussulman" which were all common in the late 1800s and early 1900s are never used by respectable news and scholarly outlets today, except in direct quotes. Thus, this work will endeavor to use appropriate verbiage wherever possible, acknowledging that the terms used may be a reflection of the history being discussed, not the author's personal feelings.

Inducing great frustration on the part of the author, the only reference to Islam in the whole of 1906, 1916, or 1926 Religious Bodies reports is the explanatory section on Baha'i and how Muslims worked to disrupt the faith's foundation. Even in the 1936 report, there is no mention of Islam in a modern, recognizable way. In this account, the closest connection is a passing reference to the "American Mohammedan Society," the "American Moslem Brotherhood" (or King Solomon Temple of Religious Science), and the "Moslem Temple, Detroit, Mich." which were listed as "small sects." The small sects table, which also included Jehovah's Witnesses, listed groups excluded from the count, because

> there are certain movements and cults which claim a number of adherents, but are not so organized as to make their presentation as religious bodies advisable. A partial list of these is given below. Because of the nature of these movements and for the reason that they do not have a distinctive membership, the Bureau did not consider it feasible to attempt to obtain any definite statistics.[9]

With respect to these three "Moslem" groups, a quick word. It is not clear from the list to what the "Moslem Temple, Detroit, Mich." refers exactly, but it is very likely a reference to the Shriners, not the Muslim mosque. An 1882 Detroit *Free Press* article reported that the

> Ancient Arabic Order of Nobles of the Mystic Shrine, [is] a secret society lately established in this city. The name of the local organization is the Moslem Temple. Though using the Arabic almanac and having among its officers certain functionaries styled "chanters of the Al-Koran," the society includes a number of

gentlemen in high standing in several Christian denominations of this city. It is therefore only seemingly a Mohammedan society.[10]

Clearly there were some who, even in the 1880s, had a hard time distinguishing the fraternal organization known as "the Shriners from religious institutions." Part of the problem regarding the history of Islam in the United States as it relates to this issue is that Detroit *did* have a sizable Muslim population. In June 1921, the Detroit *Free Press* reported on a gathering of 5,000 or so Moslem Temple Shriners and similarly reported on Shriner activities throughout the year.[11] Simultaneously, the *Free Press* discussed the celebration of *Eid al-Fitr* which also took place in June, at the newly constructed mosque in Highland Park (dubbed the only one of its kind in the United States).[12] In both instances "Moslem" is used, though in reading through the articles it is clear they are referring to very different communities. Newspapers and popular language of the day were not terribly precise in their terminology about Muslims, and it was incumbent upon the reader/listener to parse the differences.

The place of "King Solomon's Temple of Religious Science" on the small sects list is not terribly surprising. Little scholarly work exists on the organization, and even less is easily accessible in the media of the time. It does appear, however, that "King Solomon's Temple" was a storefront religion, neither uncommon in the era nor long lasting.[13]

There are those on the list, however, whose presence raises some eyebrows. Certainly, the inclusion of Jehovah's Witnesses is surprising, in light of the fact that today, according to Pew Research data, they make up about 1 percent of the adult US population.[14] The American Mohammedan Society may also fall into this category of needing further analysis. While what the society refers to is not explained, it could be a reference to that which was established by Tartars in Williamsburg, Brooklyn in 1907.[15] The American Mohammedan Society may have made this list because of its small size, but as we see in the data that is gathered, small membership numbers did not necessarily exclude populations (Table 2.1).

It is not clear why the Buddhists were removed from the Religious Bodies survey in 1926; their numbers were clearly on the rise. Although immigration laws in the 1910s became increasingly restrictive of East Asians, they did not simply disappear. The Mayan Temple, which admittedly has no direct bearing on this work, is a fascinating addition to the census data in 1936, having only been incorporated in 1928. According to the description, "The Mayan Temple is a restoration of the pristine faith catholic, practiced by the Mayas in prehistoric

Table 2.1 Selected Religious Denomination Membership Numbers, 1906–36

Denomination	1906	1916	1926	1936
Baha'i	1,280	2,884	1,247	2,584 (76)
Buddhist (Japanese Temple)	3,165	5,639	Not counted	14,388
Jewish Congregations	1,777,185*	3,300,000*	4,081,242	4,641,184
Church of Latter-day Saints (LDS)	215,796	403,388	542,194	678,217
Church of Reorganized Latter-day Saints (RLDS)	40,851	58,941	64,367	93,470
Mayan Temple	N/A	N/A	N/A	1,053
Vedanta Society	340	190	200	628

Sources: Bureau of the Census Commerce Department; *Religious Bodies 1916: Separate Denominations: History, Description, and Statistics*, Vol. Part II (1919); *Religious Bodies, 1926: Separate Denominations, Statistics, History, Doctrine, Organization, and Work* (1929); *Religious Bodies: 1936, Vol. 2, pt. Part 1: Denominations, A To J—Statistics, History, Doctrine, Organization, And Work* (1941); *Religious Bodies: 1936, Vol. 2, pt. Part 2: Denominations, K To Z—Statistics, History, Doctrine, Organization, And Work* (1941).

Hereafter to be referred to as *1916, 1926, 1936(a)*, and *1936(b)*, respectively. *According *1916*, Jewish numbers were systematically estimated for 1906 and 1916 (see page 320). In the *1926* a note is made that previous iterations data gathered by the Religious Bodies census takers only counted heads of households and was "admittedly incomplete," (see page 646). Numbers from 1906 are included in subsequent reports and can therefore be found on any of the pages in the following list (where specific numbers for the other years can also be found): Bahai, *1916*: 44; *1926*: 71; *1936(a)*: 76. Buddhism, *1916*: 185; *1936(a)*: 341. Jewish Congregations, *1916*: 320; *1926*: 669; *1936(a)*: 756. Mormons, *1916*, LDS: 329/RLDS: 343; *1926*, LDS: 647/ RLDS: 649; *1936(b)*: LDS & RLDS: 803. Mayan Temple, *1936(b)*: 1273. Vedanta Society, *1916*: 714; *1926*: 1386. *1936(b)*: 1661.

America and common to all North and South America, prior to the coming of the white man."[16] Its inclusion alongside the Vedanta Society only make the lack of data about Islam that much more puzzling. There is no explanation for the lack of substantive appearance by Muslims in the data. One plausible reason for this shortcoming is that census bureaucrats were not aware of physical spaces that Muslims occupied or utilized, to which letters or census workers could go. Sarah Howell stresses the centrality of coffeehouses as homosocial epicenters for meetings and prayers in early twentieth-century Islamic Detroit. For Muslim women in Detroit, because such spaces were male-centric they typically found their homes their spiritual loci. Such gendered roles in the development and continuance of Islam in the United States are reinforced by Curtis's anecdote about Mary Juma of Ross, North Dakota, who "preserved Islamic religious traditions. 'Syrians,' as they referred to themselves, would gather at her home for Friday congregational prayers."[17] A coffeehouse would not be a logical contact point for census workers seeking religious leaders, nor again would a private residence.[18] Even this, however, is hard to reconcile with the generally accessible knowledge about Islam in America during this era.

What do the papers say?

Both the lack of data and the suggestion of a lack of space identifiable as Islamic are not substantiated in the popular media of the time. We know there were Muslims in the United States and US territories by 1916, undoubtedly more than the 190 reported Vedanta Society adherents or even the several thousand Baha'is or Buddhists and certainly, by 1936 many more than the thousand or so practitioners at The Mayan Temple. As early as 1895, snippet reports circulated stating, "It is claimed that Hazelton. Pa., possesses the only Mohammedan mosque in America, where the Koran is regularly read."[19] In 1908, it was known that of the Syrians "working in mines near Altoona [Pennsylvania] . . . nearly all of them are from Lebanon, and, except Protestants, all sects, even Moslems, are represented."[20] This one line passage about Hazelton's supposed mosque appeared in at least a dozen papers across the country, but more recent evidence of the mosque has not been found. Another brief, though substantially longer, article in 1896 claimed that there were 600 Muslims living in New York.[21] By 1906, the San Francisco *Call* reported on fights breaking out among Hindu and Muslim immigrants from the subcontinent. In 1907, the Philadelphia *Record* reported (again, reprinted across the country) that there were at least twenty Muslims living in Philadelphia,[22] and in 1912, the New York *Sun* informed the public that "Muhammedans Now Have a Place of Worship Here," going on to recount the author's visit to a sober, unobtrusive building, on the third floor of which, was a mosque for local Muslims to congregate. The room held as many as 75 to 100 adherents on significant worship days (such as feast days).[23] In 1915, the *Farmington Times* of Farmington, Missouri, estimated the number of Muslims living in California at between 3,000 and 4,000,[24] and the 1916 Detroit *Free Press* stated that 5,000 to 6,000 Muslims were taking part in the feast of Muharram in Detroit.[25]

The frequency with which US papers discussed Muslims living in the United States increased notably by the 1920s. In 1920, the San Francisco *Chronicle* claimed that there were about 8,000 Muslims in the United States[26] This estimate was based on a census conducted by the Moslem Association of America, which was founded the previous year.[27] The 1921 report of the building of a mosque in Detroit made national news, with Washington, D.C.'s *Evening Star* reporting that it was the "first edifice of its kind in the U.S." According to the brief article there were about 60,000 Muslims in the United States and that the majority of them were Albanians, Arabs, Turks, and Persians.[28] Kambiz GhaneaBassiri has argued that between 1890 and 1924 there were about 60,000 Muslim immigrants to the

United States[29] Thus, it really makes no sense why the 1916 and certainly the 1926 or 1936 Religious Bodies censuses excluded Muslim data.

Even before the twentieth century, Muslims made up some portion of the American populous. Alexander Russell Webb, after converting to Islam known as Mohammed Russell Webb, made national news in the 1890s both as a US Consul to the Philippines and an advocate for Islam in America. When the World's Parliament of Religions convened in Chicago, in 1893, Webb was the only Muslim to present a paper. The only contribution from a native-born Muslim was a brief letter sent to the Parliament by the liberal progressive J. Sanna Abu Naddara, then residing in Paris. These two insights into Islam were not, however, the only ones offered at the Parliament.

A number of Protestant representatives presented papers, "which were biased toward Christian doctrines and values and reflected stereotypical ideas about Islam."[30] One of more comprehensive Protestant statements on Islam came from George Washburn, but as remains common today, "he denied progressive Moslems any status as real representatives of Islam and, as a result, concluded that Islam is a static religion and civilization."[31] The idea that Islam could be, perhaps even should be, viewed as a single monolithic whole is coupled with the tendency common in papers of the day to equate "Turkish" with "Islam." A *Puck* image examining the Parliament points to this tendency well (Figure 2.1).[32]

Figure 2.1 "Puck's Suggestion to the Congress of Religions," by Frederick Burr Opper. *Puck*. September 13, 1893.

The cartoon depicts many religiously symbolic people gathered around the front steps of a building. The persona which is likely the representation of Islam wears what may generically be called "Turkish garb," including a turban. He is present and relatively visible, but not named as such. It is interesting, particularly in light of the above discussion of the Religious Bodies work, that a Parsee (re: Zoroastrian) and Fakir (re: Hindu) are placed in visually more important locales than the Muslim depiction, although the (presumably) Buddhist is not.

Webb's conversion to Islam and discussion of the faith at the Parliament were not the only reasons articles about him peppered late-nineteenth-century newspapers. His plans for mosques, mass conversion, and even colonization were oft cited. *The Wheeling Daily Intelligencer*, in June 1893, argued that Webb "has virtually completed his plan for the importation of Mussulman colonists into the United States."[33] The article goes on to say that the idea is to bring them to the United States, make them citizens, and establish them in communities throughout the South. Additionally, the lengthy *Daily Intelligencer* article detailed goals for mosque construction on the part of Webb and offered insights into Islamic practices and Webb's own background.[34] Webb, it should be noted, openly declared at the Parliament (two months later) that

> I have not returned to the United States to make you all Mussulmans in spite of yourselves. . . . I do not propose to take a sword in one hand and the Koran in the other. . . . I have faith in the American intellect, in the American intelligence . . . and will defy any intelligent man to understand Islam and not love it.[35]

At the time, and in retrospect, Webb's role in US Islam was largely one of sensationalism and ineffectuality. He is mentioned in most histories, but his reach and lasting significance are negligible.

The latent concern Islam, or at least the suspicion of Islam, engendered in the United States lingered on, and in 1897 at least a few notable newspapers ran an article titled "Are Moslem Harems Possible in the U.S.?" The subtitle observed that "certainly there is no lack of Mohammedans." While the article did not give specific numbers, it did note that "of late years there has been a surprising growth of Turkish immigrants. The immigrants have been of three classes, Syrian Jews, Armenians, and Turks proper, only the latter being Mohammedan and alien in their domestic customs."[36] Two points should be emphasized here. First, the reference to "Turks proper" dovetails with the US government's own phrase, "real Turks," in talking about Turkish nationals who did not fit into other religious or ethnic groupings and the note above about the linkage between Turk and Islam. In this article the author is explicitly saying "Turks proper" are Muslims, but the use of "real Turks" in US governmental documents is less clear-cut, though it implies the idea that to be a "real Turk" is the same as being a Muslim. Second, the fascination and fear of the "harem," or more to the point polygamy, was a very real one in the United States at the time and remained so for at least another decade. While the Utah Wars (fought between the US government and the Mormon Deseret communities) were over more than polygamy, eventual statehood meant renunciation of polygamy on the part of the Church of Latter-day Saints. The discussion of polygamy in US politics was hotly contested for years to come and helped emphasis the "otherness" of both Mormons and Muslims for US audiences.

"Real Turks"

There were, we know, Near Eastern populations who came to the United States for as long as the country has existed. We know too that their numbers increased at the end of the nineteenth century, as was true for most other immigrant populations. Who they were and what their religion was are much more unclear. Sometime between 1872 and 1931 (likely before 1900 or very shortly thereafter), W. A. Rogers depicted what has been described as an Arab or Turkish colony street scene from New York City.[37] The "colony street scene" is likely a depiction of "Little Syria," a quarter in New York City to which immigrants from "Greater Syria" tended to gravitate. Rogers's depiction adds a visual layer to references of both Near Eastern populations in the United States, generally, and Little Syria, specifically.

The 1908 pulp magazine *Secret Service: Old and Young Brady, Detectives* ran an issue partly titled "The Secrets of 'Little Syria.'" Throughout the story, the Brady's interact with a variety of inhabitants of Little Syria, in both positive and negative ways. One character, who aided the Brady's in their investigations, was "Mohammed Kebda," who the reader was introduced to as "a fine, old boy, wearing a green turban on his head, which told two things to the initiated: First, that the man was a Mohammedan; second, that he claimed descent from Mohamet, the Prophet."[38] In and of itself this description is a fair treatment of a Muslim character for the time; what is really interesting, however, is the acknowledgment about the United States which follows: "If Mr. Mohammed Kebda had appeared on the street in his green turban he would have been mobbed; but in his own shop he could do as he pleased."[39] Only a few paragraphs later Kebda does leave, and in so doing "he whipped off the green turban and clapped on a derby."[40] The subtly of the suggestions in these passages can be easily missed. Islam was present, but not a matter for wide, public consumption reinforcing Haddad's assertion that pre–Second World War Islamic American communities tried to fit into the new culture.

The author of the Brady's drama speaks to the matter-of-fact nature with which Little Syria is treated, noting that "here are now hived in great numbers Syrians, Arabs, Hindoos and other Asiatic people. But about the distinction of the nationality the average New Yorker neither knows nor cares. He has chosen to dub this the Syrian quarter, consequently everyone who lives there is a Syrian."[41] This vision of the Syrian quarter was graphically interpreted in the Los Angeles *Herald* with which we began this chapter, in the illustration: "Washington Street Types."[42] The "Types" were sketches of individuals, some of heads, some of full bodies, all dislocated from their environmental context. As will be discussed more fully in Chapter 6, it is the clothing choices, not exaggerated racial features, which are significant makers of Near Eastern populations. The generalization and obfuscation implied in the Brady passage is played out further when the character of Kebda goes off on a mission for Old King Brady, "whipping off" his turban and donning the derby. This act may be interpreted as "passing," but here it indicates just how integrated Near Eastern populations were with general flow of early-twentieth-century US society. Only dress could clearly indicate difference.

In her 2010 dissertation "'Made in Massachusetts': Converting Hides and Skins into Leather and Turkish Immigrants into Industrial Laborers (1860s–1920s)," Işil Acehan examined a set of Ottoman immigrants from the Harput *vilayet*, who made their way to, and settled in, the North Shore of Boston. Acehan's work gives us a microexamination of the larger Ottoman immigrant experience. While not focusing on the religious nature of these Ottoman immigrants, Acehan offers a window into this largely invisible narrative. One point Acehan makes is that the Ottoman immigrants from Asian Turkey increased in number after 1890 and were predominantly male (84 percent) in 1899.[43] The male-female disparity holds up in Rogers' depiction where there is only one female, a young girl, in the "Colony" scene and in "Secrets of 'Little Syria,'" where female characters from the community go unnamed and little acknowledged. The greater male to female ratio is also noted in the Boston *Post* 1894 article, "Men from All Lands," which puts the number at six to one in the Syrian quarter of New York.

Government notions of "real Turks"

In December 1917, then secretary of state Robert Lansing sent Senator William J. Stone, a member of the Senate Foreign Relations Committee, a letter enclosing his memorandum on the inadvisability of declaring war on the Turks and Bulgarians, despite having declared war on their allies. Lansing's arguments were largely either economic in nature or concerned with the plight of American missionaries serving in Ottoman territory, noting,

> There is practically nothing to fear from the activities of the Turkish subjects in the United States; the vast majority of the Turkish subjects in the United States are Christians, Syrians, Assyrians, and Armenians. The number of *real Turks* in the United States is very limited. The report of the Immigration Commission published in 1911 states that only 12,954 *true Turks* came to America from Turkey during the twelve years from 1899 and 1910 inclusive.[44]

The phrase "real Turks" as used by Lansing is not a direct quote from the report he is citing, the *Statistical Review of Immigration, 1820–1910* (also known as the Dillingham Report), but it does give us some clues as to who Lansing's "true Turk" was.

The idea of nationality was more fluid in the fin de siècle than it is today. At the outset of the first volume the authors take time to discuss their usage of racial classifications. Noting that "since 1899 the Bureau of Immigration has classified arriving immigrants by races or peoples, as well as by country of last permanent residence," the Commission chose to continue this trend so as not to confuse the numbers, and thus "the Commission, like the bureau, uses the term 'race' in a broad sense, the distinction being largely a matter of language and geography."[45] This choice was not without controversy, even at the time. The problematic term "Hebrew," came under fire in the process of the coalescing the Dillingham Report's data. According to the Commission, "The practice of classifying the foreign-born by race or people, rather than by country of birth is acceptable to the people of such races in the United States with one exception. . . . The one objection to the racial classification adopted by the Commission . . . was specifically directed against the use of the word 'Hebrew' or 'Jewish' to designated a race."[46] Statesman, lawyer, and American-Jewish community leader Simon Wolf spoke at a hearing before the Commission in 1909 noting that "the point we make is this: A Jew coming from Russia is a Russian; from Roumania, a Roumanian; from France, a Frenchman; from England, an Englishman; and from Germany, a German; that Hebrew or Jewish is simply a religion."[47] In the end, the Commission chose to retain the problematic term, arguing that "the Commission is convinced that such usage is entirely justified," that the *Jewish Encyclopedia* declares Jews to be a race, and that many Jews themselves, notably Zionists, consider Jewishness a racial identity.[48]

The racial and national fluidity offered up in the Commission's racial classification system is rooted in and reflective of educational structures and institutions of the day. The 1883 textbook *A Brief History of Ancient, Mediaeval, and Modern Peoples, with Some Account of Their Monuments, Institutions, Arts, Manners, and Customs* by Joel Dorman Steele and Ester Baker Steele was used widely in schools across the United States. The causal, and blatant, racism of the text informed Americans about the nature of civilizational race for generations, as a version of the book remained in print and circulation until 1941.[49] According to the text,

> The only Historic Race is the Caucasian, the others having done little worth recording. It is usually divided into three great branches: the *Ar'yan*, the *Semit'ic*, and the *Hamit'ic*. The first of these, which includes the Persians, the Hindoos, and nearly all the European nations, is the one to which we belong. It has always been noted for its intellectual vigor. The second embraces the Assyrians, the Hebrews, the Phoenicians, and the Arabs. It has been marked by religious fervor, and has given the world the three faiths—Jewish, Christian, and Mohammedan—which teach the worship of one God. The third branch includes the Chaldeans and the Egyptians. It has been remarkable for its massive architecture.[50]

At the bottom of the textbook's page, a note distinguishes the "Caucasian" race from the "Turanian," who, the authors tell us, include "Mongols, Chinese, Japanese, Turks, Tartars, Lapps, Finns, Magyars, etc. Iran. . . . The old name for Persia (the 'land of light') is opposed to Turan, the barbarous region around (the 'land of darkness')."[51] There is a lot to unbox from this one passage of the Steeles' book, but for now we will focus on the tripartite nature of race as it was defined therein. The Steeles' book was not alone in dividing up the world into what are even more casually referred to as the "white, yellow, and black races," occasionally a "red" or "brown" grouping is added to incorporate peoples from the Western Hemisphere. While obviously dated, the delineation between the races is not uncommon even today. However, what may be surprising to the modern reader is the distinction noted here between Turkish and Arab populations. For our purposes this is an important delineation. The Turk was often rolled into the "Yellow Peril" (discussed more thoroughly in Chapter 6) and was afforded a racial distinction as "Other," which was not always assumed for Arabs, Persians, and Egyptians.

The legal groundwork laid by textbooks like the Steeles' became central to early-twentieth-century reporting. In 1909 the US Circuit Court in Cincinnati heard arguments about the "whiteness" of Turks. The *Plymouth Tribune* reported in September 1909 that "naturalization was refused to 2067 aliens during the past fiscal year," a considerable increase over the previous year. At the heart of these cases, the *Tribune* argued, was the whiteness of the applicants. The US Circuit Court case focused on the denial of a Turkish man's naturalization "on the ground that he is not a white person within the meaning of the law declaring that its provisions 'shall apply to aliens being free white persons and to aliens of African nativity and to persons of African descent.'"[52] Such reporting continued throughout the fall of 1909 as newspapers across the country ran united press articles asking, "What is a white man before the law?" It was geography, the series determined, which really counted. The article asserted that

> courts have held to the geographical distribution of races—assuming that the African was black, the Asiatic yellow, the European white and the original American red. . . . A Syrian, whose people for untold generations have not assimilated foreign blood, and who is logically the purest of Aryan stock, is held by the courts to be a member of the yellow race.[53]

In addition to informing its readers about what is and is not considered white in the law, the article discussed the creation of an organization which, it went on to note, "will this winter [besiege congress] petitioning for a change to the court's ruling."[54] Sarah Gualtieri in *Between Arab and White* writes that the Syrian American Association, founded in 1909, helped George Dow refute a judge's ruling against his naturalization by 1913. Early Syrian applications for naturalization like the cases of George Sishim and Costa Najour "emphasized the Christian heritage to distinguish themselves from the 'Asiatic' Muslim Turks who were the sovereigns of the Ottoman Empire."[55] Such a move to distance themselves from Muslim Turks was calculated especially for a moment "when the Anglo-American judiciary and the American public's perception was steeped in ignorance and superstition."[56] Once Dow's case was heard at the Federal level, the then presiding judge affirmed the idea that Syrians by virtue of their affinity with Europe "should be classed as white, they must fall within the term white persons used in the statue."[57] Thus, in the end the courts, at least in this set of cases realigned with the Steeles' racial hierarchies.

A Los Angeles *Herald*, in reporting on the case in 1909, moved quickly away from the question of Turkish whiteness to more widely discussed xenophobia, arguing that "there are certain races, notable the Chinese and the southern European, the members of which when admitted to the United States, rapidly reduce the competing white race to destitution."[58] Naturalization Division Chief Richard K. Campbell advocated a position of decisions about naturalization being "based not on science, but on 'common understanding.' The law refers to persons and confines the right to become naturalized to those who are white. . . . The average man in the street understands distinctly what it means, and would find no difficulty in assigning to the yellow race a Turk, or Syrian."[59] In comparing Campbell's statement with the notions gleaned from the Steeles' textbook, one wonders if indeed "the average man" would so easily assign a Syrian to "the yellow race."

William Dillingham, in addition to issuing the *Statistical Review of Immigration*, oversaw the creation of the *Dictionary of Races or Peoples*, which was published in 1911. The *Dictionary* identified the qualifications of immigration cases into the 1950s, when in 1951 the then chief of Nationalist and Status section H. J. Hart "concluded that continued use of the forty year-old guide 'hardly appears to be tenable.'"[60] The *Dictionary* "deemed it reasonable to follow the classification employed by Blumenbach . . . the Caucasian, Ethiopian, Mongolian, Malay, and American, or, as familiarly called the white, black, yellow, brown, and red races."[61] The racial definitions in the *Dictionary* were also used in the *Statistical Review*.

Three mentions are particularly worth noting: Arabian, Turkish, and Persian. According to the Commission, "Arabian" refers to

> one of the three great groups of the Semitic branch of the Caucasian race. The Arabians are related to the Hebrews and include Arabs proper and the wandering Bedouin tribes of the desert. . . . They are not to be confounded with the Turks . . . who are Mongolian Tartar, in origin and speech, rather than Caucasian. Neither are they closely related to the Syrians, who are Christians and Aryans, not Semites. . . . Very few come to the United States.[62]

Of the Persians less substance is offered, although the definition is pointed in declaring that "in intellect, if not in civilization, the Persian is perhaps more nearly a European than is the pure Turk. He is more alert and accessible to innovation. Yet he is rather brilliant and poetical than solid in temperament. Like the Hindu he is more eager to secure the semblance than the substance of modern civilization."[63] The Arabian definition noted few "Arabian" immigrants appear in the records, and the same is true of the Persians.

Turks, unsurprisingly, get a great deal more in definition. Beyond their linguistic and historic heritage as the ruling classes in the modern Ottoman state, the Commission notes that "to-day they are not so much Turkish by blood as Arabian, Circassian, Persian, Armenian, Greek, and Slavic. They prefer to be considered as Arabo-Persian in culture rather than as Turkish. *In religion they are almost universally Mohammedan*."[64] One really wonders why the Commission is bothering to make a separate category for Turks if it simultaneously believes they practically do not exist, at least in terms of blood or self-identification. Still, the Commission marches on, discussing the "pure Turkish" populations of the Ottoman Empire which the Commission argues is a minority of the whole Ottoman population, but it is made abundantly clear that anyone being listed as "Turkish" is "almost universally" considered a Muslim. Moreover, returning to Lansing's assertion, if we accept the assumption with which immigration officials were working that Turks are "almost universally Mohammedans" then we are led to the conclusion that the phrasing "real Turk," "true Turk," or "proper Turk" was intended to be read as "Muslim."[65]

Other Muslim-Americans?

Looking more critically at the caveat placed on the Religious Bodies census itself, that the census only measured data in the "continental United States, and does not include statistics of organizations in outlying possessions or in foreign lands," we can also push back on the number of Muslims *known* to be under American jurisdiction. The census chose to impose this restriction for two, largely logical, reasons. It was consciously not looking at data on missionary activities or those organizations with "religious affiliations," like the Young Men's Christian Association (Y.M.C.A). The second reason for this limitation is that at the exact same time the Census Bureau was being born, the US government embarked on a policy of overseas imperialism and expansion. Where then, did the peoples of Puerto Rico or the Philippines fall? Herein is the quandary. Despite the fact that the US government administered the Philippines between 1898 and 1946 (first under military administration and then by 1902 under civil administration), the noteworthy Muslim population it received, by way of the Moros, was not factored into US demographic data. Among newspapers at the time, there was a great deal of confusion as to whether these newly acquired populations were de facto citizens and, if not, what was the distinction between *citizen* and *national*. According to *The Report of the Philippine Commission* (1900–15), specifically the report on the Department of Mindanao and Sulu, the estimated population of Muslims was 313,590.[66] If this number seems insignificant against the whole population of the United States, consider that the reported number of the Church of Latter-day Saints members in 1916 was 403,388. Whether counted as "Americans" in the Philippines or not, this number and the tens of thousands of Muslims living in the continental United States were seemingly denied their existence and increasingly used as fodder for sensational media.

3

Our Muhammaden Wards

By the latter half of 1898, the United States was deeply involved in the Spanish-American War and plunging into the role of global imperialist. In the end, the United States' territorial reach extended into Cuba, Puerto Rico, Gaum, and the Philippines. Moreover, although not acquired in the same way, the United States also annexed Hawaii at the same time. Early-twentieth-century comics critiquing US imperialism made no distinction about the circumstances of the acquisitions, conflating the actions as part of the same land-grab efforts and leading to confusion in the public sphere as to how they were acquired. While it was clear that the US government was pursuing an imperialist agenda, the scope and speed of the acquisition of Caribbean and Pacific territories tested the limits of the governments' imperial resolve. Cartoonists and comic artists were quick to draw parallels between Theodore Roosevelt's administration and that of the British Empire, as in the June 1910 *Punch* cartoon "Multum Ex Parvo." The New York *Tribune* reprinted it on June 19 as part of a full page devoted to the image (or caricature) of Theodore Roosevelt in the world's press. "Multum Ex Parvo" depicts a Filipino man reading a newspaper article about President Roosevelt and the "proper management of Egypt," to which he says, "Splendid! There's nothing he don't know about Empire! And to think that he picked it all up from me!"[1] The reference to Egypt comes from such statements as Roosevelt issued in his "The Expansion of the White Races" speech, an address at the celebration of the African Diamond Jubilee of the Methodist Episcopal Church in Washington, D.C. in January 1909. During the course of the address, President Roosevelt declared, "In Egypt, in the Philippines, in Algiers, the native people have thriven under the rule of the foreigner, advancing as under no circumstances could they possibly have advanced if left to themselves, the increase in population going hand in hand with the increase in general well-being."[2] Often cartoonists directly linked the United States' empire to Great Britain's through the use of John Bull or references to India, East Africa, or Egypt.

In the years immediately following the Spanish-American War, cartoonists focused on several pointed tropes, including linkages to European empires, which underscored conscious and unconscious efforts by American policymakers. Under the broader umbrella of imperialism these recurring themes included classroom settings and the structure of education, racial differentiation, and physical labor as a metaphor for advancing Western/American notions of civilization. In both *Puck* cartoons, "School Begins" (1899) and "Visitors' Day" (1905), and *Harper's Weekly*'s cover, "Uncle Sam's New Class in the Art of Self-Government," the setting was a classroom overseen by Uncle Sam. In all three images Uncle Sam looms over the teacher's desk brandishing a pointer in two and grabbing hold of "Castro" (a reference to Cipriano Castro of Venezuela) in "Visitors' Day." In all three comics the racial distinctions are notable for establishing perceived hierarchies and problems.

In "School Begins," Texas and California sit quietly reading and are portrayed with fair complexions (Figure 3.1). The native tribes of the United States are depicted as one student sitting far removed from the rest of the class, holding an upside-down ABC book. African Americans do not appear as students but as a character washing the window and looking on. Chinese (or perhaps all East Asian) immigrants stand at the door looking in as the personification of one student clearly not allowed to attend the school's classes. The Philippines, Hawaii, Puerto Rico, and Cuba all appear as individual pupils, sitting in the front row,

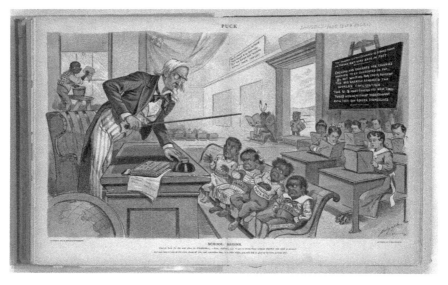

Figure 3.1 "School Begins," by Louis Dalrymple. *Puck*. January 25, 1899.

clearly unhappy or, in the case of Puerto Rico, frightened.[3] Notable is the writing on the blackboard at the back of the classroom, which reads, "The consent of the governed is a good thing in theory, but very rare in fact." The board goes on to note that England did not wait for consent and has thus "advanced the worlds civilization" and "the U.S. must govern its new territories with or without their consent":[4] A sentiment foreshadowing Teddy Roosevelt's 1909 speech (Figure 3.2). That territories like the Philippines were "in need of civilization" and that the school classroom was the best place for civilization to be learned was a recurring theme and echoed in the "Visitors' Day" comic where Holland, France, England, and Germany appear as supervisors to the general education process, much like a superintendent may visit a modern school.[5]

The *Harper's Weekly*'s cover adds an element of gendered distinction more notable than in the other two. Hawaii and Puerto Rico, both drawn as female, stand next to the teacher's desk smiling and reading, unperturbed by the commotion elsewhere. A student marked 'Cuban ex Patriot' tussles with another, 'Guerilla,' while being smacked on the head by Uncle Sam, the schoolmaster. Both the Cuban and Guerilla characters are shoeless and very dark in complexion and possess wild, unkempt hair. Similarly attired is 'Aguinaldo,' standing on a stool and becrowned with a dunce cap. Similarly attired is 'Aguinaldo,' standing on a stool and becrowned with a dunce cap. Aguinaldo, references Emilo Aguinaldo, the Filipino revolutionary who became the Philippine president

Figure 3.2 "Visitor's Day," by John S. Pughe. *Puck*. April 12, 1905.

in 1899. Scowling from his perch on the stool, he looks on as the tussle rages. Incongruous with the rest of the scene is "Maximo Gomez." Distinctly older than the other students, he sits quietly reading "his book" upon the same bench where the Cuban and Guerilla fight.[6]

The Philippines oftentimes appeared as the "example" Empire, when multiple global empires were engaged in one image. In the specific case of the Philippines, the missionary was often the personification of a school teacher and juxtaposed with the military and solider. This rhetorical juxtaposition was visually depicted, for example, in the November 20, 1901, issue of Puck, "It's 'up to' Them" (Figure 3.3).[7] Reliance on education was a central feature of both US policy in the Philippines and the comics' examination of that policy. Structured educational programs were a central feature of all imperial projects at the end of the nineteenth century, and for the United States the Philippines was no different. However, if, as suggested in this cartoon, the Filipinos do not "choose" education they will have to "learn their lesson through application of 'civilized' force."[8]

The wildness with which Aguinaldo, the Cuban ex Patriot, and the Guerilla are drawn highlights the racialization evident in these works. Cartoonist Charles L. Bartholomew's "Something Lacking" depicted a Filipino boy dressed in a grass skirt, with an earring, and distinctly dark skin asking Uncle Sam "Where

Figure 3.3 "It's 'up to' Them," by Udo J. Keppler. *Puck*. November 20, 1901.

do I come into this?" The Filipino is juxtaposed with two other boys, Cuba and Puerto Rico, both illustrated with lighter skin. Cuba is waving a flag of independence, while Puerto Rico wears a "suit of assimilation."[9] In this, and the earlier examples, the process of "civilizing" is depicted as less physically arduous and more a process of indoctrination, however the physicality of civilizing was another notable symbolic representation utilized by cartoonists. Often the Philippines is dragged, or forced, into "civilizing," by having Filipino characters physically carrying the West (personified by John Bull and Uncle Sam) as in the case of the March 1899 cover of *Life* magazine or by being physically carried by the West as in the April 1899 image from *Judge*.[10] Similarly, *Judge*'s very first cover depicted President William McKinley bathing, in a river (maybe the Potomac, with the Capital building in the background) a Filipino child. The screaming child is dressed in a grass skirt and is holding a spear.[11] Not only does this image offer a corollary to the now infamous Pears soap advertisements of the same era, with McKinley's upright stature and pale skin in stark contrast to the child's flailing body and dark skin, but it also suggests a strongly religious component with McKinley standing in for a revival minister baptizing the Philippines in the river's waters.[12] Symbolism applied in this way was hardly surprising in light of President McKinley's confession to a group of Methodist ministers that he prayed on the matter of what to do with the Philippines, but in the end decided that "there was nothing left for us to do, but to take them all, and to educate the Filipinos, and uplift and civilize and Christianize them."[13] Such striking religious overtones were echoed by Governor General of the Philippines Leonard Wood in a 1925 interview. Wood told the interviewer that the United States could not consider the idea of Philippine independence "without thinking of civilization as a whole. And Civilization, to us, is Christian civilization. . . . We are a stone, if not the keystone, of the arch of Christian civilization in the Pacific."[14]

The problem of relics

The civilizing mission to the Philippines was notably different than its practice in Cuba, Puerto Rico, Hawaii, or Guam. In looking over the examples from above, we see that rarely did the Philippines get kind treatment in the cartoons. While it was not always the problematic focus of a cartoon, it never received nice clothing or a calm demeanor as did Hawaii, Puerto Rico, or Cuba. For the Philippines there was the requisite civilizing of nonwhite populations, but the islands came with an extra layer of complexity for the US government: a sizable Muslim population. It was this population in particular that reignited controversies over the values of liberty and their application.

In 1915, John P. Finely wrote that "at the beginning of the war with Spain the United States government was not aware of the existence of any Mohammedans in the Philippines."[15] The jolt of this discovery was compounded by a general lack of understanding about Islam, particularly the nature of Islam as practiced in the Philippines. What was generally known in mainstream US press about Islam and Islamic practice focused on sweeping generalizations, assumptions, and often falsehoods. Nestled in two equally problematic frameworks, Americans frequently defined Islam through a lens of Orientalized romanticism or Oriental despotism. Of the former, adventurers like Richard Burton had solidified such narratives through travel accounts and translations of works like *1001 Arabian Nights* (of which more will be said in the following chapter). In these depictions there was a focus on the grandeur of the sultan and his harem, a sense of opulence, and of decadence verging on or plunging into moral decay. Traveling to the Philippines in 1903, Wood, along with Lieutenant Frank McCoy and Major Hugh Lennox Scott, stopped in Istanbul before traveling on to Cairo. As Walther notes, the men "were undoubtedly steeped in American beliefs about the decadence of Ottoman Muslim rule. In his diary Wood wrote: 'the Turks have done nothing here since they captured the city. Everything has been standing still or drifting backward.'"[16] Expecting to find it so, it is unsurprising that Wood's conclusions reinforced a narrative of moral decay, common in Oriental imagery. On the other hand, Islam was understood within the guise of "Oriental Despotism," heavily influenced by the narratives handed down from Medieval Europe's Crusader experiences. As we have already seen, the number of practicing Muslims in the United States was few at the turn of the century. Average Americans were unlikely to know, meet, or be Muslims, and thus their education about Islam was scant at best. Things that average Americans were likely to *know* about Islam included the practice of polygamy, closely linked to the concept of the harem, and that slavery was still practiced in Islamic cultures. As it happened, both polygamy and slavery *were* extant in the Philippines among the Muslim Moros. This revelation and the subsequent "guardianship" of the sizable Muslim population therein resurrected the words of the 1856 Republican Party Platform in the minds of many critics:

> The Constitution confers upon Congress sovereign powers over the Territories of the United States for their government; and that in the exercise of this power, it is both the right and the imperative duty of Congress to prohibit in the Territories those twin relics of barbarism—Polygamy, and Slavery.[17]

Of course, in 1856 the plank focused on the extension of slavery into Kansas or Nebraska and the practice of "plural marriage" among the newly emerging Church of Latter-day Saints community. While seemingly separate foci, throughout the second half of the nineteenth century questions of slavery and polygamy were intrinsically linked. Law professor Sarah Barringer Gordon notes that "the potential degeneration of liberty in the West was a nagging national concern throughout the Civil War era, extending well beyond the dispute over slavery."[18] The anxiety that slavery and polygamy were entwined in a degeneration of liberty followed westward expansion and did diminish with the closing of Fredrick Jackson Turner's frontier. As barbed wire encircled greater swaths of rural America there was a growing sense that the dark days of slavery were in America's past, and although polygamy remained a hovering specter of contention vis-à-vis the Church of Latter-day Saints, it appeared controllable. However, the two-faced snake of polygamy and slavery reared its head again in the US press between 1899 and 1904 (and then again around 1913), when a great deal of coverage was dedicated to "Our Mohammedan" wards, land, allies, subjects, archipelago, world, cousins, capital, and empire, in the Philippines,[19] or what was occasionally termed "Oriental America." Sensational newspaper headlines like "Faces a New Problem: United States Government Must Deal with Over a Million Polygamous Mahometans," from the front page of the *Barbour County Index*, did not help.[20]

In 1900, Major Owen J. Sweet, Governor of Jolo, said of the slavery in the Philippines: "It is a mild form of feudal bondage."[21] This dismissiveness was, as Michael Salman observes, a part of a much larger picture of US difficulties in gaining control over the Philippines. In that same year, Henry O. Dwight argued that "the course to be adopted by the United States toward Moro slavery is perhaps the gravest of the questions raised by our purchase of the Sulu Islands."[22] Dwight unwilling to discuss actual policy made the suggestion that the Moros, being different than other Filipinos, should "be classed in the same category as our Indian reservations, to be surrounded by a wall of steel for the safety of the neighboring peoples . . . until some such system of moral quarantine has educated them to new ideas of justice and equality."[23] Suggesting parallel treatment of the Moros as to Native Americans was not uncommon. In 1899 the *New York Journal and Advertiser* noted,

> We can doubtless extinguish slavery very soon, with little judicious financial assistance, but to extinguish polygamy in a Moslem community that has never known any other domestic system from the remotest generations is a different matter. The Moros are not a perverted offshoot of civilization, like

the Mormons—they are still in a barbarous stage of evolution, and we can no more civilize them all at once than we can turn the Apaches into Bostonians in a year.[24]

In an ominous analogy to the treatment of Native Americans, in 1906 John T. McCutcheon's comic "The Only Moros from Whom We May Expect No Uprising" was published in the *Chicago Tribune* (Figure 3.4). The single-panel cartoon depicts rows of Moro gravesites, overseen by a hillock on which flies the US flag. In March 1906, the Los Angeles *Times*' "Pen Points" section asserted that the "Moro seems to be not unlike the Apache. He will not be good until he is dead."[25] Such sentiments echoed infamous phrase "the only good Indian is a dead Indian," and in the cartoon the morbid counterpoints are notable.[26] McCutcheon came back to the Philippine question in 1913, when he depicted Uncle Sam and the then secretary of state William Jennings Bryan discussing "cutting adrift" the Philippines. Bryan, eager to do so, has a knife poised to slash the linking the island to the ship he and Sam are aboard. Sam declares, "Hold on there! You've never heard me say I wanted to cut 'em adrift! I've always said 'NO' when you asked me!"[27]

Figure 3.4 "The Only Moros from Whom We May Expect No Uprising," by John T. McCutcheon. *Chicago Tribune.* March 10, 1906.

Under the governorship of Leonard Wood something like Dwight's suggestion was realized. In 1903 a "separate government for the Moro (Muslim) population of the southern Philippines" was created, and "the first governor of the province, General Leonard Wood, broke with the previously lax practice of indirect rule."[28] Early on in Moro-American history Filipino Muslims were often discussed in the context of wider Orientalized romanticism, particularly as related to harems. The *New York Journal and Advertiser* lost no time in capitalizing on these sensational details. On December 4, 1898, a full page was devoted to "Real Live Mohammedan Sultan with a Harem Now Belongs to Us!"[29] It did not take too long for that Oriental romanticism to wear off as Moros were increasingly deemed dangerous, in need of subduing, as demonstrated in Figure 3.4. The *San Francisco Call*, in 1900, described the Moros as "born pirates" who "hate Christians with all of the fanatical hatred of the subjects of Islam wherever found."[30]

The questions of slavery, polygamy, and citizenship found new vent in popular discourse around the Moro example and then by extension all Muslims. The 1898 *New York Journal* "Real Live Mohammedan" article practically taunted the US populous with this new population. One picture was captioned "Headhunter's Basket in the Kingdom of Mahmoud, American Citizen," and another "Royal Yacht of Sultan Mahmoud, American Citizen." Proclaiming all Filipinos, not to mention specifically the Moros, American citizens did not make them so, but the idea was one which continued to find an audience. The *Topeka State Journal* seemed to declare with pride that "the United States now has among its citizens a genuine sultan. He has only 12 wives and the government will pay him $6000 a year to be good."[31] In 1899 the *San Francisco Call* decried relationships established by General Bates in the Philippines with Sulu leaders. A potential treaty worked out with the Sultan of Sulu, the *Call* determined, left "polygamy and chattel slavery among the Sulus undisturbed, but our jurisdiction is to be acknowledged and our flag is to fly over the islands."[32] Theodore Noyes's 1903 work *Oriental America and Its Problems*, in a chapter notably titled "Moro-Americans," focused on the two concerns of slavery and polygamy, as well, arguing that "slavery is hateful to the American idea" and "polygamy is antagonistic to American sentiment," but for both issues, Noyes advocated a slow going policy in trying to change the status quo.[33]

Abolition in the United States was not smoothly accomplished, when it came to be tied to questions of imperialism in the case of the Philippines, this complicated matters even more greatly. The vocal anti-imperialist Edward Atkinson, in his 1899 *The Anti-Imperialist* series, put forward his fight against the McKinley administration and the imperial efforts of the State under the heading

> Sequence of the Declarations and Acts by which President McKinley, with the Support of his Cabinet, has Undertaken to Destroy the Liberty of the People of the Philippine Islands and to Re-Establish Slavery and Polygamy Therein by the Force of the Army and the Navy of the United States.[34]

Atkinson lamented the reality that treaties with the Sultan of Sulu as regards the nature of "slavery and polygamy within the jurisdiction claimed by the United States" would only be fully understood when the Senate met to ratify or reject them.[35] Thus, while a much more heated battle focused on the slavery question (again), a parallel and similar fight took place over polygamy.

Less angry, more scandalous: American polygamy

Many, like Theodore Noyes, noted that

> polygamy is a luxury of the rich. Education and contact with civilization will render it more and more expensive every year, will steadily increase the discontent among the plural wives and will doubtless gradually abolish the evil of many simultaneous wives by driving men to our own superior system of many wives in succession through the operation of our lax marriage and divorce laws.[36]

Arguably, Noyes's prediction came to pass by 1921 when the then retiring governor, Frank W. Carpenter, reported that the "practice of polygamy in the Philippine Islands is being reduced through education."[37] The implication in Carpenter's report was that the Philippine peoples, specifically the Moros, had chosen the path led by the school teacher/missionaries depicted in so many *Puck* cartoons.[38]

The multifaceted logic with which Noyes viewed Filipino polygamy was very much one visible in the cultural consciousness of the day. From the middle of the nineteenth century well into the 1880s "antipolygamy sentiments were common coin among politicians, clergymen, newspaper editors, novelists, and temperance activists."[39] In an 1884 *Puck* cartoon centerfold, the artists Joseph Ferdinand Keppler, Frederick Burr Opper, Bernhard Gillam, and F. Graetz depicted "A Desperate Attempt to Solve the Mormon Question," underscoring the future polygamy questions for the United States (Figure 3.5).[40]

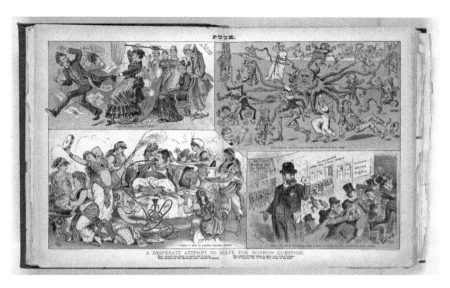

Figure 3.5 "A Desperate Attempt to Solve the Mormon Question," by Joseph Ferdinand Keppler, Frederick Burr Opper, Bernhard Gillam, and F. (Friedrich) Graetz. *Puck*, February 13, 1884.

Graetz's contribution noted Noyes's "own superior system of many wives in succession through the operation of our lax marriage and divorce laws," depicting the ease of divorce in the United States. In his panel he himself is depicted in the "foreground gesturing toward hordes of men rushing to get divorced on 'Saturday. Divorce day in Chicago,' and at places advertising 'Divorces without publicity, Divorces procured without delay. Liberal charges, [and] Divorces obtained for $5.00.'"[41]

Likewise, the motifs drawing linkages between Mormon polygamy and Muslim polygamy were explored in Keppler's contribution of an Orientalist's imagined Islamic harem and the Mormon marriage practice.[42] This comparison did not sit well with members of the Church of Latter-day Saints, however, especially as the category of "polygamist" was well established as a cornerstone of "un-Americanism." In a September 1900 *Deseret Evening News* article, the author contended that "celestial marriage, as formerly taught by the 'Mormons,' was, both in principle and practice, as different from Mohammedan polygamy as is heaven from earth."[43] The author, provoked into making this distinction, was responding to the *Sacramento Bee*, which drew strong parallels between the two faiths. Such associations, despite the efforts of Mormons, and perhaps even Muslims, did not subside. Around 1912, Bruce Kinney published a book *Mormonism: The Islam of America*. The book spawned hundreds of discussions across the country as it was taken up in church reading circles. The actual connections made between the two faiths in the work are scant at best. The foreword from the Editorial Committee noted,

> The title of this, the latest of the textbooks issued by the Council of Women for Home Missions, may need a word of explanation. It is generally acknowledged that Mormonism is similar to Mohammedanism in its endorsement of the practice of polygamy, and its ideas of heaven. Many other points of similarity between these systems have been noted by students, and the Book of Mormon has marked resemblance to the Koran. As all ancient religions have a modern equivalent, Mormonism can justly be claimed to be the modern form of Mohammedanism, and not incorrectly termed "the Islam of America."
>
> While the subject considered in this book should be approached only in the spirit of fairness and Christian sympathy, it has become of too great importance in our national life to be omitted as a topic for careful study.[44]

In fact, this is practically the only place in the book Islam ever makes an appearance. The title was merely illustrative, or enticing, not substantive. In 1869, John Shanks, representative from Indiana, drew an even more vitriolic linkage between Islam and the Church of Latter-day Saints when he declared the Ottoman Empire an "'Asiatic Mormon dynasty of Moslems,' led by a 'Mormon Sultan,' who, among other horrid defects, practiced polygamy."[45] Sentiments as these furthered the notion that there was a relationship between the Church of Latter-day Saints, Islam, and polygamy and that all of it was outside the bounds of Americana.

In 1917, a serialized short story ran in several newspapers across the country. Such fiction was not uncommon at the time and was not being touted as "truth," but it was nevertheless part of the intellectual milieu. The March 1917 portion, "Mr. Axel's Shady Past," was part of this series titled *Tracer of Egos* by Victor Rousseau. In this installment, Dr. Phileas Immanuel, soul specialist, went about solving the problems of a rich English duke's bored, debutant niece, using theories about reincarnation. In this story,

> Lady Sibyl Smith was one of England's typical new women. Seven and twenty years of age, rich, handsome, gifted, the niece of a duke and sister of a viscount, she played innumerable roles with distinction, and the craze of one week became the aversion of the next. She had been suffragette, teetotaler, Socialist, anti-vaccinationist and anti-vivisectionist, vegetarian and sandal wearer; but now she was bent upon becoming a Mormon.[46]

To "solve" the "problem of Lady Sibyl," Dr. Immanuel posits that "the Mormons are simply the ancient Mohammedans come back to earth" and that "the parallel is so close that I cannot see how any reasonable man can doubt it." Immanuel goes on,

> It holds in every instance. Mohammed came, as Smith came, at a time when the old beliefs were breaking down. Each taught a creed composed of a hodge-podge of Judaism and Christianity. Each had a special revelation from an angel, who gave him the text for his sacred book. Each was said to be epileptic. Each was driven out of his home town into a desert country and established a militant nation there. And mark my words, gentlemen, in Mormonism America and the world have to face the greatest peril that the next century will bring.

> "And each taught polygamy," said the duke thoughtfully. "But I understand that the Saints have ceased to advocate that doctrine."[47]

In time, Dr. Immanuel unmasks "Axel, the Mormon missionary," as "a certain Hadji, who in the year 689, was sent to make converts of a Christian tribe living in Lebanon, and, failing to win them, ruthlessly massacred seven hundred men, women and children, in cold blood" (Figure 3.6).[48] The accompanied image, by O. Irwin Myers dated 1914, portrays Dr. Immanuel leaning toward a tall man, with a heavy black beard, a scowling expression, and a clinched fist, presumably Axel/Hadji. The lines are heavy, and the detail is lost, but Axel/Hadji may be darker than the doctor and his companions, one of which is likely Lady Sibyl. In the surrounding room, where Immanuel is attempting to draw out the reincarnated Hadji (indicated by the doctor's raised hands and splayed fingers), there are elements of a Middle Eastern quality. On the floor, under what appears to be a bench, there is a hookah, with its pipe wrapped neatly around it. There is a curved sword hanging above the heads of all, on the wall at the back of the room. Finally, there are two octagonal end tables with something approaching arabesque styling.

The motif of the "Other" and Mormon in literature was not unique to this one piece. In 1890 the Latter-day Saint Church leadership issued a manifesto moving the Church away from the practice of plural marriage. The Immigration Act of 1891 banned polygamists in its laundry list of "excluded persons." One fear was that practitioners of the Latter-day Saints faith, who have a strong missionary component in their practice, were traveling between the United States and Europe, particularly Eastern Europe, and strengthening "the ranks of polygamists." Deirdre M. Moloney describes one case in 1883 when "Mormon 'proselytizers' arriving from Switzerland were the subject of [much discussion

"HAJIDI" SAID THE DOCTOR AGAIN, BUT NOW IN ENGLISH, "YOU
HAVE BEEN HIDDEN TOO LONG; COME FORTH!"

Figure 3.6 O. Irwin Myers image (dated 1914) for "Mr. Axel's Shady Past," in *The Tracer of Egos* by Victor Rousseau.

by those] regulating immigration at the New York Custom House. . . . The fact that the members of this group were Mormons, 'proselytizers' seeking converts, and that their religious beliefs condoned polygamy"[49] were used as rationale for prohibiting their entry. Despite the indigeneity of the Church of Latter-day Saints to the United States such anti-polygamist sentiment further helped cast the faith and its followers as un-American. Moreover, fear of polygamy, and by extension the little known faith of Mormonism underpins the literary qualities of works like Arthur Conan Doyle's *A Study in Scarlet*.

Doyle's first Sherlock Holmes's mystery added to a growing sense of Otherness about the relatively new Latter-day Saints Church in his depiction of Utah and the Church's community therein. Elder Stangerson, one of the central characters in the plot, had three wives, and the practice of polygamy was central to the story's arc. In chapter three the audience learns that in Utah, "the supply of adult women was running short, and . . . rumours began to be bandied about. . . . Fresh women appeared in the harems of the Elders—women who pined and wept, and bore upon their faces the traces of an unextinguishable horror."[50] The power of what may be deemed a "religious conspiracy" as tied to sexual exploitation, particularly "white slavery" and women ending in "harems," not only aided in the creation and implementation of domestic laws as in the case of US history but also framed a great deal of international politics as will be discussed further in Chapter 5.

In 1904, a second manifesto fully banned polygamy though rumors persisted that such marriages continued despite the Church's policy officially renouncing the practice. Cynicism followed the disavowal of the practice. In April 1904, *Puck* offered two illustrations, one of which was the cover of its 20 April issue, noting and even warning against the ties of Latter-day polygamy to the State.[51] In a more light-hearted vein Winsor McCay's short lived 1912 series, *Ain't You Glad You're Not a Mormon*, which ultimately numbered three strips, followed the daily experiences of one man and his numerous wives (all drawn exactly the same).[52] Even as recently as the turn of the twenty-first century, the phrases "Mormon" and "polygamy" are bound in the cultural consciousness of most Americans,[53] but almost equally so are "Muslim" and "polygamy." The Immigration Act of 1907 went slightly further than the 1891 Act, excluding "polygamists, or persons who admit their belief in the practice of polygamy." In neither of these Acts were Muslims specifically singled out, while indeed Latter-day Saints were uppermost in the minds of policy makers for the 1891 Act. In the case of both Acts there was a sense, a feeling as it were, about who is and is not allowed into the United States.

The February 3, 1914, article of the *Washington Herald* discussed the proposed plans to officially exclude Japanese immigrants and argued that "under the present laws the Chinese and the Mohammedans are the only ones excluded."[54] Clearly, given the data from the Dillingham Report, this was not true, but the assumption that polygamy equals Muslim equals ban was commonly acknowledged as a truism.

In the context of the Philippines, Noyes referred to both slavery and polygamy as "the Mahometan Moro . . . incidentals," but very clearly considered slavery the more insidious of the two and frequently took pains to spell out the connections between it and polygamy (and, incidentally, piracy), just as Atkinson had four years earlier. These relationships are reinforced in Moloney's "Muslims, Mormons, and U.S. Deportation and Exclusion Policy" when she notes that "polygamy was linked both to slavery and despotic rule, and to ancient Muslim traditions that were viewed by many as antithetical to democratic, civilized, and American values and traditions."[55] As far back as 1857 those linkages were codified in US statesmanship, when Vermont senator Justin S. Morrill defined polygamy as a "Mohammedan barbarism revolting to the civilized world" and "Under the guise of religion, this people [Mormons] has established, and seek to maintain and perpetuate" the practice.[56] It is polygamy, he argued, "in its most disgusting form, including in its slimy folds sisters, mothers, and daughters: and in order that no clement of cruelty and loathsomeness may be wanting, it includes facility for divorce."[57] When the Philippines first fell under American purview, *The San Francisco Call* questioned not only the rightfulness of maintaining slavery in the Philippines but also polygamy. The hypocritical attempt to protect Muslim polygamy in the Philippines and deny it to Latter-day Saints in Utah was not lost on the *Call's* author. Not that "standing upon a principle inherited in the constitution, this Government has the power to prohibit polygamy in the United States, and used that power and prohibition over Utah. . . . Yet," it cynically questions, "we cannot prevent a Mahometan from holding office in the United States though he have [*sic*] the full allowance of four wives. . . . How can we prohibit polygamy in one place, taught as religious ordinance, and permit it in another because the constitution forbids a religious test?"[58] Polygamy, barbarism, bondage, Mormonism, and Islam were welded together, intentionally or not, from very early on in US history.

The sensational qualities of polygamy certainly helped sell papers and images, for this reason alone journalists kept returning to the theme. While force was taken against polygamist Latter-day Saints' communities at the end of the nineteenth century (many polygamists were jailed), it was at immigration centers that other anti-polygamy campaigns were waged. Moloney focuses on cases of Muslim deportations taking place in and after 1910, but even before that, in November 1897, newspapers across the United States ran stories about six men, originating in the Ottoman Empire, who were to be deported back to Turkey "because they admit believing in polygamy."[59]

Several articles covered the case, but the New York's *Sun* was particularly detailed. The *Sun* argued that this was likely to be a test case, to define with certainty similar future issues. It also reported that there was at least one basis of appeal open to the men: "That merely because a man's religion makes him a believer in polygamy does not constitute him a polygamist so long as he observes the marriage laws of this country."[60] The men, including one fifteen- or sixteen-year-old, were alternately referred to as Turks and Syrians but universally understood to be Muslims. The author clearly questioned the idea that "a believer in the religious tenet of polygamy was a polygamist in the eyes of the United States immigration laws, even though the believer be but 15 years of age and never had kissed a woman save his mother."[61] The hitch in this story came when the article's author contacted the immigration official responsible for the decision to deport the men. The author noted that because the immigration official was himself an Armenian, this may have been an opportunity to "get even," even if it had little to nothing to do with the practice of polygamy.

N. J. Arbeely (Najeeb Arbeely), the immigration official in question, was one of two brothers believed to have helped found the newspaper *Kawkab America* (Star of America), "the first Arabic-language newspaper published in the United States." The Harrisburg *Telegraph*, in 1892, reported on the publication of *Kawkab America* noting that the Arbeely brothers (N. J. and A. J.) "are Christians, and expect most of their support from Syrian Christians, but will, of course, avoid anything calculated to offend Mohammedans."[62] Amid the *Telegraph's* description of the *Kawkab* offices is an accompanied illustration. The "A Glimpse of the Office" depicts a man sitting with his back to the viewer and working at a roll-top desk. The rest of the room informs us of the "Oriental" character of the office. There appear to be no less than three hookahs in the image, one absurdly left in the middle of the room, one on the window sill, and one handing on the wall. The Boston *Post*, in 1894, reported on "Gotham's Foreign Colonies," highlighting the *Kawkab* offices as well. The *Post* described them as "fashioned for comfort and repose instead of work. Divans are arranged about the walls, soft rugs strew the floor, and the walls are covered with Eastern curios—a bit of ancient Damascus set down in latter-day New York."[63] N. J. Arbeely was a noted scholar and spoke many languages, which served him well in this time working at Ellis Island. His brother, A. J., was a physician. It is unlikely their offices were anything short of work appropriate. The *Post's* insistence on highlighting the Oriental opulence of the office, as was done to a lesser degree in the illustration from the *Telegraph*, reinforces the realities of an "Us" versus "Them" narrative, in particular the hardworking white American in juxtaposition with the more indolent Easterner.

Returning to the immigration case that came before N. J. Arbeely in 1897, he presented his arguments before a special inquiry board the preceding Wednesday.

> The law distinctly states that a polygamist cannot enter, just as it bars specifically persons coming here under contract to labor, or persons suffering from foul

contagious diseases. A believer in the Koran is certainly a polygamist. He must be. I was born in Turkey and I am a student of the Koran. . . . I heard men subscribe to that faith and it seemed to me they came within the purview of the law. They are polygamists and should not be allowed here. We should remember that now there is great danger of war in the East a great many Mohammedans may try to come here to avoid military service. First thing we knew we would be having harems all over the country. And you know the Koran allows a really rich man to have even fifty wives if he supports them well. Now, that would be a nice thing, wouldn't it!

So far as I know this is the first case of its kind. The law was passed, I believe, to shut out Mormon immigration, and no doubt there are a number of Mohammedans who have been admitted. They probably were sharp enough to deny their belief in polygamy. I should be satisfied if some of these men's friends would go to the front for them and appeal the case to Washington in order that it might be settled definitely.[64]

Arbeely's assessment of the situation, aside from the faulty assertion that the religion condones as many as fifty wives, was one possible interpretation and certainly created a basis for legal evaluation.

It is unclear what happened to these six men, but it is abundantly clear that polygamy remained a feature of immigration controls. In 1902, then US Commissioner General of Immigration, T. V. Powderly wrote that "polygamists, unless practicing polygamy, or acknowledging that it is their clear intention to practice it, are not excluded" from immigrating to the United States.[65] Accordingly, to Powderly, the questions of belief in and practice of could be, and should be, two separate things. Because of the first amendment to the constitution, Powderly noted someone may not only believe in the practice of polygamy but also deny his/her own current or future participation it that practice.[66] The Immigration Act of 1907, however, more solidly sided with Arbeely's interpretation. In 1914 Senator Smoot argued, in reference to the Latter-day Saint's practice of polygamy, that "one of the articles of faith of the Church is that 'we believe the Bible to be the word of God.' The Bible particularly the Old Testament, sanctions polygamy and if a Mormon were asked, 'Do you believe in the Bible?' he would say yes."[67] Nevertheless, the Immigration Act of 1917 specifically forbade "polygamists, or persons who practice polygamy or believe in or advocate the practice of polygamy."[68]

In 1883, the US Consul at Basel, Switzerland, presented the idea that polygamy could be used as a way of excluding immigrants, being classified as "undesirable."[69] As Moloney has noted, "Widespread anti-polygamy activism emerged as a response to Utah territory's quest for statehood, but its roots were deeper."[70] Just as Senator Morrill declared "Mohammedan barbarism revolting to the civilized world,"[71] tensions over polygamy propelled the distance between suffrage reformers and immigrant rights activists. Using "anti-immigrant rhetoric to bolster their positions," pressures between the rights of, primarily elite, white, and Protestant, women in opposition to lower class, nonwhite, and non-Protestant peoples continued well into the twentieth century.[72]

In 1906, President Roosevelt's State of Union Address "declared that it was the federal government's role not the states', to safeguard 'the home life of the average citizen,' by providing 'Congress the power at once to deal radically and efficiently with polygamy.'"[73] Roosevelt's focus on "the home life of the average citizen," as being one of normative monogamy permeated journalistic understandings of the Philippines long after Utah statehood. In 1924 (and running well into 1925), a syndicated column declared, "the absence of civilization in the southern provinces of the Philippine Islands is attributed to the lack of home life and the practice of polygamy among the native Moros."[74] The notion that home life was impossible to have with anything other than monogamy suggested both a naivety on the part of the authors and arrogant ethnocentrism. It also speaks to the underlying racial concerns that circulated alongside the practice of polygamy.

What is more, the First World War did not diminish the discussion of polygamy. As will be discussed in Chapter 4, fears of polygamy becoming de facto in Western states rippled through anti-German propaganda. Similarly, in the follow-up to the war, when mandatory control was being parceled out, the United States was considered as the mandatory power for Turkey, and at least a handful of American journalists and policy thinkers spoke out against the idea contending that "we must either recognize polygamy as a national institution, or begin a Holy War and fight all Mohammadans."[75] The article stoked the fire asking, "Are we prepared to raise another army of a million or so men to prevent the Mohammedan hordes of the world from going in for the free and unlimited coinage of wives?"[76] Looking back on the United States antagonism with the Church of Latter-day Saints, the author noted, revisiting Roosevelt's normative home structure, "that marriage means a home and not a swine stye [*sic*]."[77] That there was a racialized component to all of this was never in doubt. In 1918, the Illinois based *Free Trader Journal* declared, "Menace to Caucasian Race: Practice of Polygamy in the Orient Constitutes Peril Which Must Not be Underestimated." The article fed on race fears observing that "the Caucasian population of the world is doubling its number once in a hundred years; the dark-skinned races, which now outnumber the white population two to one, are doubling their numbers every twenty-five years."[78] Oddly, the focus of the article's data came from Korea, and particularly on the idea that the "oriental demands male children, as many of them as he can produce."[79] In light of the fear of polygamy and even race wars brought on by population increases, it was hardly surprising that the pictorial embodiment of polygamy, namely the Harem, became so central in portraying Islam in US media at the turn of the twentieth century.

Harem Peeping

Dane Kennedy has observed that, for Victorian Britons, "Islam remained a strange and menacing faith . . . , known mainly in terms of Orientalist stereotypes about polygamy, harems, and other exotic practices."[1] The same may be said for Americans at the fin de siècle. Through popular culture, US audiences became cognizant of what the Orient was *supposed* to be, having been trained by adventure tales, travel memoirs, and artistic representations. C. W. Kahles, the author and illustrator of the *Hairbreadth Harry* comic series, dipped into this font of knowledge for storylines. In one series, we find Harry's beloved, Belinda, in the clutches of the dastardly Rudolph, Harry's nemesis. Belinda must tell Rudolph a story each week to keep him from killing her.[2] The Scheherazade frame used in this series, which ran in the *Washington Herald* between October and November 1922, was not unique to Kahles's comic. It was a common formula for authors and artists at the turn of the twentieth century and before. In 1888, Nikolai Rimsky-Korsakov produced the symphonic suite *1001 Arabian Nights*. From there the ballet adaptation, *Scheherazade*, opened in Paris in 1910. The tales and their reimaginations were very much present in the cultural consciousness of Western audiences. What is perhaps more interesting is how Kahles and other cartoonists added layers to the Orientalist genre.

Kahles's *Arabian Nights* and *Scheherazade* series included the following:

1. "The Story of Rudolpho and his Forty Yeggs"
2. "A Story of A. Laddin and the Wonderful Lamp"
3. "The Story of Inbad the Jailor, the Country Maid, and the Wicked Rudolpho"
4. "The Tale of Bel-in-dah and Blue Whiskers"
5. "The Story of the Magic Camel"
6. "Story of the Genie and the Magic Trumpet"

Each of the stories in the series, as well as other adventures set in Kahles's Orient, drew heavily from common tropes of the time. Tales like "Bel-in-dah and Blue

Whiskers"³ allow us to look more deeply into the nature of the female/feminine Orient in US cartoons and popular culture.

"Bel-in-dah and Blue Whiskers" begins with "a guy with eight wives" who one day "got kinda soft hearted and took 'em all . . . out for an airing" (Figure 4.1). The "guy," Blue Whiskers, is dressed in what may be termed "Oriental attire"— he is beturbaned, wearing billowing pants and long jacket, and is replete with scimitar. It is cast as perfectly normal for Blue Whiskers and his attendant guard to walk the streets with their scimitars unsheathed. The wives too are dressed in an Oriental style—harem pants, vests, and wispy veils. In the process of directing his wives about, Blue Whiskers's gaze falls upon "the beautiful princess Bel-in-dah" who he declares shall be Mrs. Bluebeard number nine.⁴

The assumption in the "Bel-in-dah" story, as in most harem-based narratives, is that women are easily procured, and they exist without agency or free will of their own. This masculine access and control over feminine bodies and spaces is a common component of Orientalized fiction but may simultaneously fly in the face of interpretations intended by authors like Richard Burton, who wrote one of the most celebrated translations/adaptations of *1001 Arabian Nights*. According to Kennedy, Burton "vigorously objects to the view that such women are chattel intended to gratify the desires of men, condemning [this belief] as a Western misconception about relations between the sexes in Eastern societies. He believes Muslim women enjoy freedoms all but unknown to their Christian British counterparts, especially regarding property and inheritance rights."⁵ As Kennedy further acknowledges, "One of the most noteworthy features of [Burton's translation of] Arabian Nights is the independence and influence of its female characters."⁶ This independence, not to mention outright power, is important to bear in mind, particularly as the Arabian Nights get blended with other, generally European, fairy tales.

We should not overemphasis Burton's progressive insights into feminine matters. Burton was a paradox on the question of equality among the sexes, especially in seeing women as sexual objects. This makes him a fascinating corollary to William Moulton Marston, the original author of *Wonder Woman*. Burton, who appears to have had at least a passing fascination with bondage and slavery as a device for understanding sexual relations, is just as much a contradiction as Marston, who, in 1937, "predicted that women would rule the world."⁷ Despite this deep-seated feminist leaning, however, when directed by the publisher of the *Wonder Woman* comic series, Max Gaines, to reduce the use of chains and ropes in binding characters, particularly women, Marston refused. The fear, expressed in reader letters, that Wonder Woman was playing right into

Figure 4.1 "Hairbreadth Harry: The Tale of Bel-in-Dah and Blue Whickers," by C. W. Kahles. *The Washington Herald*. October 29, 1922.

the hands of men interested in bondage as a sexual fantasy, bothered Marston very little, declaring "Harmless erotic fantasies are terrific."[8] Both Marston and Burton struggled in their works to define the lines between sexual control and sexual freedom. Neither accomplished the task of understanding his own position vis-à-vis women, sex, and control, but in both cases their work had a tremendous impact on the cultural assumptions about women, sex, and control, in both Western and global settings.

The specific case of the "Bel-in-dah" story has yet another aspect which needs elaboration. In this particular episode, Kahles conflates the *1001 Arabian Nights* and the seventeenth-century French fairy-tale *Barbe bleue* (*Bluebeard*). Originally set in France, *Bluebeard* is the story of a young woman married off to an aristocratic, wealthy, older man. The husband, who had a history of serial marriages, all ending under mysterious circumstances, brought his newest wife home and gave her the keys to the castle. He bid her to explore to her heart's content with the one exception that she never goes into one room/closet. The wife's curiosity gets the better of her, and one day while Bluebeard is out, she opens the room only to find the mutilated bodies and heads of the previous wives. Before Bluebeard helps her to join them, the wife is saved by her brothers and male cousins.

In George Colman the Younger's stage adaptation (1798), *Blue-Beard; or Female Curiosity!* the story was relocated "to the Orient, and Blue-Beard became Abomelique, a Turkish despot."[9] Bluebeard, after the staging of Colman's play, became synonymous with Ottoman, or Oriental, despotism. He was "the stereotype of an oriental stage tyrant," while the story continued to be a tale of violent misogyny. Casie Hermansson argues that the Oriental Bluebeard is the "most enduringly popular English Bluebeard, perfectly poised as he was to become the blundering buffoon . . . of nineteenth-century harlequinade and pantomime, the endearing butt of the lovers' joke."[10] The further evolution to which Hermansson refers, with Bluebeard becoming a buffoon in later iterations, helps underscore the significance of the "sidekick" depictions of Turks in the First World War era cartoons.

The unification of *Bluebeard* and the *Arabian Nights* is aided by the nature of the husband in both stories. The king, Shahryar, of the *Arabian Nights*, having once been betrayed by a wife, takes a new wife every night for three years, executing her in the morning because of this ingrained mistrust of women. This murderous legacy comes to an end when he meets and marries Scheherazade, the daughter of his vizier. For 1001 nights, Scheherazade tells a story to Shahryar ending on a cliff-hanger every morning, which encourages him to keep her alive for one more night, so he can hear more of the story. Unlike Bluebeard, however, Scheherazade's tales lead Shahryar to becoming a better man, a better ruler, and more trusting of women. Through Scheherazade's actions, Shahryar is redeemed. Through the actions of Bluebeard's wife, Bluebeard's homicidal tendencies are revealed, but there is no redemption.

In Coleman's play Bluebeard's wife is named "Fatima," but she is not clearly named in the original story. The reader is informed that she is the youngest daughter of her family, and her sister Anne is identified, but she herself lacks even the simplest marker of identity—a name. That the Bluebeard and Scheherazade's stories should be conflated is telling not only of the Orientalization undergone in the evolution of the tale(s) but also of the distinct parallel between murderous, serial-monogamous husbands.

Interestingly, Kahles's Bluebeard straddles the violence of the French tale and the hedonism of the Western interpretation of the Arabian Nights. Even though Blue Whiskers's wives seem physically unharmed and do nothing other than trail around after him (one even saying, "Gee! This is a dull life!"), we get a sense of the more sinister nature of the man, but only when the rescuer, "El-Hari," notes that "a lot of dames have been strangely disappearing in here."

Between 1880 and 1920, the term "Bluebeard" emerges in several places in US newspapers. A brief glimpse at the Google n-gram generator indicates that, in the case of American English, the term "Bluebeard" reached a peak in about 1900. In general English usage, the term peaked once in about 1900 and again about 1923. This second peak is likely connected to sensational case in France, which papers, even in the United States, were avidly covering. Dubbed the "French Bluebeard," Henri Landru was tried, convicted, and executed between 1921 and 1922. The fact that the papers referred to Landru as the "French Bluebeard" or the "Bluebeard of Paris" suggests that significant disassociation had taken place between France and the Bluebeard legend.[11]

In 1903 a single-page-paneled comic "The True Story of Bluebeard's Forbidden Room" made light of the domestic abuse/murder inherent in the tale and simultaneously derided the vanity and despotism of the "wrathful Turk." The Fatima/wife character entered the forbidden room to find her husband's beard dyeing paraphernalia, his hair being naturally red. Just on the point of his discovering her and being near to killing her, police officer Brother Stephanapolos arrives with an arrest warrant for Bluebeard, alias "Red-Whiskered Abdullah." Bluebeard/Abdullah being naturally redheaded suggests a parallel with the common assumption of negative traits foisted on redheaded historical figures, most notably Judas Iscariot, and thus anchoring it in traditions the audience is likely aware of. One may read into this closing scene an added element of geopolitical interpretation, either of Greco-Turkish, or perhaps Christian-Muslim, antagonism in the arrival of Brother Stephanapolos (perhaps even named for Saint Stephan) as the wife's rescuer.[12]

The disturbing imagery of a violent, and typically Oriental, husband married to a fair, young woman found expression in other cartoons of the era as well. In the *Tacoma Times* January 1, 1904, issue, "Miss Bluebeard, 1904" became the poster woman for the ominous potential of a new year (Figure 4.2). Her depiction, arm linked with an aging Oriental man, indicates the freshness of the New Year, but the line of disembodied female heads behind her, tacked to the wall under their corresponding years is an ill-omen of how her own year will end.[13] There is no context for this cartoon, beyond the newspaper being a New Year's Day publication. Unlike its paneled mates, "Miss Bluebeard" does not provide much internal context either. Still, despite the traditional narrative of the story

Figure 4.2 "Miss Bluebeard, 1904," by Walter C. Kledaisch. *The Tacoma Times.* January 1, 1904.

focusing on the marriage of Bluebeard to his various wives, the creator titled it "Miss" Bluebeard, and not "Mrs." One wonders if "Miss Bluebeard" is aware of her choice, if indeed she has a choice, as it appears from the cartoon that she and Bluebeard have just had a leisurely stroll through the room of the disembodied ex-wives' heads. Her face is upturned, and her eyes look almost happy, certainly not demure or apprehensive. Is 1904 cognizant of its predecessors or moving forward/away from what has come before? Alternatively, the "Miss" may indicate that we are being introduced to Bluebeard's daughter. Perhaps the artist is suggesting the callous, murderous nature of Bluebeard is being handed down to the next generation. If this interpretation is to be taken seriously, one may ask too if the artist is suggesting a negative interpretation of rising feminist power.

In 1920, John Sheldon, for the *Washington Times* (D.C.), reported on three cases of men acting out the Bluebeard account in real life. Despite the fact that Sheldon's article highlighted the original story's French heritage and the cases of at least two Anglo-North Americans, the newspaper ran an illustration which included the then commonplace Oriental despot, complete with turban, scimitar, and a scantily clad woman on her knees at his feet (Figure 4.3). Sheldon's article does include one case which brings the reader to Egypt: the story of a man named Ben Husof, who allegedly beheaded twenty women "of good families" outside of Cairo. It is possible this one portion of the article is the reason for the nearly full-page illustration, but it is just as likely that American audiences were well trained by 1920 to expect the Oriental Bluebeard in depiction alongside any Bluebeard or Bluebeard-like tale.[14] Indeed, of the 8,506 pages returned on the Library of Congress's Chronicling America database (of a potential 12,252,412), for the term "Bluebeard," associated images come in three categories.[15] The first are photographs, either of actors playing parts in Bluebeard plays and films or of men accused of being modern-day Bluebeards and their victims. The second is a void of a category, most pages returning no associated images. The third and final category is accompanied by *illustrations* in Orientalist taste and tone.

The Bluebeard and Arabian Nights motifs went beyond a purely entertainment quality as they were frequently employed for explaining political events and personalities. Kaiser Wilhelm, for example, was often "Orientalized," particularly by *Punch* cartoonist Bernard Partridge. In one such cartoon, which was reproduced in the US *Cartoon Magazine*, the reality that the First World War had reached its one thousandth and one day fed into the general *Arabian Nights* thread, as the "official story teller" (re: Scheherazade) explains that she is out of fairy tales but offers him a "true" one instead.[16] Similarly, in November 1894, the Parisian periodical *La Silhouette* ran a cartoon called "William Bluebeard," later

Figure 4.3 "Modern Bluebeards" image alongside John Sheldon's "Unearthing the Crimes of Modern Bluebeards." *The Washington Times*. June 6, 1920.

reprinted in US literary periodicals like *The Bookman*.[17] "William Bluebeard," discussed in *The Bookman*'s "The History of the Nineteenth Century in Caricature," depicted Wilhelm II "warning Hohenlohe and pointing to a closet in which are hanging the bodies of Bismarck and Caprivi robed in feminine apparel." Wilhelm says, "My first two wives are dead. Take care, Hohenlohe lest the same fate overtake you!"[18] We have already seen this Orientalization of Wilhelm, as in the Kaiser's tour "Around the Orient Circle." The difference in these two cases is who is doing the Orientalization. In the examples like "William Bluebeard," the cartoon's creator has taken away Wilhelm's choice, foisting on him the appeal of the Oriental Bluebeard. In the "Around the Orient Circle," the creator gives Wilhelm the agency to choose to bedeck himself in Oriental costumes.

Such use of *Bluebeard* and *Arabian Nights* motifs extended well back into the nineteenth century. General Benjamin Butler was "Orientalized" a number of times, most notably for our purposes, on a visiting card held at the Library of Congress, which is a depiction of Butler, military governor of New Orleans at the time, as Bluebeard "for challenging the behavior of the city's Confederate women toward Union soldiers. 'John Bull' looks on in horror as Butler holds a woman by her hair in one hand and a large bloody cutlass in the other."[19] Butler's Orientalization is clear in his "Turkish attire" and cutlass, reminiscent of the scimitar so frequently equated with Middle Eastern and Islamic peoples.[20] Similarly, in 1906, Udo J. Keppler produced for *Puck* "A Tip to Fatima Ted," with Fatima Ted being Theodore Roosevelt and Bluebeard the "Protected Monopolies." Playing on the nature of Coleman's Bluebeard characters, this Bluebeard holds "Keys to Rate Regulation, Meat Inspection, Pure Food and Anti-Trust Laws" and informs Fatima Ted that he (she) may go as far as he likes, just as long as he does not go into the room marked "Tariff Revision."[21] In both the Fatima Ted and William Bluebeard pieces men cross-dress to carry out the story, suggesting that the power dynamic between the masculine "Bluebeards" and the feminized wives is being challenged. Unlike the original Bluebeard wife, both Hohenlohe and Roosevelt are named, but neither is successful in their associated efforts. Unlike the typical end to the Bluebeard story, these "wives" did not both satisfy their curiosity and get away with it.

The Shriners and male space

The "feminine" and "masculine" tropes we see illustrated in *Arabian Nights*– and *Bluebeard*-inspired cartoons further situate them in a period noted for shifting cultural sensibilities on questions of gender identity. In other parts of popular culture, the broadly constructed Islamic world acted as a means of redefining gendered expectations for US audiences. According to William D. Moore, the relatively new Shriners fraternity, a derivative of the Masons, "viewed the Arab world as being both alien and without chronology. Within Shrine circles no distinction was made between the worlds of nineteenth-century Islam and

Pharaonic Egypt. 'Isis' and 'Mecca' were equally valid Oriental names for Shrine temples."[22] According to *A Short History: Shriners Hospitals for Children and Shriners of North America*, the membership numbered about 55,000 in 1900; by 1919 that number had grown to 363,744.[23]

Susan Nance maintains that, of Shriner Temples and adherents, "American fraternalists sought to enjoy two identities at once: authentically masculine wise man of the East and successfully affluent man of the West."[24] This distinction between Eastern men and Western men finds a corollary in Susan Kollin's *Captivating Westerns* through her examination of Christine Bold's "frontier club." In works like Kollin's, Bold's, and G. Edward White's, elite men of the Eastern United States were shaped in their formative years by the region's economic development but chose to leave the East, to go West "in order to experience a new start." This resultant "frontier club" of "self-made men" like Frederic Remington, Theodore Roosevelt, and Owen Wister "worked hard to shore up their influence, not only by managing public opinion but also by directing federal policies in the areas of land use, race relations, and popular press," largely as a response to "threats from new immigration and completion from new wealth."[25] This playing Eastern, Nance goes on, "like the arts of blackface or playing Indian, in which whites performed in hybrid guises, wise men of the East wore a guise that similarly adapted Arab and Middle Eastern masculinities to Anglo-American identities in ways that 'mediat[ed] white men's relations with other white men.'"[26] While Kollin et al. are seeking rationale and codification of the genre "Western" their insights are reinforced on a more localized scale by the Shriner's temples, as places where the New American Man can build his identity through a process of acquisition and appropriation. Moore reasons that "the spaces utilized by the Ancient Arabic Order of the Nobles of the Mystic Shrine to assist individuals in playing the fool and thus to embrace a new masculinity based on personality, rather than upon character."[27] Moore's work reinforces the idea that negative stereotypes played out in the popular press of the day, and that "the Arab, [was] artificially conceived as without the need to work and unfettered by Christian morality, and thus living in a state approximating perpetual boyhood, proved a perfect foil for the conception of masculinity that American men were attempting to discard in this period."[28] There is a gulf of difference between Moore's and Nance's interpretations, but what both argue together is that the *actual* Arab, Egyptian, Muslim, and so on are nowhere to be seen. Ironically, however, an 1893 *Kawkab America* article suggests there may be more to the story. The *Kawkab* article describes the evening's events of "The Carnival of the Mystic Shrine," held at Madison Square Garden, in the same detail other newspapers of the era afforded Shriner gatherings. There is no spoken judgment in the English language piece, but one cannot help but wonder if there is some cynicism with which the topic was approached.[29] None of the named participants appear to be from the Syrian or Arab communities; thus, it is likely that the spectacle was just an interesting piece to cover, and yet again just as in so many of these comics, Muslim and Middle Eastern personages and styles are plot devices in the background, not active participants in the fore.

The harem and female space

The issues which arise in Moore's discussion of space and the construction of masculinity are also significant in examining cartoons of the era in the projection of the harem and the bath as both feminine and violable. Unlike the Shriner's temples and other men's clubs of the era which prided themselves on their exclusivity, and centrality as a male domain, the harem was accessible, a Mt. Everest for the adventurous man.

In the *Jerry MacJunk* series, as syndicated in *The Ogden Standard* in 1918,[30] the comic's protagonist sets sail on something like a "Grand Tour," much like Kaiser Wilhelm's 1898 travels in the Levant and Egypt. Less formal than the travel writing of the nineteenth century, in particular, the subgenre of travel writing about Palestine, MacJunk's series plays with many of the same tropes. The experience allows MacJunk to learn about guidebooks, art, and dining in foreign locales. The thread of this series ran in Ogden throughout spring 1918 and took MacJunk to Italian settings and desert or Oriental destinations where he said, "I can get a peep at an Arabian harem."[31] The series appears to have been printed out of order, bouncing between Near Eastern or North African and Italian settings in an unnatural way. This was probably not done intentionally, nor was it the only instance of a misprinted series. The disorganized issuance coupled with its syndicated lag time had the unintended consequence of further emphasizing the "Otherness" of the Mediterranean world. By conflating Italian experiences with Levantine and North African ones the comic informs the general US populous that all Mediterranean cultures are essentially one in the same. Locating where MacJunk is in the region is made difficult by the lack of clear visual cues, and readers are forced to rely on his commentary to get a better sense of location. In one of the more clearly "Oriental" locales, buildings have a vague Middle Eastern look with domes and crescent moons, and there are camels, palm trees, and prickly pear cactus to indicate the desert, all very like

Moore's description of the Shriner Temples. We are only certain of his location when MacJunk clearly states, "So this is Algiers."

To cap his travels in Algeria, MacJunk convinces a local man (as he refers to him, "an Arabian coffee drinker") to help him sneak that peek at a local harem (Figure 4.4). In the style of the adventurers Richard Burton or Johann Ludwig Burckhardt, MacJunk disguises himself as "an Arab," and his guide says, "I've advised lots of Americans on this trick—the main idea is to act as much like an Arab as any Arab can talk Arabic—that'll fool them."[32] Clearly Walter Hoban, MacJunk's creator, understood harem peeping to be as much a part of the Westerner's tour cycle as a museum or a set of ruins (both of which MacJunk takes in in due course in Italy, Spain, France, and Germany). Just as the artist of "the Kaiser's Swing around the Oriental Circle" offered up a vignette of the Kaiser glimpsing a harem, the expectation was that such a scene is essential to travel narratives of the Orient. When MacJunk enters the harem and spies a woman he loudly proclaims, "Hello Kid—How's the chicken?" When he is kicked out of the harem by the guard, the last panel has him cursing in what we are supposed to believe is Arabic, but is just nonsensical squiggles.

By the fin de siècle there was an expectation that wealthy, even moderately well to do Americans and Europeans were to travel the world in search of experience and education. That the harem and the women of the "Orient" were

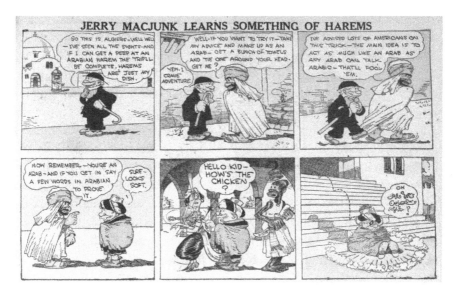

Figure 4.4 "Jerry MacJunk Learns Something of Harems," by Walter Hoban. *The Ogden Standard*. April 27, 1918.

a part of that education, for male travelers in particular, was assumed as well. As Rana Kabbani notes in her work *Europe's Myths of the Orient*, "Europe was charmed by the Orient that shimmered with possibilities, that promised a sexual space, a voyage away from the self, an escape from the dictates of the bourgeois morality of the metropolis."[33] By the turn of the twentieth century, the mystique of the Orient, in particular the harem, was equally "charming" in American discourse. An equal element in "knowing" the world through travel was the aspect of "conquering" it, and in the cartoons at least, the pantomime nature of the characters tended to satirically question the "conqueror" narrative. MacJunk, for example, fumbles his way through his travels and although he gets into a harem he is quickly rushed out again, because of his loud and brash (one may argue stereotypically American) self.

In a similar vein, *Mutt and Jeff* took their turn peeping into harem life and exploring the Ottoman Empire, in "Mutt Finds the Scenery Annoying" (Figure 4.5).[34] The keyhole view of a harem Mutt acquires from the less than scrupulous guard is both reminiscent of Jean Auguste Dominique Ingres's "The Turkish Bath" (1863) and the theoretical concept of the imperial gaze. The fanciful harem and the associated bath were common tropes not only in cartoons but also in general newspaper discussion. *The Ladies' Home Journal* reported that "'The Book of the Thousand Night and One Night,' as translated by Sir Richard Burton, gives us pictures of the bath we would find it impossible to equal to-day. Not only was the bath a means of luxury in those days, but its hygienic value was known and appreciated."[35] A 1908 newspaper article, the "Joy of Bathing," described the "Harem Bath," verbally, in the same sexualized, and racialized, tones artists like Jean-Léon Gérôme painted:

> The Mohammedan bell bathes amid all the mystery suggested by those of her pictures which we see adorning the inner sanctuaries of our frisky old bachelors and widowers. Attended by her black slave, she cools herself in the harem pool,

Figure 4.5 "Mutt Finds the Scenery Very Annoying," by Bud Fisher. *El Paso Herald*, February 20, 1913.

hidden in the inmost of inner courtyards, and around which—'tis said (the writers has never been admitted)—loll other fair creatures, combing their hair and painting their eyebrows.[36]

The harem was integral to Western conceptions of the East

The harem, the bath, and perceptions about race and racial divisions were also intrinsically tangled in these productions. The harem guard in MacJunk is depicted in much the same way other black characters were drawn at the time. The Algerian helping MacJunk is slightly darker than MacJunk, though not as dark as the guard, and has a scraggly beard and enormous nose. MacJunk and the harem woman are drawn with light skin, with the woman featuring a petit nose and a figure reminiscent of Betty Boop. A white- or light-skinned harem girl (or, more correctly, woman), like many of the other motifs at play in these comics, was not surprising for the era. Orientalist artists almost universally depicted the women of the harem with "pure white" skin, and other individuals *in* the harem, but not necessarily *of* the harem, with varying degrees of darker skin depending on their station. These ethnic clues are similar in the Blue Whiskers's issue of *Hairbreadth Harry*. The Blue Whiskers's harem ladies, as best as we can tell from the drawing, are all light-skinned, whereas Blue Whiskers himself is slightly darker, and the guard is so black he lacks nearly all facial definition. This racialized understanding of the Orient, and particularly the harem was thoroughly incorporated into US media. In an 1882 advertisement for Belle of Nelson whiskey the advertising company lifted liberally from Jean-Léon Gérôme's *c.* 1876, "Pool in a Harem," in part because of the artistic beauty of the piece, in part because Orientalist art work, motifs, and tropes were pervasive and well understood.[37] The Belle of Nelson ad may too have used the Oriental setting, complete with racialized hierarchies, as a way of inspiring nostalgia in some of its drinking audience. As we have seen elsewhere, there was a general uneasiness with the practice of slavery when it came into contact with modern American structures, as in the case of the Philippines, but there was an almost equal desire to excuse slavery in Islamic settings as being somehow different, less morally problematic, and even "quaint."

The visual and literary depictions were not alone in their commodification of the idea of a harem. Irving Berlin's 1919 "Oriental foxtrot," *Harem Life*, is another example of an avenue through which the harem was embedded in US popular culture. The song's narrator sings:

> While trav'ling through Turkey in my dreams
> I chanced to stray
> Right into a harem.[38]

Much like the comics of the day, traveling in the East was frequently done by Westerners in their dreams. The Orient, more to the point, the harem, in dreams was another well-established motif by the time Berlin was writing. Jacques Bousquet's examination of the historical change in dreams over time noticed "a frequency in those dreams [between 1830 and 1870] depicting harems and orgies, where the dreamer could possess a multiplicity of women."[39] Kabbani observes that "this type of dream came to be transferred to the artistic *oeuvre*" which by the 1910s was well beyond the canvass, on the silver screen and in the gramophone.

As discussed in Chapter 2, N. J. Arbeely's insistence on the nature of "rules" governing the number of wives in a harem was often dismissed in favor of more fanciful visions. As Berlin's narrator says,

> I wanted to know how many wives The Sultan had
> She answered each day a wife arrives Fresh from Baghdad.[40]

The assumed fluidity of the harem's existence is evident in both the song and artwork. The song's narrator "stumbles" into the harem just as Gérôme appears to be granted full and unguarded access to the most private of all spaces in Islamic, or any, households. Only the author of "Joy of Bathing" admits to not actually being allowed into the harem baths and acknowledges his reliance on these other sources. Despite reality, illustrations and cartoons, like the cover of *Life* magazine from 1912, continued to indicate that accessing the harem was fairly easy for a plucky (white) man.[41]

It is doubtful that the guard of the harem Gérôme is depicting and the guard of the harem on *Life* cover are the same guard as in Irving Berlin's other harem song: *I'm the Guy Who Guards the Harem*. In the song, the guard declares,

> I'm the guy who guards the harem
> When the Sultan goes away
> I'm a conscientious Turk and my heart is in my work
> The Sultan tells me that I earn my pay
> While he's gone I keep them happy
> And it keeps the wheels a-working in my knob
> If the Sultan ever saw the way I guard his harem, he
> Would go out and engage someone to stand guard over me
> I'm the guy who guards the harem
> And I wouldn't take a million for my job.[42]

Berlin's harem guard achieves personal satisfaction from his employment by keeping a secure lock on the harem doors from all but the Sultan . . . and himself.

Amid all of this discussion of the harem we should note that the harem at the fin de siècle really cannot be divorced from the broader depiction of the "Turk," Islam, or the average person from what would today be called the Middle East. Returning to *Mutt and Jeff*'s Turkish escapades, we find the notion that the harem was a feminine counterpoint to the masculine "unspeakable Turk" in the general analogy that polygamy is to harem as Mormonism is to Islam. In "Jeff's Bump of Caution," Jeff gives up his Oriental attire while on vacation in Istanbul, only to replace it when he hears of further massacres of Christians, presumably Armenians. This coupled with the aforementioned "Mutt Finds the Scenery Annoying" spell out US popular perceptions of physical distance from the Orient while active engagement with the Orient through gazing upon it and acquiring its *accoutrement* of culture.

The Harem and its cultural significance *in* American settings

As is suggested by all of the harem peeping, the Orient was a place of unbounded opulence and exoticism, not to mention eroticism. In this regard, the Harem and the Turkish bath played heavily into imagery associated with the Turk. Amid this discussion of the masculine/male image at odds with a feminine/female image. The male Turk is blood-thirsty, barbarous, and public. The female Turk is civilized (cleanliness is next to godliness, after all, and no harem depiction was complete without an associated bathing scene), beautiful, and secluded, if idle. Implied in the female imagery is the idea of oppression, that Turkish women are so oppressed, it is the duty of the civilized Christian Man to save her. Here the modern audience is reminded of G. K. Spivak's "white men saving brown women from brown men."[43] Ironically, as this antagonistic relationship between the Ottoman state and the American depicters of the Ottoman state continued, particularly through the masculine line of imagery, the Ottoman woman, and the harem more specifically, infiltrated the US consciousness as not only acceptable but at the symbolic heart of female liberation.

As discussed in the preceding chapter, the Republican Party platform of 1856 asserted that slavery and polygamy were the "twin relics of barbarism." It was not Islamic polygamy which occasioned such rhetoric but the Mormon practice of plural marriage. Separating Islam and Mormon philosophy was never really a goal of anti-polygamy campaigners, nor for that matter, was the idea that a "harem" simply referred to a space. The harem was rarely seen as an institutional practice, a natural part of any household, whether that household practiced polygamy or not. The "Otherness" of both Mormons and Muslims was reinforced though anti-polygamy laws and rhetoric in the United States throughout the late nineteenth and early twentieth centuries.

The "barbarous" nature of polygamy carried on as cultural *caché* well into the First World War, and there the discussion became even more tangled. The United States fought the First World War against the Germans, not the Ottomans, and as a result the very notion of the harem was imposed on the "Hun" and manipulated to further alienate "right thinking American's" from the German cause. Helen Ring Robinson, the first female state senator in Colorado, offered up, in the November 1918 *Pictorial Review*, the article "Making the World Safe for Monogamy." In this piece, Robinson argued that "the ideal of the German marriage as it has been shaped by militaristic madness is cannon-fodder . . . . So William the Prussian, in order to provide cannon-fodder for his next war, has frankly instituted in his Empire a system of 'secondary marriages' which is only another name for polygamy without the decencies of the Turkish system."[44] Robinson even closed the article with the sentence, "So my thoughts turn again to the men of the Allied armies, holding the line against the Hun and the Harem."[45] Polygamy, as expressed by Robinson, was un-American. Many papers reported on the idea of "secondary marriages," no matter how unlikely the concept was, and argued its un-Christian-ness.[46] The notion that Germany engaged in "secondary marriages" added to the antithetical nature of German sociopolitical structures as compared with US ones; reinforcing the very "otherness" anti-German propagandists sought to instill. Even the illustration which draws the eye to the article directly links Germans and Turks by depicting a male form representative of each standing above groups of women, shown with staring, horror-struck eyes or downcast expressions, very much evoking the feeling of the women being herded like cattle.

The view that Germany was creating an environment fertile for polygamous households was, however, rarely taken at face value. One 1918 Oklahoma newspaper succinctly gets at the jumbled nature of anti-German rhetoric and its manipulation in other ideological debates:

> Indeed, we are disposed to question reports from Germany of the spread of Brigham Young's favorite occupation in that country. There is little chance that it will find favor in any of the warring countries, except Turkey, where the harem is regarded as an inalienable right.[47]

This snarky little tidbit in an article, deriding the mild hysteria circulating around the idea that polygamy may even come to the United States as an outcome of the

First World War, encapsulates so well these themes. Once again not only are Germans and German leaders encircled by the symbolic imagery of Oriental tropes but even the institution of marriage and homelife had to be "Othered" in the name of the First World War effort.

Puck's Harem Girl

Much of the narrative we have seen thus far in the manipulation of the harem has taken a male-centric orientation; yet, as much as polygamy and harem were linked in defining Islamic and non-Islamic men, so too were the harem and suffrage linked in defining female tropes, particularly in the guise of fashion. Oriental style not only was a "source of commercial kitsch especially in the 1920s," but also helped more than one population reestablish or reorient their identity. Sally Howell, in focusing on Detroit, contends that for "many southern black migrants to Detroit" there was a general appropriation "of clothing, religious trappings, names and identities."[48] It is, therefore, hardly surprising to see Oriental inspired fashion reshaping gender politics.

In 1911, the illustrated American magazine *Puck* ran a cover image entitled "Harem Girl" (Figure 4.6).

Puck's cover is a fascinating look into how the United States was coming to terms with changing ideologies and styles. The "harem pants" were a convenient step between the skirt and the trouser, aided in part by their association with the ultimate(ly) feminine "harem" origins. Simultaneously, their association with the Orient and the harem and their nature as essentially pants made them equally revolutionary, as understood by the aghast reaction of the gentleman in the background of the image. The fact that the cover is a cartoon is in and of itself yet a further statement about the role the medium played in developing national (and international) norms.

On April 11, 1911, the *Tacoma Times* ran an article about British cartoonist Harry Furniss, claiming that as "the greatest of English cartoonists now doing active work, [he] is an ardent defender of the so-called 'harem skirt.'"[49] The harem skirt, called by many variations on the name, was ridiculed by segments of society who found them unbecoming or "un-lady-like." This ridicule occasionally extended to legislation, as in March 1911, when one New Jersey assemblyman sponsored a bill prohibiting the wearing of the harem skirt anywhere in the state. Assemblyman George B. Cole was prompted to this action on hearing a *rumor* that a harem skirt was spotted at the shore destination of Asbury Park.[50] Furniss's

Figure 4.6 "The Harem Girl," by Bert Green. *Puck*. March 29, 1911.

work, as discussed the following month, turned the perceived negative traits of the look on their head. The article's author points out, after including a selection of Furniss's London *Mirror* work, "This cartoon makes the conventional skirt look positively indecent, as well as extremely ugly."[51] This of a woman exposing herself while carrying out daily activities and wearing a traditional skirt illustrated one of the increasingly attractive aspects of the harem skirt's design.

Puck's "Harem Girl" is further illustrative of two additional points, hinting at the increasing complexities in American society. The fashion and style component opens a window onto a question of cultural appropriation. As *The Lake County Times* noted in 1913, "The orient this spring is the source of inspiration for builders of costumes. You may be oriental in any way you please and affect in your raiment the East Indian, the Chinese, the Japanese, the Mohammedan or the Egyptian, anything at all that is eastern."[52] Susan Nance argues that the American populous and media producers were not "a uniform, unthinkingly racist mass public somehow timelessly 'obsessed with the Orient.'"[53] However, manufacture of how the Orient in everyday life, as the article from *The Lake County Times* indicated, pervasively underscored a uniform Orient. Moreover, the power dynamic between West and East allowed for a fluidity of movement for Western "builders of costumes" through global markets, if not vice versa.

The "Orient" and the "harem" continued to dominate style pages, appearing as perennial favorites of designers throughout the First World War and into the 1920s. With regard to what connections the "harem" dress had with actual harem garb, few attempted to say. One satirical opinion piece in *The Seattle Star*, again in April 1911, stated,

> It is obvious to persons who have studied this matter of costume, that the ordinary bell skirt was, so to speak, the original "harem" skirt, for it was once the livery of the concubines in the courts of Eastern potentates.[54]

Both Gayle V. Fischer and Valerie Steele argue that "the 'notorious . . . harem trouser-skirt of 1911' caused a scandal, in part, because it indicated the legs."[55] While Oriental inspired fashion waned during the war years among British and French audiences,[56] American consumers never really broke from it. Shortly after the US entrance into the First World War, in June 1917, fashion columnist Lucy Duff-Gordon noted that Turkish trousers continued to be favored for the "double reasons of their grace and utility."[57]

A second illustrative component of the *Puck* cover is the young woman's *châtelaine*: "An ornamental appendage worn by ladies at their waist, [which is] supposed to represent the bunch of keys, etc."[58] In 1921, Tansy McNab's "Fairy Tales for Grown-Ups" played on the narratives of Bluebeard and prohibition, while its associated illustration, done in a Bakst style by illustrator Sophia T. Balcom, paralleled *Puck*'s Harem Girl.[59] Balcom's illustration includes a harem-pant-clad woman dangling a sizable collection of keys. These keys, in both the illustration and the *Puck* cover, as well as their mention in the Bluebeard story more generally, are of great significance as symbols both of power and of submission.

One aspect to the châtelaine detail is its suggestion of normative femininity, in much the same way the pants themselves fit into a narrative of "fashion fantasies," which Steele argues by the 1910s, "Women seemed to picture themselves as 'the favorite of the harem,' through their Orientalized wardrobe choices."[60] The idea that there was a slave/master component to the choices made in styling finds some of its roots in Richard Burton's "myth of the Orient that derived from a 'master-slave relationship' between the sexes, with women serving as 'chattel and sexual convenience.'"[61] However, the *Puck* color choice of yellow for the background is subversively significant. Yellow was a color of the women's suffrage movement. (A number of articles ran at the same time talking of the "Real Yellow Peril" and disparaging the movement.[62]) Keeping in step with fashion color choices of the 1910s, "'clear, true colors' appeared in 'reaction'" to the muted, pastels of the earlier era. The yellow chosen here was not an accident. It reflected both a political and cultural shift.

A flurry of controversy followed the harem skirt, not only because of its suggestive legs (or suggestion of legs) but also because of its direct association with suffrage. In 1911, newspapers around the country ran articles declaring that suffrage leaders were promoting the purchasing of harem skirts, "for the cause," while many of those same leaders were quick to disassociate the skirt with the cause. Leaders who sought to distance suffrage efforts from the harem skirt did so out of a fear that the ridicule (and laws) against it would be transposed on the effort to secure the vote.[63] There was too, as much as the movement of leg was empowering, a suggestion of that master-slave relationship in the garment, the very antithesis of what suffragists were working so assiduously for.

Just as much as fashion and the right to vote were increasingly intertwined in the United States' context, a parallel relationship between fashion and suffrage was evident elsewhere. As US women were increasingly donning harem pants to march for the vote, American newspapers were filled with stories of Egyptian, Turkish, and Persian women "stepping out of the harem" and into "Paris fashions" in their own political advocacy.

In December 1912, Ivan Narodny wrote "The Vanishing Harem," contending that

> what attracts the most attention of a foreign traveler in Turkey is its women. Like shadows in an atmosphere of secrecy and silence, these veiled phantoms arouse in the heart of a stranger a feeling of pity and curiosity. Not only the stories of the Arabian Nights, but the romantic mystery that surrounds oriental life, have been the cause of the eagerness of the Western imagination to know something of the harem, the real home of Turkish women.[64]

Reinforcing the contention that Turkish women were tourist destinations, not fully realized humans, Narodny laments the harem's passing as "modern" or "revolutionary" ideas find their way to the Ottoman Empire and balks at the idea that women of Turkey have issued the battle cry "Down with the harem! Down with the veil!"

> Turkish women are fundamentally the same as all other women, which is shown by the *contagion* that ensued a few days [after the efforts of feminist Mirhi Nissa Hanoum], when women of the upper class unhesitatingly walked unveiled in the streets of Constantinople, chatting freely with their male companions. It caused a sensation such as the ancient city had never experienced before, and gave a shock to custom that marked the final change to modernism.[65]

Narodny's use of "contagion" leaves no doubt in the readers mind about his attitude toward feminist movements and the not so subtle notion that they were disease-like in their effects on society.

Still, one of the fun things about history is pointing out the illogical workings of our predecessors. The era of the First World War is nothing if not rife with this opportunity. It is hard to not be struck by how amazingly illogical the American populous was in the 1910s and the 1920s vis-à-vis the harem skirt. Historically, a parallel can be drawn with coffee's introduction to European palates. Before 1600 many Europeans objected to coffee because of its Islamic associations; in time of course this gave way, but these objections which focused on a perception of Islam as heretical, even demonic, appreciably slowed coffee's adoption. Working with the knowledge Europeans had at the time, while it seems absurd to the modern viewer, there was a least an internal logic to anti-coffee sentiment.[66]

The type of logic that appeared in anti-coffee sentiment before 1600, however, is noticeably different in the question of "harem style" and its associations with women's liberation at the end of the nineteenth century. It is clear that many worked very hard to equate polygamy, the harem, and Islam to the evils in the world, if not outright declare the harem the reverse of the suffrage movement, yet nearly no one seems to have seen the harem pants, and the whole harem style, as a problematic symbol of the suffrage movement itself. When we do have dissent against harem pants along "heathen" lines, it is against women's emancipation more generally.

In April 1911, the *San Francisco Call* asked readers what they thought of "Dress Reform." Mrs. A. J. Baird had very little sympathy for the harem skirt. She declared that "any female appearing on the street in a harem skirt should be arrested, heavily fined and fed on bread and water for 90 days," and went on,

> We send missionaries to foreign countries to enlighten the poor, degraded heathen now, are we to become a degenerate race and follow the dress of the inhabitants of the stone age, and call for dress reform? Now I feel that I have done my little toward helping in the work of sending the shameful and infamous thing back to the harem where it originated.[67]

Mrs. Henry M. Moreno agreed with Baird that "the unspeakable harem skirt, the very name of which should preclude the possibility of any respectable woman ever wearing the thing."[68] The irony is that while those who advocated against the harem skirt did so with the same internal logic of seventeenth-century anti-coffee campaigners, they did so at the peril of forcing the harem skirt more firmly into the arms of the suffragists. Declaring it the duty of every woman "to be as attractive as possible" and that the best way of achieving such beauty was by donning the "civilized fashions." These "civilized fashions," pro-Dress Reform advocate Esther Purvis noted, "robs her of muscles of free play, robs her of the privilege of enjoying, with her brother, the full measure of health and happiness, untrammeled; not to speak of overwrought nerves that are taxed the very limit of endurance."[69] And this is perhaps the most salient point: the Turkish harem, as it was seen in American popular consciousness was an "inhuman" establishment, in much the same way the "Western practice of wearing physically restrictive clothing" was seen as "inhuman" by women like Purvis. That women were restricted the world over was not lost on the suffragists, if the irony of their clothing's history was. In 1928, well after our period of discussion, Rosalind Toynbee wrote,

> We commonly assume that wherever there is a difference of custom or expectation, we Western women hold the more enviable position . . . [and yet] I remember my own surprise on hearing a rather violently Nationalist Turkish girl inveigh passionately against the humiliating position of Western women, "who are always called by the name of some man they belong to! We have our own names," she said, "we are not called by the name of our fathers or husbands, our names do not change simply because we marry. How can you bear such a humiliating custom?"[70]

In the context of this chastisement, it is worth noting that the two ladies who spoke out so vehemently against the harem skirt in the *San Francisco Call's* discussion were identified only by their marital status and their husbands' last names. Conversely, the example of a pro-Reform advocate was named of herself, her marital status not being discernible.

Suffrage, as much as it was a movement about creating more space for women in the public arena, was an awakening of "Self" in the world. The fusion of the harem in the midst of the First World War, with the movement to gain the right to vote, was not accidental. Western women used the symbols of the harem, of the perceived seclusion of the female world to shake up the perceived realities of the male, but at the same time, if they flew too close to aligning with Oriental tropes their efforts were "Othered" by those who wished to maintain the status quo.

Conspiracy at Scimitar Point

On April 6, 1917, the United States entered the First World War. On April 7, Happy Hooligan was still on his honeymoon, exploring Egypt (Figure 5.1).[1] He fell into the Nile River and rode a crocodile to shore, where he was captured (again) and held for ransom. More darkly, just before the United States entered the First World War, on April 1, Rudolph—Hairbreadth Harry's nemesis— promised to turn over a new leaf and atone for his wickedness, declaring his previous life too influenced by "the little black man from Egypt!"[2] depicted as a devil on Rudolph's shoulder. Of course, Rudolph does not repent and is soon back to his dastardly ways. By April 15, he capitalizes on general assumptions about the Orient to prey on people and their pocketbooks. As a "swami," the "Allah Achbar Bazoolah," Rudolph hypnotizes the "mentally sick" to get them into their "proper aura," all the while stealing from them as they remain entranced (Figure 5.2).[3] While the United States only hotly *debated* declaring war on the Ottoman Empire, conventional wisdom, as explored by comics, alleged that the Orient was a place of danger, trickery, and untrustworthiness. The United States never went to war against the Ottomans, but cartoonists of the era did.

Bluebeard, as we have seen, was one manifestation of disinclination toward Oriental men. While he was a useful tool for discussing murderous husbands, his visage was also a common device used to mark Ottoman Sultans, or Islamic leaders more generally, with a despotic moniker. Moreover, as seen in previous scenarios, physical attributes of race cued readers into who had power in the comic version of the world. By the time US soldiers were mobilized, the "Unspeakable," "Terrible," and "Bloody" Turk were well nestled into popular consciousness. Given this, it seems all the more surprising the United States did not go to war against the Ottomans. In a 1916 snippet, about the "Unspeakable Turk," the Kentucky newspaper *The Citizen* wrote that no "glimmerings of honor, or even 'enlightened selfishness,' seem to affect the Turk . . . seemingly enjoying

Figure 5.1 "Happy Hooligan's Honeymoon," by Frederick Burr Opper. *El Paso Herald.*
April 7, 1917.

the exercise of cruelty as other men enjoy eating or doing good."[4] The article
highlighted the slur-like nature of "Turk" in the United States, noting that "we
have Turks in America. The man who cheats in a bargain is a small Turk. The
man that betrays a woman is a Turk. The man that exults in any meanness of
which he should be ashamed is a Turk."[5] The *Citizen* concluded with thoughts on

Figure 5.2 "Hairbreadth Harry: The Omnipotent Oom Gets Two Costumers," by C. W. Kahles. *The Washington Herald*. April 15, 1917.

how the Turks (Ottomans) should be dealt with in response to their treatment of the Armenians:

> Can the Turks be converted? If they are not to be converted they ought to be hanged. President Wilson asks us to pray for the Armenians, and send money to feed the women whom the Turks are keeping in pens. . . . And we are sending some money, but we had rather send some missionaries or some battle ships to bombard the Turks.[6]

Leading up to 1914, characterization along these lines reflected the irredeemableness of the "Turk"; however, during the First World War, Turkish characters were oftentimes demoted to a sidekick's role and largely denuded of such power as they had previously been granted. Not the archvillain, the Turk became the sidekick of the more sinister German/Kaiser/Hun. On some level, pre–First World War comics (and journalism in general) were much fiercer critics of the Ottomans than those during the First World War.

At the point of a scimitar

If the scimitar seems a narrow symbol for indicating Islam, the Turkish Empire, or Muslims, considers the ubiquity of Edward Gibbon's assertion that "the Arabs from the desert, with the Koran in one hand and the scimeter [*sic*] in the other, swept out the remains of the fallen Lower Empire."[7] Even in the 1990s, the connective tissue between Islam and the scimitar rankled Muslims. In 1997, a coalition of Muslims from across the United States pushed for a "depiction of the Prophet Muhammad etched on the marble inside the U.S. Supreme Court chamber" to be "sandblasted into propriety."[8] The frieze, erected in 1931, depicts notable characters of history including King John of England and Charlemagne, alongside the Prophet Muhammad. The objection that the coalition raised focused on the depiction of the Prophet, a topic which we will address elsewhere, but it is significant to note that the "bearded Muhammad is shown clutching a scimitar in one hand and the Koran in the other." That Islam spread by the sword, specifically the scimitar, is a long-held, if barely creditable, belief in the West. While not likely his own invention, Edward Gibbon's testament that early Muslim conquests were achieved by the Qur'an in one hand and a scimitar in another certainly solidified it in the mind of most Westerners.[9] Thus, the history presented by Gibbon, alongside the narrative history of the Crusades pitted the West verses the East in a myriad of cultural imaginings. Textbooks like Joel and Esther Steele's *A Brief History* . . . (discussed in Chapter 2) did not help to disassociate the scimitar and the faith. On page 407, of their 1883 edition, there is an image, "Mohammedan Emblems." The "Emblems" include at least five weapons, a battle standard, and the crescent moon. The scimitar is front and center in the image, only overlaid by the crescent moon. Fascinatingly, at about the same time that the Steeles were reinforcing the scimitar-in-hand imagery, Moulavi Cheragh Ali published his *A Critical Exposition of the Popular "Jihád."* Ali's stated purpose was to remove the general and erroneous impression from the minds of European and Christian writers regarding Islam, that Mohammad waged wars of conquest, extirpation, as well as of proselytizing against the Koreish, other Arab tribes, the Jews, and Christians; or that he held the Koran in one hand and the scimitar in the other, and compelled people to believe in his mission.[10]

Jihad, while often used as a synonym for "holy war," simply means "struggle." In a fascinating twist on the history of appropriation, the common spelling of "jihad" at the turn of the twentieth century was "jehad," and some US labor unions and activists co-opted the term into their slogans. These examples from 1913 to 1914 suggest a sophisticated understanding of the nature of "jihad" as being more about "struggle" than "holy war."[11] Despite efforts like Ali's, however, jihad as an all-encompassing anti-Western holy war remained (remains) a constant in Western imaginings of the East.

Narrative traditions which produced menacing, scimitar-wielding Turks or Muslims pitted in eternal battles against Christian Western Europe permeated the ways in which "the West" understood Islam and the Islamic world. Still, this was simultaneously bigger than the Islamic world; the "everyone else" included a fluid number of parties as either insiders or outsiders depending on that particular zeitgeist. Catholics and Jews, for example, both took turns as foils to Protestant European heroes, and Africans, Asians, and Native populations of the Americas were pitted against the White European in greater or lesser roles throughout the centuries (see Kollin's and Walther's works for further examples). Just as the "Other" was fluid, so too was what defined the hegemonic center. The rhetoric used in the process of "Othering" was applied freely to justify colonial, imperial, political, social, and wartime needs as seen by the creators of hierarchy. Those tropes and identifiers that were in fashion as defining one group of "Others" were easily transposed onto "new Others," just as we have seen in the Orientalization of German leadership. Societies like those of Great Britain or the United States, which had at one time applauded their Germanic roots, erased German names and imagery with abandon when the First World War was declared. What is more, because the process of "Othering" necessitates stark comparative juxtapositions, this left little room for nuance in distinguishing Germans from Turks, from Chinese, and so on. In the examples we have already seen, German leaders were Orientalized when their bellicosity stepped beyond what hegemonic powers deemed proper. For comic artists and authors, Othering European or American leadership was a way to censure and seek corrective measures on behalf of society. This idea is seen in Henry James's approbation of *Punch* (Chapter 1) as a "mirror to this institution" which he further noted "can hardly fail to be instructive."[12]

There was less room for those who were "Othered" for longer periods of time, to "redeem" themselves as had been done by Scheherazade's Shahryar.

During *Mutt and Jeff*'s 1913 Ottoman adventures, Jeff made light of the massacres of Christians which dominated US public understanding of Ottoman practice at the time[13] and simultaneously reinforced the notion that these cyclical forms of violence in Anatolia were "natural" and immovable. The massacres were themselves common features of US newspapers, magazines, and journals. The fourteen-part serialization of Aurora Mardiganian's autobiographical, *Ravished Armenia*, was a celebrated and ubiquitous conduit for the public to access the topic.[14] *The Washington Times*, October 1918, two-page spread for part eight, "My Two Years of Torture in Ravished, Martyred Armenia" is a useful example in terms of its visual rhetoric. Even without delving into the details of the portion's content the reader can take away several important impressions, allowing him/her to form assumptions about the Ottoman world and Islam more generally. First, part eight appeared just before the "Women's Section," which included standard articles on fashion and advertisements for beauty aids, and right after a full-page article: "The Kaiser's Last Cruelty to the Little Luxembourg Princesses." Second, the article is adorned with photographs of a peacefully sewing Aurora and a quiet Armenian church on the first page which is contrasted forcibly with a woman obliged (at the crack of a whip) to pray in an Islamic fashion, as other women cower in the background and rigid, presumably Turkish, soldiers oversee.

Tensions between the United States and the Ottoman Empire, on the eve of the First World War were greater than just the Armenian question. Long-standing frustrations between the two states over the rights and sovereignty of Greece and Greek Islands stretched throughout the nineteenth century, a point made clearly in Karine Walther's *Sacred Interests*. Extensive coverage in Western media not only of the atrocities carried out against Armenians but also of the massacres and deportations of Greek Christians, by fall of 1914, drove Ottoman ambassador Rustem Bey to obverse that these acts were no different than other forms of imperial violence carried out when "political agitators engaged in undermining" imperial structures. Rustem referenced French actions against Algerians, British responses to the Great Rebellion of 187, Russian pogroms against Jews, and even the "extrajudicial violence regularly committed against African Americans" (lynchings) in the United States.[15] When Rustem was called before William Jennings Bryan, then secretary of state, he

> attacked the American press and accused it of having over a period of years
> viciously maligned the Ottoman Empire, "Her religion, her nationality, her

customs, her past, her present are reviled." This hateful press coverage was responsible for "poisoning public opinion" in the United States to such a degree that Turks were "seldom thought or spoken of in this country otherwise than as the 'unspeakable.'"[16]

As with Fredric Wertham's work, nestled inside Rustem's diatribe were hard truths that Woodrow Wilson and Bryan were unwilling to face. In drawing comparisons between lynchings of African Americans in the United States and United States' treatment of Filipinos, Rustem was speaking perhaps even more accurately than he intended. Rustem was largely declaring that only "he who is without sin should cast the first stone," but the fact that such violence is inherent in imperial endeavors does not excuse it. To this day some politicians and scholars insist on viewing Ottoman history of violence against minority groups as one of political necessity. Others maintain, as many did at the time, that violence, wherever it occurs, is not inherent in "civilized imperial practices," but the result of corrupted political systems uninterested in the best interests of *all*.

The actions carried out against Armenians were, and often still are, distilled into two sets of illustrated reflection: gendered violence (specifically of Turkish men against Armenian women) and the juxtaposition of peaceable Christianity with militaristic Islam.[17] Despite the nearly forgotten nature of those atrocities, by the end of the twentieth century in US popular consciousness, their existence was one of the main arguments *for* declaring war on the Ottomans in 1917. Cartoons like the November 1917 "And All Those Dead of Belgium and All That Mighty Procession of the Slain in Armenia—How If All These Hosts Still Live?" that focused on the crimes against humanity perpetrated in Belgium and Anatolia linked the perceived despotic nature of the German and Ottoman states, similar to how placement of the two articles discussed earlier did in 1918. In "And all those dead. . ." a German solider waves off the ghostly army of those who have been massacred. The cartoon expresses the reality that for the United States, while it was aware of Ottoman atrocities, it was only *officially* at war with the Germans.[18] Aside from their role as the German allies, Ottomans were often depicted as scimitar-wielding, blood-thirsty, morally bankrupt demons. A series of cartoons by Clifford Kennedy Berryman illustrates well this point.

Berryman, the cartoonist responsible for the "Teddy Bear" during Teddy Roosevelt's tenure in office, produced several cartoons for the *Washington Evening Star* dealing with the First World War, in particular drawing the relationship between the Kaiser and the Ottoman state. In each of these cartoons the German character (either the Kaiser or, in one case, Ambassador Bernstorff) is drawn in great detail. The Turkish character lacks clear identity, perhaps the Sultan, perhaps Enver Pasha, it is unclear. In the cartoons while the Turkish character is clearly an unlikeable figure (blood dripping from his ubiquitous scimitar) he does at the same time have an element of uncertainty, even apprehension in his alliance with the Germans.

Berryman's September 1, 1914, cartoon "September Morn" is perhaps one of his most symbolically complicated of the series. In the cartoon, the Turkish character has waded out, perhaps into the Bosporus, up to his ankles (Figure 5.3). He looks apprehensively across the troubled waters of "European War." Both the title and the Turk's stance indicate that Berryman was playing with the imagery of Paul Émile Chabas's 1911 oil painting of the same name. In the Frenchman's work, the focal point is a young girl or woman who has ventured into a lake naked. She is depicted in a position of modesty, perhaps bathing, perhaps protecting herself from a chilly morning and the cold water. While Berryman's Turk is fully clothed, the fact that he is depicted in the same posture is clearly indicative of

Figure 5.3 "September Morn," by Clifford Kennedy Berryman. Ran in: *The Evening Star*. September 1, 1914.

an act of feminization or emasculation or simply straight up dismissiveness. He is exposed, the European War figuratively washing up on him. That Chabas's female muse and his depiction of her have raised more than a few eyebrows over the years, particularly around questions of innocence and the fetishization of innocence,[19] only deepens the feminization element of Berryman's work.

By May 1918 Berryman's Turkish character is quite literally chained to his German, Bulgarian, and Austrian allies, his face clearly indicating a wish he had never joined them (Figure 5.4). By September 1918 the Turkish and Bulgarian characters are finding paths of escape: racing from missiles, jumping from ships, evacuating burning buildings, and alighting from moving trains. The Austrian character, even more shapeless as an idea than the Turkish character, appears in all of these depictions to be a bit slow, as if he is saying, "Oh, that's a good idea," as he watches his fellows get away.

Cartoonists were quick to pick up on the Turko-German theme in their works. In November 1915 the *Aberdeen Herald* (Washington State) published a cartoon (originally published in Cleveland) depicting Turkey's allies' desires to literally stab Turkey in the back.[20] It is an oversimplification, but when we look at the portrayal of Turks, and if we argue this means Muslims more generally, at the

Figure 5.4 "The New Teutonic Alliance," by Clifford Kennedy Berryman. Ran in: *The Evening Star*. May 19, 1918.

end of the nineteenth century and beginning of the twentieth century in Anglo-American cartoons, we have two things happening. On the one hand there is the harem, the Turk as feminine. On the other hand, there is the bloody scimitar, the Turk as masculine. Increasingly, as the First World War progresses, the Turk as the wielder of the bloody scimitar disappears. The scimitar is transferred to the hands of Wilhelm and the Hun, and the Turk becomes merely sycophantic.

Nestled in the more melodramatic bloody scimitar imagery of Turks, the cartoonish, as it were, element of this narrative is a much more sinister paranoia about the conspiratorial nature of Islam. Casie Hermansson's discussion of the pantomime, even buffonishness, butt of the lovers' joke coincided with the emasculated, sidekick depictions of the Turk, but there was another end of the bloody scimitar spectrum, one that dominated pre–First World War depictions of the Islamic world. This retrospective trend of identifying the "Turk" and Islam more broadly in a global focus was a counterpoint to the increasingly caricature nature of the sidekick. In this narrative the Islamic world, and the potential it had of global unity, focused much more on the supposed sinister, conspiratorial nature of Islam. This is at the heart of Rustem Bey's attack on US media, in particular, in its tendency to view Ottoman actions as "the result of primitive Islamic fanaticism."[21]

Vast conspiracies

At the close of the nineteenth century, and the beginning of the twentieth century, fear of "vast" religiously guided conspiracies was common in media across the globe. Perhaps the most significant, and sadly enduring, of these conspiratorial narratives was the forgery turned propaganda *The Protocols of the Elders of Zion*, which among its many failings purported to unmask the international network of Jewish bankers controlling trade and global politics. *The Protocols* were touted by Nazis and car manufacturers alike, and despite having been debunked time and time again they continue to pop up in bookstores and on websites as "evidence" of the conspiratorial nature of the Jewish community. Jews, however, were not the only group to suffer under such unsubstantiated presumption. In the case of *The Protocols*, the conspiracies were largely sociopolitical or socioeconomic in nature, while other conspiracies echoed these themes and/or introduced layers of gendered and sexualized elements.

In the United States, and Europe, members of the Church of Jesus Christ of Latter-day Saints found themselves the focal point of salacious fascination and granted cult status by large segments of society and the media. Much of what drove the popular discourse in literature and news about the Latter-day Saints' community was that they were deemed to have values "outside the norm." *A Study in Scarlet* simultaneously used and added to a growing sense of the "Otherness" of Latter-day Saints in his depiction of Utah and the community therein. Elder Stangerson's oppressive hold on Doyle's Utah community, mixed with poor understanding of Church of Latter-day Saints' doctrine, added suspense and fear to the story's arc. The equation made in *Study in Scarlet* between the Latter-day Saints' faith and Islam through the use of the word harem is, as we have seen elsewhere, deliberate. Often religious conspiracies were tied to sexual exploitation, of "white slavery" and of women ending up in "harems" or otherwise disgraced in the eyes of the native faith or country. Conspiracy narratives mixed with very real events to further exacerbate the fear. The violence perpetrated against Armenians and Greeks in the Ottoman Empire may have been born from conspiratorial visions of those populations, as held by Ottoman elites, but the violent aftermath flipped the narrative in the minds of many Western creators of popular culture. In Ottoman hierarchies the violence was justified as a necessary measure to Armenians, for example, from conspiring against the Ottoman state (as we saw in Rustem Bey's arguments). However, in the West the brutality of the violence of the events was coupled with an older fear of racial loss. Armenians, by virtue of their Christianity and their geographic heritage, were granted white status in the minds of Western creators of popular culture. Thus, in accounts like Mardiganian's, where she purports to be "one of the 18,000 Armenians of the town of Tchemish Gedzak who were carried away by the Turks to be slaughtered in trackless wildernesses and secret places or condemned to slavery in the harem,"[22] Western popular culture sees the conspiracy as one of evil, *brown* or *yellow*, Turks against the innocent white Armenians.

In fiction, such stories were sensationalized for the masses in popular media like dime novels. *Sold to the Sultan, or the Strange Adventures of Two Yankee Middies* was published in June 1914. In the story, the pretty faced singer Christine Ajarian (an Armenian Christian) lamented her fortune when she was "seized by those dreadful men and dragged into this dreadful place." Ajarian telling the novel's male leads that this turn of events means she has "been sold to the Sultan . . . [to] be locked up in the Imperial harem."[23] Ajarian's potential sexual loss is not explored in the novel, but the driving force of the story's arch is to see her rescued from the harem/prison.

Similarly, one article from the Indiana *Plymouth Tribune* reported on forty-nine "American girls" having been "sold into white slavery in harems of interior

China belonging to wealthy Chinese mandarins."[24] Likewise, abductions of heroines and fear for their virtue and safety drove many illustrated works of fiction and eventually films. In Edgar Rice Burroughs's *The Eternal Lover*, Burroughs's most famous character Tarzan, under his title Lord Greystoke, discovered that "among the other prisoners of the Arabs was a young white woman. Instantly commotion reigned upon the Greystoke ranch."[25] Gender, as Mrinalini Sinha has contended, "was an important axis along which colonial power was constructed."[26] In the context of British India, "Any real or imagined threat to white women was perceived as a threat to the prestige of the entire British race."[27] While the white woman did not carry all of the burdens of colonialism in the context of the United States, which she carried in British India, this racial prestige, particularly as a means of controlling and understanding nonwhite populations, was significant as a trope of late-nineteenth- and early-twentieth-century literature.

Between 1879 and 1921 stories circulated both as fiction and as current events focusing down on other fanatical and conspiratorial natures of Islam. The well-known history of the Revolt in the Sudan, of the Battle of Khartoum, and of the Mahdist agenda in the region was only one of these accounts. The framing of these other reports as somehow linked or akin to the Sudan must be noted, but the *actual* connection between the Mahdi and the other "vast conspiracies" is not always, if ever, present. The conspiracy of Islam was not always global in scope, oftentimes significance rested on the perceived impact Islam would have on European imperial powers or states, or even on the US Empire through the Philippines.

Jihad

One of the more significant perceived threats came from the newly emergent Senussi. In modern texts the Senussi receive very little coverage. In Marshall G. S. Hodgson's three volume tome on Islamic history, *the Venture of Islam*, only a phrase is devoted, not even a full sentence, to the Senussi. Frederick Mathewson Denny says of the Senussi that it "used social action to combat European colonialism . . . a combination of Sufi organization and a free-ranging though basically orthodox Sunnism."[28] First hints that the Senussi were of importance to US audiences began circulating in 1885, when snippet articles articulated the notion that the recently deceased Mahdi of the Sudan appointed various leaders to carry on his mission against European imperialism. The Senussi founder,

Muhammad ibn Ali as-Senussi, was supposedly tasked with Egypt as his center of focus.[29] In 1907, *The Literary Digest* condensed H. A. Wilson's *The Nineteenth Century* piece about the Senussi and Islam in Africa, highlighting Wilson's assertion that "it is my absolute and certain conviction that the Senussia is a far more mighty force than we in Europe have any conception of, . . . that the day is drawing steadily nearer when we shall stand face to face with a wave of Mohammedan fanaticism, universal throughout the continent."[30] Wilson went on to contend that "so great is the unrest and discontent among *all* native races of Africa that it needs but a spark to set the whole continent ablaze from end to end."[31] By the time the First World War was in full swing, such articles as these made increasingly common reports of Senussi efforts to unseat Britain in Egypt more believable to US audiences.[32]

The Senussi were not alone. In 1879, a Wilmington, Delaware paper discussed the "East Roumelian police . . . [unearthing] a great Mahometan conspiracy"[33] and the Yankton (Dakota Territory) paper of 1881 focused on the "vast moslem [*sic*] conspiracy against the French in Africa."[34] Further conspiracies included those in Java, India, and Somaliland.[35] An 1885 report from near Lake Tanganyika spoke of 3,000 "fanatical Mohammedans" armed with modern rifles and the intention of driving out Europeans. According to the article, "It is feared that the Mohammedan races throughout the entire equatorial belt will be induced to join the fanatical movement which promises wealth and power from them."[36] Young Turk leadership, largely secular in intellectual roots, had de facto political power in the Ottoman Empire by 1914, but nevertheless "followed German guidance and convinced a group of its highest religious leaders to call for a global jihad in November 1914."[37] Despite the widespread fear among Western statesmen, the "global jihad delivered no tangible results." Still the specter of jihad remained a strong motivation in calls for international action. In the 1917 "New Fears of Holy War," the author contends that "the peril of the Jehad has not entirely passed away." A new potential for jihad, the author goes on to observe, is kindling in Baku, "the center of the great oil-fields of Russia . . . [and] 'a surprisingly modern, prosperous, and alert city."[38] Here, the author reports, "nationalism and religious zeal are practically one and the same." More than the religiosity of these movements, it was the nationalist sentiment which provoked panic in the West. Nationalism meant anti-imperialism, which spelled loss of power, prestige, and control if successful. Inciting feelings against these movements by playing up their Islamic nature was helped by tropes long understood in the West.

Crusader imagery was common in cartoons of the First World War. Coupled with the Orientalization of Kaiser Wilhelm the British capture of Palestine in early 1918 further heightened its usage. John T. McCutcheon's "The Holy City" depicted "The Turk," guarding a crusader era building, presumably in Jerusalem. From an upper window of the building a woman reaches out, the personification of "Christianity." In the distance, as the Turk looks on, scimitar stashed in his belt, a battle rages between British and Ottoman forces distinguished by their respective flags.

In fiction a perceived uniformity of the Muslim world, not unlike that which underlay *The Protocols* vis-à-vis Judaism, was reinforced in an effort to underscore the potential power of global jihad. John Buchan's 1916 *Greenmantle* centered entirely on the fear of holy war, as the main character Richard Hannay says, "It looks as if Islam had a bigger hand in the thing than we thought. . . . I fancy religion is the only thing to knit up such a scattered empire."[39] His compatriot responds, "You are right. We have laughed at the Holy War, the Jehad [but] . . . there is a Jehad preparing."[40] That Buchan was presenting fictional accounts of the war, and the prospects for the future of the war, in the very midst of the war is one thing, but that Buchan was a member of the British war propaganda bureau, generally known as Wellington House, added a whole other dimension to the story. In 1917, Buchan, as a member of the bureau, wrote a confidential memo describing the House's efforts in terms of literary and pictorial propaganda.[41] Of the pieces described, two posters stand out as significant: one referred to as the "Moshi Poster" and the other the "Sherif of Mecca Poster."

The "Moshi Poster" was

> a reproduction in Chinese of a German document found at Moshi by General Smuts in which Mohammedan worship amongst East African natives is condemned and orders are given to encourage them to keep pigs—unclean animals. A translation is given in Chinese and the photographs are of Dr. Schnee who signed the order and Moshi fort and town where the document was discovered. 50,000 of these posters were printed for the benefit of the Chinese Moslems who live mostly in the provinces of Kansu, Hsin Shiang, Chihli, and Yunnan.[42]

The "Sherif of Mecca Poster," which was later known to have been turned into a pamphlet as well, was

> a poster which reproduces the Declaration of Independence made by the Sherif of Mecca, now King of Hejaz. It is of great interest to Chinese Moslems, and the idea is to have it circulated in the four provinces mentioned above, but since the materials used in the compilation of the poster were sent out to Shanghi Committee their request, that they might make up their own poster from them,

the situation of the poster which we have had printed can be utilised in China proper. We should like to know the exact situation and to be informed whether the Shanghi Committee could make use of a certain number of these 25,000 copies, some of which are being distributed in places outside China, such as Hong Kong and Siam and the Straits Settlements.[43]

While unpacking all that these posters, and the other Wellington House products, would be a worthwhile endeavor, for now we will just focus on how the British government actively chose to pursue propaganda developed out of Middle Eastern and African Islamic contexts for use in China, Thailand, and the Straits Settlements. As overseeing the largest number of Muslims of any empire in the world at the time, the British government, and thought-creators like Buchan, found it utilitarian to view the Islamic world as a monolith, that what was significant for one group of Muslims was significant for another.

These assumptions about the global nature of Islam and the power of unity it could provide to the right ally were deeply entangled with Germanaphobia. In his *The Unseen Hand: Adventures of a Diplomatic Free Lance*, first published in *Blue Book Magazine* 1916, Clarence Herbert New wrote,

> The great trouble in Turkey, just now, is to know who may be trusted! When you complicate Oriental intrigue with German propaganda, one scarcely dares to trust his own eyes or hands. "If we could bring about some incident or coup which would galvanize every Mohammedan in the Empire—unite all the Mussalmans in one great wave of religious frenzy?"[44]

As in Buchan's work, the real power, or fear, was not so much the Islamic connection, but how Germany would benefit from a united Islamic world. The basis of *Greenmantle* rests on a prophet or leader, who the Germans are courting to unite the Islamic world. One of Hannay's comrades notes that

> he must be something extra special if he can put a spell on the whole Moslem world. The Turk and the Persian wouldn't follow the ordinary new theology game. He must be of the Blood. Your Mahdis and Mullahs and Imams were nobodies, but they had only a local prestige. To capture all Islam—and I gather that is what we fear—the man must be the Koreish, the tribe of the Prophet himself.[45]

In the end, the man referred to as "Greenmantle" is essentially castaway as insignificant enough to be the main villain. The real adversary is a German woman, as Hannay's friend Sandy, reflecting on Nietzschean thought, observed, "There never has been, and there never could be a real Superman. . . . But there might be a Superwoman."[46] As it happened, the woman, as antagonist worked to the detriment of Buchan's American character Blenkiron, who declared,

> I guess we Americans haven't got the right poise for dealing with that kind of female. We've exalted our womenfolk into little tin gods, and at the same time left them out of the real business of life. Consequently, when we strike one playing the biggest kind of man's game we can't place her. We aren't used to regarding them as anything except angels and children.[47]

The interplay between a female intelligencer, the Ottoman state, the German state, and the future of the First World War finds a fascinating analogue nearly a century later in the feature film *Wonder Woman*, wherein one nemesis Wonder Woman must face is Dr. Poison, stationed in the Ottoman Empire, developing new, deadly chemicals for the German war effort. In this rendition of *Wonder Woman* Dr. Poison, a woman too, operated alongside a fictionalized Ludendorff to fend off Wonder Woman and her team, just as von Eniem, Hannay's villainess, worked alongside the martial Colonel von Stumm to aid the German war effort.

Such themes of global Islam and conspiracy were not unique to the immediate First World War years. In an earlier work, No. XI "The Mohammedan Conspiracy," from February 1912, Clarence Herbert New presented a different, yet similarly conspiratorial version of the Islamic world. Struggling to see the Islamic world as both uniformly structured and richly diverse, New opens this issue with thoughts on the complexity: "Egypt isn't really the Orient, to be sure; but it is one of the Occidental gateways to the East, and its people, manners, architecture and customs are largely those of the 'Arabian Nights,' with the spell of mystery of a far older civilization in the background."[48] *The Mohammedan Conspiracy* went on to be adapted for screen and played to audiences across the country. This struggle to see the East as both uniformly understandable and richly diverse led a number of authors and artists to preform stylistic gymnastics.

In nonfiction, these acrobatics are visible in works like Lothrop Stoddard's 1922 warning of "war between Christian Europe and Moslem nations" within ten years' time or Europe will be compelled to withdraw their troops from presiding over Muslims subjects.[49] In his book *The Rising Tide of Color*, Stoddard questioned the centrality of leadership like Sultans and Caliphs, but reinforced the hysteria of the conspiratorial nature in Islam contending, "Pan-Islamism's real driving power lies, not in the Caliphate, but in institutions like the 'Hajj.'"[50] Stoddard presented a racist vision of the world's future, a Klansman, eugenicist, and prolific author, his work was found in papers across the country. Articles written by him or about his books were conveyed in an approving tone and with reverence for Stoddard as a scholar. His views were published in newspapers and magazines across the United States, including some of the most prestigious of the time. His vision of race in the world, and for our purposes Islamic politics, were considered mainstream in the early 1920s, and articles applauding his work like "'Mohammedan Peril Threatens New World War,' Eastern-Expert Says" and "See Mohammedan Threat of New World War: Expert Predicts Revolt!" are just two examples of Stoddard's presence in popular media.[51] Visually the audience was clued into to Stoddard's sentiments, before even reading the words. Accompanying these articles was a map flanked by "sinister" Muslim, male, faces. The map is painted with a swath of black across North Africa, the Middle East, and deep into Asia, and it dominated the space just below the headline. Without even reading the article, the impending doom was made clear.

As with the case of the Mormon and Jewish examples, it was in fiction and film that these visions of Islam gathered their greatest followers. In examples, the perceived uniformity of Islam was reinforced in an effort to underscore the potential power of a global jihad. The sense of imminent danger around the idea of a global holy war rippled through American newspapers between the 1880s and the 1920s (as it does with disturbing frequency to this day). During the First World War a great deal of ink was spilled, as we have seen in both fiction and nonfiction, agonizing over the German's ability to capitalize on Islamic unity. In one case, the Paris, Kentucky *Bourbon News* reported on German attempts to incite Muslims to global jihad. Some alleviation to the anxieties this notion was sure to produce is also noted in the article in which the Sultan of Sulu was both the second most important leader in the world *and* "a protégé of the stars and stripes."[52] A number of sources at the time argued that the Sultan of Sulu was particularly important to the global Islamic community, stating, "In tables of precedence at Mecca, the Holy City of the Moslems, the Mohammedan ruler who ranks next to the Sultan of Turkey as the greatest power among the Prophet is this same Sultan of Jolo."[53] Like so many other attempts to prove the global uniformity of Islam, the *Bourbon News* article belied the notion that global jihad was even possible, as the author noted the great lack of unity of Muslims across the world, divided as they are by sect, geography, class, and political persuasion.[54] Still, neither the significance of the Sultan of Sulu being under US jurisdiction nor the great diversity of Islam was enough to stem the tide of the underling dread.

If in 1914 the German and Ottoman states were able to create the wave of pro-Central Power sentiment they sought, then perhaps those stories that followed would have been more justified, but even as late as March 1918, American newspapers continued to foretell the coming Islamic tidal wave. The *New York Tribune* dedicated a full page to the article "Can the Kaiser Explode the Mahometan Bomb?" Focusing on the potential power of central Asian Muslims to unite and bring together the continent's believers under the guidance of the Central Powers, Adachi Kinnosuke, the article's author, declares, "Mahometan Asia is the next on the Kaiser's programme. Not the conquest and occupation of it, but the turning it into a monstrous bomb—just for the gentle humane work of exploding the whole of Asia with it."[55] Accompanying the article is another map, this time of Asia colored in where significant populations of Muslims live. Surrounding the map are six disembodied heads and at least ten identifiable weapons. The heads, all male, are supposed to be representative of various Islamic populations. One of only two faces viewed straight on is of a Turkish man, adorned with a fez and neat curling moustache. The other is of a man, perhaps North African in origin. He is depicted wearing a burnoose and full beard. The remaining faces regard the map and are likely representative of Arabs, Sub-Saharan Africans, Muslims from the subcontinent, and Central Asians. The weapons, few of which are shown in full, include daggers, swords, spears, halberds, and rifles—an echo of the "Mohammedan Emblems" in the Steeles' textbook.

None of these narratives are rational. They were representative of a general fear of imperial and racial loss and the linked concern that Islam could become paramount over Christianity. In reviewing the work of Cardinal Charles Lavigerie (founder of the White Fathers), one 1890 article in the New York *Sun* ends with this: "As soon as the second part of the Cardinal's memoirs, detailing the grand Arab conspiracy against Europeans and Christians on the African continent appears in print, I shall give your readers the substance of it." His book on the "Arab Slave Trade" informs its readers that "the first great lesson they bring us is that our greatest danger arises from the secret spread of fanatical Moslem associations."[56] Visually this sentiment was explicit in the April 25, 1897 *New York Journal and Advertiser*'s "American Magazine." The full-page article "The Shadow of the Turk on the Cross of Christianity" took up the cause of Greek efforts to push back against Ottoman control and end massacres of Greek Christians. In the opening paragraph the author asserts, "It is a struggle between the cross and the crescent. The one represents Christianity, civilization, and human love. The other represents Scio [Chios] and Marash [Kahramanmaraş] and Diarbekir [Diyarbakır]!" (representative towns where violence against Greeks was carried out). Even if a reader did not bother to look into the article's anti-Turkish stance, the narrative was writ large across the page. A hollow cross transected the article. Embedded inside the cross are images of Greeks and Turks firing at one another in battle, of cities being ransacked, of women being carried off, and of a general sense of violence and destruction. A shadowy silhouette of a Turk's profile under/overlays the image. The silhouette's hand is raised, holding aloft a scimitar.[57] Similarly, the marching Turk with raised scimitar graced a 1922 advertisement for the *Saturday Evening Post's* upcoming articles (this one published in the *Richmond Times-Dispatch*). The ad foretold the coming work of Lothrop Stoddard, who, the ad tells us, wrote those "brilliant books, The Rising Tide of Color, The New World and The Revolt Against Civilization . . . will visit the Balkans, Turkey and the Near East generally, and analyze the new and acute problems they present." The image associated with Stoddard's work is one of a Turkish man, arms raised in anger (and carrying, of course, a scimitar) striding across a globe, positioned in such a way as to step on Europe.[58]

Racial loss narratives did not uniquely focus on the Islamic world but did embed Islam in larger racialized discussions, like those surrounding the "yellow peril" message. In 1909 the *New York Tribune* reported on Pastor D. B. Thompson's charge that

> the danger of the white race lay in the union of the all the Tartar and Mongol races if un-Christianized. . . . The Turks are a part of that great Mongol race of which the Japanese, Chinese, Tartars, Tibetans, Magyars or Huns, and to a large extent the Cossacks, are a part. The sympathies of those people when it comes to racial affinities are very strong.[59]

The Presbyterian of the South, in reproducing James L. Vance's (the powerful minister of Nashville's historic First Presbyterian Church) address to the General Assembly Meeting on Foreign Missions, echoed the sentiment that Islam, a religion practiced at the time by millions of people across all continents, was a *racial* concern. Vance declared, "Islam challenges Christendom with its menace. It is a race peril. The things which blight and cripple and curse humanity march under the crescent. Mohammedanism is a cancer."[60] Like Vance, other significant thought-leaders of the time railed against the "Islamic peril," persuading US audiences of impending doom. William Jennings Bryan took his own stand against Islam proclaiming, "Mohammedanism is propagated by force, while Christianity rests upon love and is spread by moral suasion."[61] With such powerful leaders of cultural production proclaiming such "facts" as these about the faith and practitioners of Islam it is hardly surprising Islam faced uphill work in the United States in countering such thought. Still, as the comics of the era indicate, the cultural perception of Islam and Muslims, while one unified whole at a macro-level approach suggested a much more nuanced understanding on the microlevel.

Disguise or Acculturation

In the January 31, 1909, issue of the *Old Opie Dilldock's Stories*, the eponymous character partook of "competitive exhibitions of equestrianism" on the "plains of Arizona." Over the course of the nine panel issue, Dilldock displays his equestrian prowess "in Cossack costume . . . in all the pomp and regalia of the Bedouin" and as a cowboy on a "splendid Indian pony."[1] In this episode of the Dilldock series the Cossack, Bedouin, and cowboy are presented as interchangeable disguises; ones even natives, we are informed, cannot see through. In this comic iteration, the persona of the Bedouin is a part, a disguise to tell a story. More often than not, such depictions of Muslims or peoples from the Islamic world rose only to this level of depth and nuance, in US comics of the turn of the twentieth century.

If one did not read the Dilldock strip mentioned above, but simply glanced at it, the reader may be forgiven for thinking the story was one of three separate persons. In such a ready, the second character, the Bedouin, could be additionally read as Muslim, replete as he is in the iconographic trappings so often associated with Muslims characters at the time. However, identifying who is and who is not Muslim in comics from the fin de siècle is largely guess work reliant on context and association. Costuming and dress, in particular, are often key identifying features, but they can be equally misleading. Veiled women almost universally indicate Islam, and as we have seen the scimitar has often been associated with Muslim men. Identifiers such as these do not give us a sense of the character's religiosity so much as a sense of the intended religious identity as racial identity. It is always important, moreover, to be mindful of the context and how the assemblages are constructed. We gain variation of characterization, but sometimes add to confusion, when harem pants, turbans, and fezzes are used. These are common choices not only in depicting Muslim peoples but are often simultaneously used for American Suffragettes, Sikhs, and Shriners. When taken in whole, with environmental or verbal cues, dress and costuming add additional layers of data to our work.

It is not so simple as to say a turban or scimitar means the character is intended to be Muslim, but it does open up the conversation. The power of dress and costuming is vital to underscoring how creators of popular media of the time conveyed meaning to the masses and in so doing constructed archetypes of Islam and Muslims. Lines are not always clear. Sometimes the indigenous character is depicted in local attire, and the Westerner is dressed in Western styles. In other moments the Westerner dons native apparel as an act of deception or appropriation, an action well documented in the history of Orientalism. It was, after all, explorers like Burton and Burckhardt who "went native" to observe the "mysteries of the East." But what of the Western character who dresses in local attire not in a duplicitous way but as an act of acculturation, maybe even assimilation? What of the non-Westerner who, when in the West, dons the derby hat to walk the streets un-accosted?

War Puzzles

During and for some time after the First World War, the series *War Puzzles* was produced for the International Syndicate. The most likely author/illustrator of the work was W. Charles Tanner, who already had a long résumé as a cartoon puzzle creator. *War Puzzles*, like his previous historical series and light-hearted children's puzzles, were detailed single-panel illustrations with a brief comment about the image and a hint for finding a hidden object.[2] Running in a wide variety of newspapers across the US Tanner's *War Puzzles* is useful as a cache of archetypal images of Muslims, representative of trends common in US comics of the era. Of eighteen *War Puzzles* illustrations of people we are led to assume as Muslim, only one is explicitly identified as such. The December 15, 1917, "Sheik-ul-Islam" image informs readers that the Sheik is the "Head of the Mohammedans at Constantinople, [who was] proclaimed a holy man, two years ago today" (Figure 6.1).[3] The Sheik wears a long robe, suggesting a *thobe, bisht* (a cloak), and a *ghutra* (the rectangular scarf) under a tight fitting cap. Eight of the *War Puzzles* offer another costume ensemble which we have seen a number of times already: a fez and a moustache (often with pointed tips or curled up ends) (Figure 6.2). These characters often wear a cropped jacket or vest and voluminous pantaloons, not unlike the harem trousers discussed earlier. When the image is more cartoonish or caricature-like the shoes worn are almost always an adaptation of *juti* (a style of shoe common in the Punjab region of the subcontinent). The particular version of *juti* depicted in these situations

WAR PUZZLES

SHEIKH-UL-ISLAM
Head of the Mohammedans at Constantinople, proclaimed a holy man, two years ago today, November 16, 1915.
Find another Mohammedan.
YESTERDAY'S ANSWER
Right side down under elbow

Figure 6.1 "Sheik-ul-Islam." *Honolulu Star-Bulletin*. December 15, 1917.

is of a style known as *Salim Shahi Juti,* named for the Mughal emperor Jahangir. In modern US parlance this style of shoe may be called "Aladdin" or "Genii" slippers and are notable for their curled toe point. The counterpoint to this footwear choice, often apparent in more realistically drawn images, are either military-style boots or Western-style footwear.

War Puzzles in offering us some archetypes for Muslim men do offer one option for Muslim women. Unlike so many other women we are intended to view as Islamic in cartoons of the era, this is one instance of a Muslim woman depicted in a fairly realistic manner. The February 11, 1918, issue "Drive to Palestine" is foregrounded by a British solider, perhaps General Allenby (Figure 6.3). Over the soldier's left shoulder is the image of a veiled woman. Wearing a full covering *abaya* and face veil her features are completely obscured, but that she is present at all is an interesting indicator of the story that Tanner is trying to tell. Over the soldier's right shoulder is a male counterpart, dressed in a style reminiscent of the Palestinian *fellahin* (a Levantine agricultural laborer or peasant). Both background images represent native Palestinians in a much more

Figure 6.2 "Turkey Declared War." *Honolulu Star-Bulletin*. December 14, 1918.

precise manner than the generic "Muslim" or "Turk" present in so many other comics. To this, they also add nuance to the story of who lived in Palestine at the time. While Zionist and non-Zionist communities in the region were small, the Balfour Declaration issued by Britain had just declared support for establishing a Jewish national home therein. As seen in McCutcheon's "Holy City" cartoon, there was general knowledge that Palestinians included Christians as well. While we cannot identify the religious choices of these two background figures in "Drive to Palestine," the visual cues suggest they are supposed to be read as Muslim. Intentionally or not, Tanner is establishing an identity for the people in Palestine when the British took control.

Old Opie Dilldock and cultural curiosity

Just as *War Puzzles* gives us a selection of images from which we can draw archetypes of Muslims in US cartooning, the *Old Opie Dilldock* series offers

Figure 6.3 "Drive to Palestine." *Honolulu Star-Bulletin*. February 11, 1918.

insights into how important dress and costuming are for developing the narrative of the story, and the character of the personifications. First published in 1907, Dilldock was created by F. M. Howarth when he began his tenure at the Chicago Tribune Syndicate. Howarth's time as Dilldock's creator was short lived, dying of pneumonia in 1908. The eponymous character lived on under the hand of W. L. Wells until 1914, but the tenor and scope of the stories was very different in each incarnation.

All Opie Dilldock stories were framed as a narration of his past adventures in stories told to his nieces and nephews, "Tilly, Billy, and Philly." In time, this framing became looser, sometimes never even mentioning the family. Under F. M. Howarth's direction, Dilldock explored global themes and played, if only narrowly, with a form of cultural curiosity. Dilldock ventured into foreign lands, aided Sultans and Maharajas, explored jungles and deserts, and preformed superhuman feats of strength and cunning. When W. L. Wells took over the comic, the artistic rendition of Dilldock stayed largely the same, but the story line took a dramatic turn inward, nationally and culturally speaking.

Between March 31, 1907, and September 20, 1908, Howarth produced seventy-five episodes of *The Old Opie Dilldock Stories* between October 18, 1908, and February 27, 1910, and W. L. Wells created another seventy-five. Comparing these two datasets allows us to see some interesting themes in terms of America's place in the world, artistic interest, and racial hierarchies. Of the seventy-five Howarth issues, Dilldock leaves North America fifty-four times, or about 72 percent of the time, but in Wells's seventy-five, Dilldock only leaves North America thirteen times, or about 21 percent of the time. This distinction in setting is not only striking in the raw numbers, but even evident in flipping through the strips. Both creators relied on a jumble of fictional and real locations, but nearly always identifiable enough to know where Dilldock is intended to be. In Howarth's work, for instance, Middle Eastern or Central Asian settings are identified as such by special architectural details (e.g., arabesque styling), environmental clues (e.g., deserts and palm trees), "Middle Eastern" sounding names like "Bey of Tinnkahn" or "the Great Desert of Dustarah," and character costuming. Both Howarth and Wells readily identify places as being in Africa, Europe, South America, and East Asia, leaving "deserted islands" and the "frozen north" as the only truly undefinable locales (Figure 6.4).

Costuming, not only important for helping the reader identify the setting, was a noticeable dissimilarity between Howarth's and Wells's work. In Howarth's comics, Dilldock often dresses as do the locals. When he is not dressed as the locals, he is attired in contemporary American, big game hunting, or sailor's style. Of the times Dilldock appears in the Islamic Orient, seventeen times in all, he is dressed in local style eight times; in Europe—sixteen times—of which he dresses as a local half of the time, again. Outside of these two regions (and North America) Dilldock only dresses as do the locals in two more instances: when he is at the North Pole, where he is sensibly dressed in the style of the native inhabitants, in furs and skins, and in South America where he wears gaucho attire. Conversely, when Wells's draws Dilldock's adventures, he only dresses Dilldock in local fashion five times total, of those first seventy-five issues: once is in "the land of the midnight sun," twice are in unidentifiable locals, but likely Mediterranean Europe, and twice are montage episodes. Of these last two examples one reflects 1908 and includes pieces from both Howarth's and Wells's work. (It was a Christmas reminiscence piece.) The other, which introduced this chapter, is set at a rodeo in Arizona, during which Dilldock dons the riding habits and dress of a Cossack, Bedouin, and cowboy. Wells's Dilldock is playing parts, not integrating himself into a culture, whereas Howarth's Dilldock was often immersive.

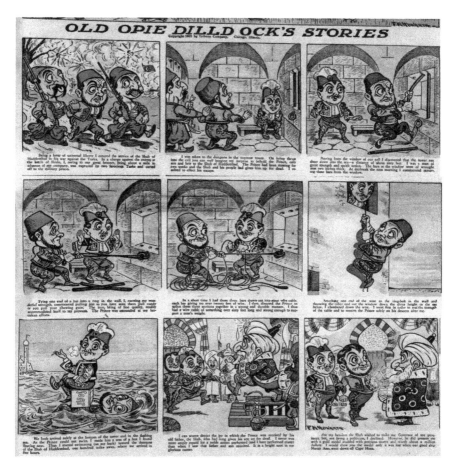

Figure 6.4 "Old Opie Dilldock's Stories," by F. M. Howarth. *Chicago Tribune.* May 12, 1907.

There are no clear signs that explain the differences between content choices in Howarth's and Wells's work. Perhaps one excuse is apparent in the artists' backgrounds. Howarth is clearly identified as a cartoonist, whereas Wells is more widely acknowledged as a traditional artist and naturalist. Howarth had an extensive cartooning background before he joined the Chicago *Tribune*, having contributed to *Puck, Truth, Judge,* and *Life* at various points in his career. He is since known for both his "big heads and little bodies" style and as "one of those who [gave] 'serial' pictures a distinct popularity."[4] In recent years scholars have argued that, influenced by work done in Germany (e.g., Wilhelm Busch) and France (e.g., Théophile Steinlen and Adolphe Willette), "Howarth fractured the single panel that had previously dominated the form in the United States"[5] and is considered a founding leader in American comic form. Wells, on the other hand, is often described as an artist and naturalist.[6] This portrayal fits well with his depiction of Dilldock and his adventures. Whereas Dilldock took to the world to test his prowess under Howarth, under Wells he turned to the "Wild West" and dressed as a cowboy no less than thirteen times. Moreover, Wells's Dilldock focused on "manly" activities like hunting, fishing, horsemanship, wood-cutting, and other sporting activities (e.g., boxing, racing, and golf).

Wells's preference for the cowboy, over Howarth's preference of the sailor, is telling of the global and local nature of the Dilldock personifications. The more nuanced relationships between Dilldock and "the locals," whether they be in North America or out, reinforce the distinctions between the two artists. Howarth's Dilldock suggests a racial and cultural familiarity and comfort. The fact that the Dilldock strips were produced at the same time as questions about Arab and Turkish whiteness were raised (see Chapter 1 and Sarah Gualtieri's *Between Arab and White*) adds potential depth to how we may read Howarth and Wells's choices. Howarth's depiction of Dilldock as nearly indistinguishable from his European and Middle Eastern counterparts signals that there is merit in the argument for racial similarity or kinship between the two regions. Couple this with the fact that in a number of the "Middle Eastern" settings Dilldock claims a role as a member of the state's apparatus, as "in the service of" or as advisor to, the local leadership.

Further to the point, Howarth further signals his understandings of racial hierarchies by not depicting Dilldock in Chinese or African attire, cuing the readership into a distinction between some sets of races. Still, even in this more distanced framework, Howarth's Dilldock does continue to create close relationships with the local populations, for example, by staying with local families and bringing the children special gifts.

In contrast, Wells's Dilldock lacks this ease with locals almost entirely. In the few times Wells's Dilldock leaves North America, he maintains a distance from local populations. In Africa, for example, he is an overseer in a South African mine and spends the entire strip pointing and directing only to step in, in the last panel and use his superhuman strength to break the stone which no other man or machine can break. In North America, in his few encounters with Native Americans, they are the enemy (unless one is female, and she is in need of rescuing).[7] Wells's Dilldock is much more comfortable in the seat of power, above the other characters of the narrative, even at home among those who should undoubtedly be his socioeconomic or cultural equals. Wells's separation of Dilldock from locals, changes the narrative of the series. He lacks the ease with the world, which had so marked Howarth's Dilldock.

Howarth's fluidity in expressing Dilldock's adventures as those of a man comfortable in the world suggests a sympathy or even equality with what we may call the Middle East. Such treatment is uncommon in comics of the era. For example, Howarth's Dilldock interacts with Middle Eastern characters as he does with Europeans. He wins against the "bad guys" and succeeds in righting wrongs (bringing children home to their families, joining star-crossed lovers, and protecting kings from assassination). There is no mockery in Howarth's

Figure 6.5 "The Evacuation of Sambo." *The Topeka State Journal.* August 26, 1911.

Dilldock, unlike that which we see in *Sambo*. In at least one strip, Sambo and his friends not only openly mock an Arab/Bedouin man but also take advantage of his preforming prayer as an opportunity to steal from him (Figure 6.5).[8] Sambo, himself, as a character comes from a place of mockery. He is intended to be read as childish and ignorant. Howarth's Dilldock on the other hand is mature and experienced; whereas Wells's is mature, he is significantly more arrogant.

That Muslims were presented in cartoons as a hodgepodge of archetypes is apparent in a January 1916 issue of *Mutt and Jeff* (Figure 6.6). In "Yes, indeed, these Mohammedan troops are very fierce. Oh my yes!" Mutt attempts to play a prank on Jeff, describing to him how fierce some of their own allies are. Mutt says,

> Yes, France and England made a big mistake in bringing these native African troops over here. These Gurkas are good fighters but they are Mohammedans and are religious fanatics. Now their religion calls for the sacrifice of human life at various times and these Gurkas are natural born murderers.[9]

Assuming Mutt knows that Gurkhas are not (1) Muslim, (2) African, and (3) ritual killers, the fact that he is able to frighten Jeff with this string of nonsense indicates a strong proclivity to accepting the universal assumptions about the Islamic world as embedded in the comic. The character who Mutt convinces to be the actor in the final stage of his effort to frighten Jeff is one of the colonial troops to whom his story supposedly refers. The man, drawn with a dark complexion wears military-style shoes and pants, carries a riffle, appears to be wearing a poncho and has a head piece that may a turban or a fez. Since Jeff nonchalantly knocks the man on the head with a stone in the midst of Mutt's storytelling we are left wondering who the prank is on; Jeff, Mutt, the audience, or the poor colonial knocked senseless by the rock?

Figure 6.6 "Yes Indeed These Mohammedan Troops are Very Fierce," by Bud Fisher. *The Seattle Star*. January 17, 1916.

On American soil

There really are very few instances of Muslims in comics appearing on US soil, with the obvious exception of the Philippines, when the Philippines were still a US territory. Reflecting on the example from the *Old King Brady* series, as discussed in Chapter 2, we can see how identifying characters through their dress carries a variety of pitfalls. As the author noted in describing the character of "Mohammed Kebda," his dress was important in not only identifying him as Muslim but also indicating that he comes from the family of the Prophet. Still, when Kebda left his shop to go on an errand for Brady, he whips "off the green turban and clapped on a derby."[10] One implication of this interaction with a member of Little Syria is that, perhaps unlike those who lived in Harlem or Chinatown, the inhabitants of Little Syria could navigate the racialized structures of New York City by changing their attire. Sarah Howell reinforces this point by noting that American Muslims were relatively invisible in the first half of the twentieth century, "which eased their incorporation in many ways."[11] Artists and authors used dress to single out racial identity, but they had to simultaneously contend with the very fact that dress was easily adaptable. Just as Burton or T. E. Lawrence could don the dress of the *fellahin* to pass as a local, so too could a denizen of Little Syria purchase a three-piece suit and bowler hat to walk unremarked upon by the average New Yorker. In some cases, however, the authors and creators of these works purposefully kept their Islamic or Middle Eastern characters in "native" dress, to continue forcing the distinction between themselves and their North American surroundings (Figure 6.7).

In "How They Got Rid of the Rajah Abul Khan—The Story of a Bloodless Revolution," which first appeared in *Puck* in 1896, F. M. Howarth presented a full-page cartoon narrative of the tyrannical Rajah of Kanikapoor and the efforts of his "leading Mugwumps" to overthrow him.[12] Typical of Howarth's "Middle Eastern" settings Kanikapoor is fictional but indicated as Middle Eastern by the style of dress the characters wear, the architectural details we are given, the hookah pipes, and, of course, the ever-present harem. In "How They Got Rid . . ." one of the Mugwumps declares,

> I have traveled in the Occident and know a Western game
> I want but three short days, my scheme will then be proved,
> And this odious, cruel tyrant shall be from hence removed.

The Mugwumps hire for the Rajah a "fair-haired Western maiden who on lettered keys did pound."[13] The Rajah, it seems, fell for the secretary, much to

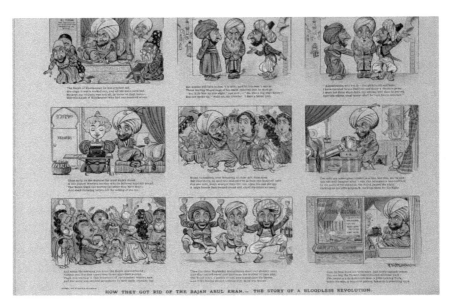

Figure 6.7 "How They Got Rid of Rajah Abul Khan," by F. M. Howarth. *Puck.* 1896.

the chagrin of his numerous wives who spotted on his coat "a large blonde hair twined round and round his collar all awry." In the end, the Rajah fled with his secretary, to the delight of the Mugwumps and the despair of his wives and children. The last panel informs us that the Rajah, now only Abul Khan, has set up shop in the United States:

> Now, in New York is a little store, just lately opened, where
> You can buy the Turkish cigarettes and Oriental ware;
> The owner is a dark-skinned man, a jolly-looking Turk,
> While his wife, a blue-eyed person, takes in typewriting work.

In this last panel, Abul Khan sits smoking his hookah, legs crossed, and wearing much the same type of clothing he was wearing before. His now-wife sits at the back of the shop busily typing on her typewriter. Howarth's Abul Khan appears to be wearing the ornate attire associated with Sultans, as seen in a variety of imagery of the day. Like the *War Puzzles*'s less realistic depictions, he is also wearing a pair *juti* style shoes. Unlike the *War Puzzles*, however, he retains his elaborate turban. The turban is one of the few indicators that Abul Khan has changed rank. In all of the previous panels his turban had a gold crescent moon and a star affixed to the front. In the last panel, in New York, it is plain white. As Abul Khan is inside his shop in this last scene we do not know if he, like Mohammed Kebda, would leave wearing different head gear or not, but, as King

Brady's narrator suggests, appearing on the streets of New York so stridently "foreign" may cause new problems for the former Rajah.

The camel, the cowboy, and the myth of the frontier

That the stories of Dilldock in Howarth's Orient could so seamlessly transition to stories of cowboys in the Wild West under Wells's pen is a testament to a fluidity between the two regions which needs further elucidation and which offers insights into the construction not only of what a Muslim was perceived to be but also of what an American was being established as. We have seen how urban Islam manifested itself in the lifestyle accoutrement of US households through the acquisition of harem pants, for example, but in rural, frontier America, Islam wove itself even deeper, underpinning the very structures of what became *Americana*. Susan Kollin's work *Captivating Westerns* delves deeply into this phenomenon, observing that even globally there is an interconnectedness between the Arab world and the "Wild West." Then US Secretary of State, Condoleezza Rice, in 2007, was confronted with this global dialogue on a visit to Ramallah, in the West Bank. On arrival "she was greeted by Palestinian protesters dressed as Native Americans and carrying signs that read, 'Mrs. Rice, The Indian wars are not over. We are still here too.' The continuing critiques of U.S. frontier discourses in new contexts speak to the powerful ongoing nature of settler colonial projects."[14] The US frontier and its relationship with the Islamic world most clearly develop out of a narrative centered on the camel driver's, the closing of the frontier, and advent of the cowboy, in particular, with the, ultimately unsuccessful, attempt to incorporate camels into the logistics apparatus of the US Army in the middle of the nineteenth century.

The US Army Camel Corps, while an otherwise brief moment in military history, was avidly followed by US newspapers in the 1800s and fueled a romanticized Orientalism that wove well with the emerging Western narrative and landscape. The camel corps, and more specifically the camel driver, was a near perfect alignment for the cowboy. The camel, the camel driver, and romanticized Orientalism entwined themselves throughout the narrative of the West, and with this came a subtle but nevertheless widely understood notion of Islam.

According to Charles C. Carroll, in a 1903 Bureau of Animal Industry report,

> In the early [1850s] the Government was sorely beset with difficulties in protecting the vast frontiers of the country from the ravages of hostile Indians.

The transportation of men and supplies of the great reaches of plain, mountain, and desert that stretched between the Mississippi River and the Pacific coast was a problem that swallowed liberal appropriations of money and used up thousands of mules.[15]

To this end, "it occurred to the military officials that the use of the camel might at least aid them in preforming the difficult duties of protecting the expanding frontier and of keeping open a line of communication between the Mississippi and the coast."[16] After much discussion it was determined in 1852–53 that the Secretary of War should have thirty camels and ten dromedaries (the former referring to those with two humps and the latter with one) imported, "together with 10 Arabs to look after them."[17] The US officials traveled to Tunis, Malta, Smyrna, Constantinople, and Alexandria, first choosing about three dozen camels and dromedaries. In 1856 they returned to obtain another four dozen. "Among the handlers were two men who would become well-known figures around postwar Arizona and California: the Syrian Hadji Ali, a colorful, moderately successful businessman better known to Americans as 'Hi Jolly;' and George Caralambo, a similarly colorful rancher who was renowned as 'Greek George.'"[18] Beyond this, what we know of the handlers who came back with the US officials is scant and perfect for the stuff of legends.

At first the camels, more so than their drivers, became minor celebrities. Between 1855 and 1860 newspapers in Cincinnati, New York, and Chicago (as examples) ran articles discussing their arrival, their movement to Texas (from which they were to be based), and their intended uses. Even years after the corps' disbanding and the scattering of the camels to the four winds, they popped up in the occasional newspaper account. Lone wondering camels, forty, fifty, even sixty years after the fact, were "spotted" in the deserts of Arizona and New Mexico. As for the drivers, two became widely known themselves in the 1880s and the 1890s. One of these, "Hi Jolly" was recognized with a monument and makes an appearance in a variety of pieces of Western fiction.

"Hi Jolly" is the most well remembered of the camel herders. His name, Hadji Ali, was "anglicized" into Hi Jolly by American soldiers, probably in Texas, and he later (re)changed his name to Philip Tedro. Evidence suggests that Hi Jolly was born to Christian Greek-Arab parents, converted to Islam as a young man, came to the United States and eventually became a citizen, converted back to Christianity, and long remained active in US military supply endeavors. A monument was erected to Hi Jolly and his fellow camel drivers in Quartzite, Arizona, in the 1930s, and at least one work of fiction, *Dead Man's Journey* by Jon Sharpe, and one film, *Southwest Passage* (1954), were produced with some reference to Hi Jolly and the camel corps. All of these pieces of popular discourse reflect the cultural fascination with camel drivers among US audiences.

The mystique of the frontier: Camel drivers and cowboy poets

The rugged individualism of the cowboy, ranging across the plains, is an important trope in the development of American identity. That the cowboy recited the poetry Omar Khayyám is perhaps less well understood, but nevertheless essential. Mukhtar Ali Isani notes in his 1977 work "The Vogue of Omar Khayyám in America" that "according to a report current in the 1890s, even a frontiersman striking a remote camp on the Great Divide was heard murmuring a quatrain from the *Rubáiyát* of Omar Khayyám."[19] Khayyám's work became central to American cultural consciousness:

> Americans quoted the *Rubáiyát* from memory, . . . publically debated the philosophy of Omar, and copied the Persian's manner and method either in admiration or to heap satire upon the events and personalities of their time. Some of the "Omarism" of the 1890s was a fad, but evidence of a serious and lasting American interest is now spread impressively over the span of a century.[20]

Khayyám, as himself, and in his work, appeared not only in the recitation of his poetry and through the guise of the Omar Khayyám Club but also in the vernacular of the day: comics. The 1904 single-panel cartoon, "The Omar Khayyám Cult Up to Date," took to the satirical bent that Isani observed. The image depicts Khayyám sitting under a date palm, a camel dutifully waiting behind him, a book resting on his knee, while he listens to a gramophone.[21] The cartoon, produced by James Gilbert, an early illustrator of the translations of the *Rubáiyát*, reflects Gilbert's own humor and his illustration "Here with a Loaf &c." The cartoon, first published in *The Tattler*, found its way into a variety of American publications soon thereafter. The original quatrain read,

> Here with a Loaf of Bread beneath the Bough,
> A Flask of Wine, a Book of Verse—and Thou
> Beside me singing in the Wilderness—
> And Wilderness is Paradise enow.

This appeared alongside the image, but the addition of the gramophone suggested the changes apparent in society, moving from the spiritual to the superficial. By the 1920s, Omar Khayyám's words reached a newer level of kitsch, represented by cartoons like *Omar Jr*, a serialized single-panel cartoon which featured a caricature of Omar Khayyam offering pithy witticisms. Similarly, capitalism flourished in the wake of Omarism. The Omar cigarette company, named for Omar Khayyám, exploited the popularity of his work by serializing the *Rubáiyát* in its early advertising campaigns. The *Rubáiyát* campaign began as early as 1910, but by the time the First World War was underway, the opulence and splendor of the advertising reached a zenith. The *American Magazine* ran at least two in the series in 1914, depicting a rotund male character enjoying the pleasures of life with a fair-skinned, usually seated beneath him, woman, named "Angel Shape," also bedecked in "oriental costume."

The Omar cigarette company's advertising campaign focused on lines from the *Rubáiyát*; underscoring the themes of pleasure, leisure, and luxury, with the occasional adventure thrown in. In one advertisement from 1913, Omar rescues Angel Shape from a burning hotel. When he is asked how he could breathe with all that smoke, he nonchalantly claims that Smoke is his middle name. The campaign took a notable shift when the male character who was depicted as chubby (occasionally downright obese) and jovial became substantially svelter and evolved into a character for romance. As Omarism waned the company took the cigarette out of the Orient and planted it in "traditional" and notably "masculine" Western settings, for example, the male club, the battlefield, a tennis game, and camping/hunting/fishing. The Omar "fishing" advertisement harkened back to the associations between the outdoorsman imagery of Arabs and Bedouins, as suggested in the imagery of the Wilderness being Paradise, melded with the rugged individualism of American identity. The assumption of a masculine identity wrapped up in outdoors, nonurban settings, is reinforced in Wells's cartoons as well. While Wells did not highlight the Oriental underpinnings of the cowboy's identity, the fact that one of his rodeo personas was a Bedouin nods to this history. In the work *The Poetics and Politics of Desert* the author acknowledges the construction of the American Southwest "as [a] domestic Orient." It was the camel, and the camel herder as symbols of the freedom of wide open spaces that helped Orientalize at home the West and the cowboy in the United States' very own "domestic Orient" as well as informing the masses, at least in one sliver of knowledge, about the nature of Islam and the centrality of the camel to it.

Omar Khayyam's legacy and significance in American popular consciousness helps us elucidate the masculine and feminine place of these narratives as well. *The Ladies' Home Journal*, among others, quoted liberally from Khayyam's poetry, although his legacy was not always considered appropriate for women. The article series "A Plain Country Woman" first published in 1915 referred to

Khayyam's work as "despondent," admonishing readers to be more concerned with the here and now, less with the ephemeral what-might-be. In 1916, the article series continued that theme, charging readers with learning to "reconcile yourself to the present, . . . not as you would have made it if you had, as Omar Khayyam blasphemously puts it, the power to shatter this sorry scheme of things to bits, and then remold it nearer to the heart's desire."[22] *Good Housekeeping* informed its readers that they could, host an "Omar Khayyam dinner" by creating place cards with "Persian designs in Persian rug colors, each bearing an appropriate quotation from the *Rubaiyat*, which abounds in them."[23]

Is the Muslim woman veiled?

As indicated by the *War Puzzles*, women, particularly women dressed in modest Islamic fashions, are fairly uncommon in US comics between the 1880s and the 1920s. In the *Opie Dilldock* series, for example, although there are a large number of women in Howarth's stories, especially in lands we are led to believe as Islamic, no woman is veiled. Similarly, in Howarth's 1896, Rajah Abul Khan's cartoon none of the women are veiled, although it is worth noting they are only depicted inside the harem and would not necessarily be veiled there anyway. One could argue that there is much less indication of Islam, among the female Howarth characters than the male. Whereas men are often suited in the tropes of Islam, Howarth's women are more often than not wearing formfitting clothes, ornate jewelry, and the occasional hair ornament. Aside from the fact that in 1896 American women were not yet wearing harem pants, most of Howarth's ladies would have been interchangeable with American women.

Still, the veil was often an indicator of Islam in illustrations and comics of the day. In 1913, Lady Duff-Gordon thrilled at the coming of "Harem Veils" to Paris fashions. She noted, "We Occidentals are ever interested in the Turkish women, in the women of the Seraglios, and we avidly copy them when we may. I am indeed glad that we have elected to favor the veil rather than the trousers of the Seraglio!"[24] Not long thereafter, of course, those same trousers became the center of the harem aesthetic. Like so many other pieces of fashion Western designers acquired the veil, but not the sentiment. "Veils," Duff-Gordon noted, "so provocative of mystery, so associated with charms, are rapidly becoming a craze."[25] Despite discussing the *yasmik*, "the soft, transparent veiling that all well-born Turkish women wear to hide the lower part of their faces from the vulgar gaze," none of the images flanking Duff-Gordon's article offered face concealing veils.[26] The pictured examples were of draped shawls and wraps, but nothing concealing anything more than some hair or a shoulder. If this is how the West understood the Islamic veil, it is perhaps less surprising then, that most examples of veils in cartoons of the day were flimsy, if at all existent.

One opulent example of the variety in veils Western audiences came to expect was from "The Widow Wise," a poem and series of illustrations for the *Washington Herald*. In the story, a Turkish man by the name "Mohammed Mulai Hassan Bey" courted a European or American woman, the "Widow Wise." Nearly convinced by the man's keen attentions, the Widow turns down the man's advances when his numerous wives visit her in turn. At the end we hear,

> "Wives!" cried the Widow, "And you come to ask I wed him, too!"
> "Of course," the gentle ladies said, "as all good wives should do!"
> The Widow flushed. "No thanks!" she said, with scornful, flashing eyes,
> "I'LL NEVER JOIN A SYNDICATE!" exclaimed the Widow Wise.[27]

The women who visit the Widow are all clad in dress "of the harem," including Turkish trousers, but they each have a different take on the veil. Some appear to have no veil at all, others are pulling down the lightweight veils over their mouths either to smoke or to speak with the Widow. One is playing with what might be a veil; others are wearing solidly shaded veils concealing the lower half of their face. Behind the throngs of wives, but distinct as her own being, is a woman wearing what appears to be a veil, and perhaps even as mask. She looks more like she is headed to a masquerade, but this may be the artist's attempt at indicating something more akin to a *niqab*. What is particularly striking about the wives in the scene is the rest of their attire. All appear to be wearing harem pants, with a significant amount of ankle exposed, most are wearing tight fitting hip sashes that accentuate their curves, and at least one may have an exposed mid-rift. Their style is an interesting juxtaposition to the Widow, who wears an admittedly formfitting, full dress that effectively covers her shoulders and chest.

Of course, real Islamic veils come in a wide variety of styles themselves. Covering one's face is only a portion of the forms taken up by Islamic women. The modern *hijab* serves to cover a woman's hair, neck, and shoulders, but do not necessarily cover any part of her face. In recent years, rebellion against women's Islamic dress in countries where it is mandated has taken on the exposure of hair and even the neck, as a way to fight back against rigid demands. Far more conservative trends, such as in the *burkah* or *niqab*, are less common but far more concealing. In both of these examples, women conceal their entire face, exposing only portion of their eyes in the case of the *niqab*.

Figure 6.8 "Jeff is Some Escort," by Bud Fisher. *El Paso Herald*. March 6, 1913.

In the March 6, 1913, issue of *Mutt and Jeff*, "Jeff is Some Escort," Mutt has procured a "swell job" for Jeff "escorting ladies from the Sultan's Harem out for their morning walks" (Figure 6.8). Mutt duly warns Jeff that he "must never speak or get fresh to 'em. It means sure death." Jeff assures Mutt he can handle the charge, and we see three intervening panels when Jeff is walking alongside a woman in *juti* shoes, harem pants, a cropped vest, and a face veil that obscures the lower half of her face. In the third of these panels Jeff is seen making eye contact with the lady and the questioning is situation. In the last panel Jeff races toward the Bulgarian border, the place Mutt assured him was the "only one chance for anyone to live who gets fresh with the harem."[28]

Jeff's escapes, both inside the harem and out, not only explicitly defined the place of Muslim women in US cartoons at the fin de siècle but also helped draw distinctions between female spaces and male spaces in an era and society struggling to define its own parameters on the matter. The Widow Wise, herself, establishes this distance as well, creating an "Us versus Them" dialogue. As suffragettes won the vote and took up a place in public service in greater numbers than ever before, their shifting status was redefined, and non-American women became foils to the New Woman of North America.

Echoes of the Past, Shadows of the Future

When Marc Singer, in 2002, wrote about the reductionism dominant in superhero comics, his focus was on the fact that those characters "are wholly externalized into their heroic costumes and aliases."[1] Arguably, in the last twenty years, superheroes have become increasingly more complex personifications of the reality about which their story lines are supposed to be allegory. The idea that comic characters "are continually reduced to their appearances," however, was especially true of non-European or North American, nonwhite character depictions at the turn of the twentieth century. Comics inherently distill narratives to tropes and archetypes to meet the constraints of panels, making them not only readily accessible to a broad readership but also potentially dangerous by oversimplifying a complex reality. As Wertham noted, pre-1950 comics had a tendency to create an expectation of what a "regular-featured and 'an athletic pure American white man'" was, contrasted dramatically with the villains who were often "foreign-born, Jews, Orientals, Slavs, Italians and dark-skinned races."[2] The exaggerated and deeply racialized comics of the turn of the twentieth century have, thankfully, increasingly been replaced by more nuanced articulations of race, gender, and ability, although much work is still necessary. Female characters, in particular, remain the focus of the male gaze and are often depicted in hypersexualized ways. Just as the harem, into which so many characters peeped, was articulated as a domain intended for the enjoyment of male onlookers, the female superhero's costuming offers nearly nothing for protection and nearly everything for fantasy, leaving very little to the imagination.

In the case of Muslim characterizations, the key has changed, but the song is still recognizable. The fanciful Orientalization, which incorporated Scheherazade and sumptuous, exotic settings, by and large, fell out of favor with cartoonists after the turn of the millennium. Reflecting an ever globalizing world, comics, while still dominated in the industry by US, French, and Japanese production, is becoming increasingly decentralized. In the case of specifically US productions the events of September 11 absolutely impacted portrayals of Islam and Muslims, but this is not the only influence on the market. The world is hyper-connected, and emergent social media and information sharing platforms allow for a broad range of voices to be heard. There is much more variety today, than one hundred years ago, in how Islam is depicted, even within the confines of the United States. None of this is to say that the old tropes, types, and formulas have been dismantled or even rendered unusable. Works like Craig Thompson's *Habibi* are a modern example of that opulent past being carried forward. When reviewed by *The Guardian*, Thompson's work was described as "an orgy of art for its own sake," but one depicting "a timeless Middle East that fuses exotic legend with grim modernity."[3] The fact that the Islamic world, and there is no doubt here that Thompson is setting his work in an imagined Islamic world, remains timelessly caught in a world of harems and despotic sultans, of slave traders and of desert nomads is more telling of how deeply embedded these tropes are in American cultural consciousness than their utility for telling a good story. Thompson's vision with *Habibi* was not to offer up a real-life story of the early modern Middle East but to emote through the legacy of Orientalist artwork a feeling of that "timeless" land. Thompson, who is at the heart of the work telling a love story, does not shy away from the brutality of humanity, using well-established tropes to lend an air plausibility, if not authenticity, to his narrative. Aside from works like Thompson's, however, largely gone is the scimitar, inexhaustibly dripping with blood, it was increasingly replaced by the AK-47, just as the fez was replaced by the ski mask. Some tropes of the early twentieth century have receded on a significant scale, others have emerged into more prominent roles.

Depicting the Prophet

Modern discussions around depictions of Islam and Muslims, especially in comics, inevitably turn to the specific question of depicting the Prophet. This conversation is not surprising in light of works published in France's *Charlie Hebdo*, Denmark's *Jyllands-Posten*, and by the so-called "American Freedom Defense Initiative" for their "Muhammad Art Exhibit and Contest." The cartoons and images published and produced for these organizations were not, nor were intended to be, reverential. While they may have been intended as thought-provoking and an exercise in free speech, for many iconoclastic Muslims, and not, they were simply abhorrent, hurtful, and blasphemous.

Violence, to varying degrees of severity, followed the images created for these outlets. Thus, in modern popular culture, the question emerged by what right is there to depict Muhammad. The animated TV show *South Park* grappled with this, in the wake of the *Jyllands-Posten* cartoons, centering its "Cartoon Wars" episodes on the question of American purveyors of popular culture depicting Muhammad. Critique and discussion of this episode largely focused on the rivalry between *South Park* and *The Family Guy*, not engendering the much needed national discussion on religious iconoclasm.

The idea that Islam is iconoclastic is an accepted truism in the West, but it is a perceived fact that needs to be challenged more thoroughly. Certainly Islamist groups like al-Qaeda and ISIS perpetuate prohibitions against depicting the Prophet and other central Islamic figures, or even other religious figures, as noted by the Taliban's destruction of the Buddhas of Bamiyan, but when the Western media frames anger over *Jyllands-Posten* cartoons or *Charlie Hebdo* caricatures as Islamic iconoclasm, it negates the very real frustration Muslims feel that their faith is not being taken seriously and is distilled to the punch line of a joke. To continue to insist that all of Islam is iconoclastic is to further perpetuate an Orientalist vision of the unchangeable/static Islamic world.

The larger history of Islam is much more dynamic. Muslims and non-Muslims have, for centuries, depicted the image of the Prophet despite prohibitions against doing so. As early as the thirteenth century (and perhaps even earlier) Muhammad's visage (veiled and unveiled) adorned Middle Eastern artwork. Christiane Gruber tells us that there exists "a notable corpus of images of Muhammad" particularly from the "Ilkhanid (1256–1353), Timurid (1370–1506), and Safavid (1501–1722) periods."[4] "The earliest extant paintings of the Prophet Muhammad depict him as a fully visible corporal figure, whose facial features or *shamā'il* are neither hidden beneath a veil nor engulfed by flames."[5] The flames in these images are similar to halos in Western iconography, suggesting spiritual significance. Since those days, Muhammad has made cameo appearances not only in "high art" and literature but also in a longish history of comics as well.

Depicting Muhammad has varied tremendously over the religion's 1,400-year history. Artists who depict the Prophet use(d) a variety of "motifs and techniques to communicate visually the Prophet's exceptional status. In turn, such explorations crystallized into specific pictorial traditions that could be given new meanings in different contexts, be these Shi'i, Sunni, Sufi, or some combination thereof."[6]

"Sufi writers discussing the subject in particular believe that the Prophet had both human (*nāsūt*) and superhuman (*lāhūt*) nature united into one being."[7] For theological reasons this sums up the crux of some fundamentalists definitions of Islamic history and in part what leads to iconoclasm more generally among believers of the faith. Like debates between Nestorians and other Christian sects over the nature of Christ as Divine and human, some Muslims (mostly Shi'a and Sufi) asserted a divinity of Muhammad that others feel uncomfortable with or outright denounce. Iconoclastic tendencies, moreover, are not unique to Islam; Christians themselves flirted with their own moments of anti-imagery rhetoric at various points over the centuries. From the point of view of a comic scholar, however, this is a clear indication of Muhammad's possibilities in sequential art.

Outside of his appearance as a provocative instrument for those aggressively testing the limitations of freedom of speech and press, Muhammad's most common part in comics was in that of a comic-cum-education guise. In 1925, the comic series *High Lights of History* began to offer a cartoon interpretation of world history, in particular major turning points. In June 1928, a two-issue set offered a narrative of Islamic history. The first, from June 10, openly depicted the Prophet Muhammad, and what is more interesting, even his (first) wife Khadija.[8] On June 17, the next issue picked up with the story of Islam after Muhammad's death, tracing the faith's spread across the Mediterranean and Asiatic worlds.[9] Nearly twenty years later, *Picture Stories from World History, Vol. 2* duplicated the efforts of *High Lights*, and depicted, once again, Muhammad and the story of Islam's founding.

Echoing the pre–First World War fascination with Muhammad's camel driving past, a cartoon depiction of Muhammad in the *Evening Star's* "Uncle Ray's Corner" from 1932 and issue #74 of *Thrilling Comics*, from 1949, reemphasized this as a crucial component in understanding Islamic history.[10] Non-Muslim US audiences may not explicitly understand why the camel driving tidbit of information retains its relevancy over the years, although the cowboy-philosopher angle may explain why it still resonates. Yet as almost all Muslims know, God has one hundred names. Humans know only ninety-nine of those names, the camel knows the last, and this is why the camel smiles with that enigmatic smile.

Islam, and Muhammad specifically, continue to be depicted in the pages of graphic novels and comic books, but like the artists of the thirteenth through the fifteenth centuries, illustrators and authors are playing with the medium in order to fully articulate the story the nature of the faith and its people. Gruber tells us that Islamic artists of earlier eras tended to portray the Prophet in one of three divergent and at times overlapping ways: veristic, inscribed, and luminous.[11] The first of these, veristic, depicts "the human form as it is visible to the human eye, by including such details as facial features, bodily limbs, and other physical characteristics."[12] The inscribed method contained "inscriptions either below or above a painted surface—usually the Prophet's white facial veil—and thus reveal the painter's processual approach to image making and / or the viewer's active reception to it."[13] The final method, luminous "paintings adopt metaphorical language of the golden aureole to convey the Prophet's sacred, primordial, and creative light, called the 'Light of Muhammad.'"[14] Over the course of the thirteenth through the fifteenth centuries representations increasingly became more metaphorical, not so much "attempts to prohibit or eradicate his depiction" this "being only one facet of a distinctively modern phenomenon."[15]

Muhammad, and Islam, continues to be a conduit through which artists explore these reverential concepts, even in comics. The most obvious example of this is superhero series *The 99*. Naif al-Mutawa, creator of *The 99*, used the ninety-nine names of God to describe each of his superheroes. These names are attributes that, al-Mutawa points out, are qualities shared by all of the world's faiths (generosity, intelligence, love, etc.), "basic human values."[16] While these attributes are certainly not unique to the Quranic tradition, some conservative Muslims disagree with al-Mutawa's efforts. One Saudi cleric issued a *fatwa* in 2014 calling on the people to "shun this series, both on television and in the comic books."[17] While al-Mutawa and his team of artists and writers are not actively depicting God or Muhammad, they are metaphorically depicting them, and many others, through these attributes. Al-Mutawa's purpose in creating *The 99*, "to give Muslim children, especially young boys, characters that they could really look up to and dream about," echoes the results that Oya Pancaroglu has offered based on twelfth-century Persian scholarship, that images of the Prophet were more often than not "instruments in ethical instruction rather than traps leading to idolatry."[18]

Comics then, in the example we have before us, are doing exactly what Gruber argues the high art of the Islamic world was doing:

> Depicting persons as rich and complex entities blending presence and essence—not just material fact . . . the general shift from understanding a portrait as a simple likeness to perceiving it as a procedure that aims to describe an individual's entire character has led to new discussions that highlight the deep divide between *vision*, as a scientific mechanism linked to the production of sight, and *visuality*, which encompasses the many culturally contingent modes of seeing.[19]

In this context, in seeing comic depictions of Muhammad, at least the ones intended as educational, if not overtly reverential, opens up a depth of analysis in the philosophical underpinning of the nature of God and God's works.

Superheroes and women

As we have had reason to discuss before large communities of people have been forced into background roles in comics. In the case of Muslim women and women in Islamic-style settings, at the turn of the twentieth century, they too played a role largely as plot devices or extraneous characters. In Howarth's "How They Got Rid of the Rajah Abul Khan—The Story of a Bloodless Revolution," the women, all, are devices used to move the plot and Rajah along. The wives pester and demand, which acts as the final motivator in sending the Rajah packing. The blue-eyed secretary never speaks but is the means for their survival when the Rajah and she settle in New York City. The sexual availability, and even downright ownership of women in comic settings like these, was presented in a light manner but created an undercurrent of unease for women worldwide advocating for greater rights. Craig Thompson's *Habibi* not only harkens back to the sumptuous style of Orientalist art, through the medium of sequential art, but does so exploring, perhaps too deeply, sex and sexual pollution. Michel Faber's otherwise laudatory review of Thompson's work bluntly derides Thompson's handling of sex as "problematic," and that "scenes of self-loathing, castration and post-traumatic angst, piled on top of Dodola's frequent relapses into sex slavery and starvation, raise the suspicion that the author is compelled to be crueller than his narrative demands."[20] Thankfully, there is a distinct shift afoot among comic authors and artists to move away from such narratives. This trend is increasingly coupled with more creators being themselves women, and/or people from historically underrepresented communities of color or faith.

As much as Muslims inhabited limited spaces in comics generally, they inhabited very few spaces as superheroes more specifically. In 1944, *Bomber Comics #1* presented Kismet, the first, as A. David Lewis has stated, "genuine" Muslim superhero. Much like the Muslim characters in the pre–Second World War era, most of the evidence we have about Kismet's Islam is suggestive. Lewis notes that "there are superficial signs, certainly, such as his prohibition against drinking alcohol ('When the brain is soaked with wine, the fist is not obedient to its master,' he said) as well as his exclamations of 'By the beard of the Prophet!'

and 'By the star and crescent of Islam!'"[21] Lewis applauds Kismet's creator(s), Omar Tahan, who was likely himself fictional, for choosing to ignore Kismet's backstory. According to Lewis Kismet's garish costume, cape, gloves, and fez

> act as markers for concealing an identity that is never explored—much to one's relief! In all likelihood, the mind(s) constituting "Omar Tahan" did not have the background or personal knowledge to flesh out a believable, nuanced Muslim character. So, rather than his being burdened with stereotypes and excessive orientalism, Kismet was able to remain an unfettered and attractive character.[22]

This may be a rosy interpretation of Tahan's choice; it suggests a thoughtfulness among the creators that was uncommon of the era. It could be just as easily argued that a too clearly identifiable Muslim character was a potential non-seller, leaving Kismet's backstory to the imagination added both mystery and distance between him and the reader. Again still, Kismet's creators could have felt that no backstory was needed because enough stereotypes and tropes were established in popular consciousness to simply just rely on those.

The evolution of Muslim *women* in sequential art took significantly longer to gain traction. The first substantial entrance of a female Muslim voice into sequential art did not come until 2000, and even then it came from outside the United States. Marjane Satrapi's seminal work *Persepolis* garnered international acclaim, not only for the material it covered but also for the very style in which it was produced. While Art Speiglman's *Maus* was in circulation for at least a decade, Satrapi's work reinforced the utility of the graphic novel style while simultaneously centering the narrative on the female voice. Her 2005 work *Embroideries* delved even deeper into the lives of women in Iran, and the navigation they undertake through the cultural mores of an Islamic (in this case, Shi'a) state. Satrapi's work is autobiographical and exposes and explores complexities of religion, culture, and global citizenship.

In terms of fiction, it was not until 2002 when Marvel, in the series the *New X-Men*, introduced Sooraya Qadir, also known as Dust. Qadir, is a niqab-clad mutant, Afghani immigrant to the United States. While powerful as a superhero, she nevertheless embodies many of the tired Orientalist tropes of the twentieth century. She was, according to Marvel's own website,

> sold into slavery in her native Afghanistan at a young age, [and] . . . liberated by Wolverine of the X-Men. Subsequently enrolled as a student at the Xavier Institute, Sooraya was originally placed in the Special Class to allow her time to acclimatize to her new environment.[23]

Unsurprisingly, given the unabashed conflation of peoples and cultures within the Islamic world by those outside it, Qadir, despite being from Afghanistan, speaks Arabic, not Pashto or Dari which are more likely choices for the region. Moreover, just as Belinda was saved at every turn by the Hairbreadth Harry, so too is Qadir saved by a male lead, before she can be empowered as her own character. Belinda did stave off Rudolph's advances, but in the end it was Harry who remained the central character of the narrative.

Qadir's backstory suggests less intensive research on the part of her creators than simply falling back on old tropes. Dust's choice in wearing a *niqab* not only rankled conservative comic readers but also those Muslim girls and women who looked to her as a guiding force in superhero comics. In 2018, Sara Alfageeh reimagined Dust after looking at her depiction and wondering: "Who looked at a niqabi character and still gave her the latex costume treatment?"[24] Alfageeh offered an updated look for Dust, reflecting modern Islamic dress sensibilities, modesty, and a decidedly freer movement of limbs than what one twitter described as "vacuum sealed."[25] Just as dress was telling in early twentieth century the role of the veil and women's Islamic style in particular have become central to modern conversations about Muslim depictions in comics.

In 2008, Marvel, in its *Captain Britain* series, introduced Faiza Hussain, a London-based medical doctor of Pakistani background, as the wielder of Excalibur. Hussain, depicted wearing a hajib, was certainly a breakthrough character for many, but as the Captain Britain title did not circulate as widely as others, her reach and influence were limited. In 2010, and with a great deal of controversy in conservative comics-reading communities, DC added Bilal Asselah, also known as Nightrunner, to the *Batman, Inc.* series. Asselah challenged a number of traditional Orientalist tropes and drew attention to the complicated history of colonialism. He is a citizen of France (of Algerian descent) and a practicing Muslim, who lives in the community Clichy-sous-Bois, a neighborhood noted in real life for being the scene of racial and economic tension. His mother, unnamed and apparently single (perhaps widowed), is a source of moral fortitude for Asselah. When Asselah and his best friend run afoul of police officers who confuse them for rioters, it is Asselah's mother's calm and thoughtful manner that helps give him strength to do the right thing. Throughout our first introduction to the Asselahs, the mother is seen in six of ten pages. We do hear her voice, calmly asking her son, literally and metaphorically, to "step away from the edge,"[26] but the greater sense of her as a person is in her actions. In these ten pages, we see her pray three times, give comfort twice, and sleep once. At least while at her prayers, Asseah's mother is left in peace, unlike the Bedouin in the *Sambo* comics. Superhero comics, and comics more generally, have a tendency to be secular in scope. Seeing faith not only expressed but also even explored in these comics is surprising. The fact, however, that the importance of faith is transmitted through the mother's character is much less astonishing. She is not the central character, but her actions and depictions as an Islamic woman suggest another trope, that of the dutiful, pious, mother character. Asselah's mother is much like other notable mothers or parental figures in comics. Like Aunt May in Spiderman, she is the moral compass for his future undertakings, but she lacks much depth as a character of her own. The space she inhabits is not one far removed from the expectations of mothers and the pious in the wider world. They are not endowed with avowed superhuman qualities, but anyone familiar with the family members of superheroes know that their fortitude, patience, understanding, and resilience is in and of itself superhuman. These non-super actors reflect real-world human actions, and their role in comics is symbolic praise for those real-life mothers and pious leaders who exhibit these traits in the real world .

In 2013, the global community began to push forward new Muslim female, cartoon voices. Pakistani pop star Aaron Haroon Rashid's *Burka Avenger* and Egyptian art student Deena Mohamed's *Qahera—the Superhero* recentered female-centric Muslim superheroes in much more empowering narratives. While neither of these was produced for or by Americans, they were certainly both consumed by Americans. The *Burka Avenger* a children's cartoon starring a teacher who fights injustice and extremism with knowledge, literally turning pens and books into weapons, is widely accessible and is translated in a variety of languages. The idea that "bad guys" want to shut down schools may be foreign to American or British children, but the thought of it is not so wholly unfathomable as to not be relatable. School, especially for the youngest children, retains the magic that more cynical adults associate with Christmas or Hogwarts.

The United States, finally in February 2014, received its first full-fledged, empowering Muslim female superhero. Marvel returned to the idea of women and Muslims in its comic books by recreating Ms. Marvel as Kamal Khan, a sixteen-year-old girl of Pakistani origin living in Jersey City, New Jersey. Marvel tapped author G. Willow Wilson to write the story line, she herself playing an important role in the evolving landscape. Wilson, a practicing Muslim, has lived extensively in Egypt and the United States and navigates the complexities of those cultures in all of her work. In terms of sequential art, before writing *Ms. Marvel*, Wilson authored *Cairo*, a magical realist story blending modern tropes and concerns with the images of Middle Eastern lore (e.g., jinn). She is well versed in the hackney tropes of Orientalism, the deep rich history of the Islamic world, and the complex realities of popular culture and its shifting nature, all of which she brings to her work in a critical, introspective, and circumspective manner.

Both Deena Mohamed and G. Willow Wilson offer similarly pointed interpretations of the role of women in comics, in particular, Muslim women. Unlike authors who have presented Islamic, and female, characters in the past, both Mohamed and Wilson represent these much needed intersections of comic material. Their characters are reflective of the communities from which they come and with whom they speak. As Gloria Steinem noted, in reflecting on Wonder Woman, "Women and girls, more than boys, need superheroes because women face the greater majority of violence in the world than do men and boys."[27] This element, of violence faced why women and girls in particular, is, by their nature as Superheroines, a significant point of discussion in both Mohamed's Qahera strips and Wilson's Ms. Marvel. Superheroes are inherently the righters of wrongs, particularly the wrongs perpetrated against the weakest in societies. Both Qahera and Ms. Marvel are positioned as advocates for those suffering the ramifications of asymmetries of power.

Interestingly, both Kamala Khan and Faiza Hussain come out of another population that unites them with their audiences, but without ethnic identity or religious background: that of the "fan-girl" community. In both instances, Khan and Hussain become cognizant of their powers after having lived lives minutely following the doings and happenings of superheroes. With Khan, this personality trait is less jarring than it is with Hussain. Hussain, already a medical doctor, not a student, is a well-established, independent adult. Her child-like joy at not only meeting but also getting to work with superheroes like Black Knight is meant to be humanizing, but it has the effect of infantilization. In the audience's first meeting with Hussain she trips over her words, blushes, and giggles, all the while working triage on a battlefront. While Hussain acknowledges this and chastises herself for it, the act itself weakens her credibility as a potentially strong female lead and leads us back to gendered formulas of women superheroes as not equal to their male counterpoints.

Imperial legacies

In two significant ways modern US comics are boldly facing the legacies of imperialism and an increasingly globalized world. On the one hand, the relationship between conservative political elements and comics has become much more complicated than they were in the early 1900s. This complex relationship, moreover, leads to an understanding of the second legacy, the advent of a more diverse comics' universe and community of creators.

For the first of these two points a minor story that broke in the wake of events in Charlottesville, Virginia, in August 2017 is indicative of the whole. At the heart of this subtheme in Charlottesville was a question of who "owns" a *Captain America* title, "Secret Empire." Some elements in far-right communities took the series as a token of their own sentiments and ideologies being writ large in mainstream media. Even, at the riots, clothing and gear that reflected an alliance to the story line was proudly worn by alt-right, and other right-leaning, extremists. Still further, some on the left took aim at Nick Spencer's story arc for feeding into far-right sympathies and are deriding "hydra cap for Nazis in America."[28] Spencer, in response, took umbrage with his story line's usage by the right and blame leveled at him for other people's actions, citing right-wing websites which condemn his work as leftist propaganda. Whatever Spencer may feel on the subject, there is a vocal element of far-right US communities who take quite seriously what they perceive to be an attack on *their* cultural heritage in the shifting nature of comic story lines. What this community sees as the usurping of their cultural heritage often falls under the guise of their disdain for "political correctness," that adding diversity to comic book story arcs somehow weakens or delegitimizes those stories' power. In 2010, Andy Khouri wrote, in response to anti-*Nightrunner* sentiment, that what those individuals and groups, like the Council for Conservative Citizens, "don't care to understand is that by sheer force of will, superhero comic books and animation have amassed a significant amount of political and cultural capital with which to reflect and impact" complex religio-sociopolitical themes.[29] In considering this from the vantage point of this book, moreover, that amassing began well over a hundred years ago.

The interconnectedness of politics and social constructions with comics and cartoons, of course, are at the very heart of this book, and these modern shadows of past events indicate just how intertwined this history is. At the turn of the twentieth century the United States was only just embarking on a global imperial agenda, and, by the end of the period with which this book is most concerned, the United States began a process of drastically restricting immigration into the country. Asian and Southeast European immigrants were primary targets of Nativist and isolationist efforts. A subsequent outcome of these laws and changes was that far fewer Muslims found their way to the United States before the 1960s than may have otherwise. Despite the isolationism with which policy like immigration restriction are associated, however, the United States was simultaneously deeply embedded in a global narrative of cultural adaptation and change. We saw this set of themes developed unconsciously by Howarth and Wells in the *Opie Dilldock* series.

The 1965 Immigration and Nationalities Act reversed previous immigration practices in the United States, ending the National Origins Formula. While the number of Muslims in the United States has not skyrocketed, it has certainly grown since the 1910s. Kamala Khan and her family are reflective of the much more diverse United States that resulted from the 1965 Immigration Act, just as postwar immigration to France and Great Britain dramatically altered the ethnic and religious diversity of those countries as well. For far-right, conservative groups, however, this immigration, which is vital to a thriving economy, was decried as detrimental to their supremacy. Their invasion of the pages of comics only further inflamed their ire.

Kamal Khan, Faiza Hussain, and Bilal Asselah share a number of attributes that make them effective representatives of their communities, while at the same time initiating a conversation on globalization. Khan, Hussain, and Asselah all appear to be first generation citizens of the United States, Britain, and France, respectively, but their families come from Islamic countries notably changed by colonial heritage (Pakistan and Algeria). While the United States was not an imperial power in the Indian subcontinent like Great Britain, or as France was in Algeria, the experience of colonialism dramatically shaped the lives of people who both stayed and left. We are not given a great deal of detail about Khan's, Hussain's, and Asselah's parents, but we can assume that they came to their respective Western countries sometime between the 1960s and the 1980s. As characters of Marvel and DC story lines, their inclusion and their global impact suggest that American power to sway and define global popular culture is the modern equivalent of high imperialism at the end of the nineteenth century. Like *Punch* and *Puck* cartoons, which reached across the world, embedding themselves in local versions, critiquing the enterprise of imperialism, the very enterprise that makes their cartoons accessible to the world, Khan, Hussain, and Asselah critique a patriarchal, Western-dominated, White-centric worldview, using the medium of superheroes, a product of a patriarchal, Western, White system.[30]

Imperial heritage does not always so obviously reflect direct history, as in the case of *Nightrunner* or Kamala Khan. As we saw in Chapter 4, Bluebeard evolved away from his French background to that of an Ottoman one, over the course of the nineteenth century. Since the 1920s, while Bluebeard has not had the centrality of fairy-tale characters of Snow White or Cinderella, he has not been altogether forgotten and indeed seems poised on a resurgence in the wake of #MeToo.[31] As hinted at in earlier discussions of Bluebeard's depiction, he has always been, no matter his national origin, the epitome of a manipulative and violent husband. That in 2018, Kelly Faircloth was able to write "of all the echoes of fairy tales, the loudest of all is the story of Bluebeard," screams the power of stories to elucidate present narratives as well as past.

> A door that locks without anyone touching it . . . . A large man who overpowers, beast-like. A man who wears a mask of virtue that he removes behind closed doors. These striking and grotesque images could have sprung from fairy tales, but they didn't—they are from real testimonies by real women, over the last year of reckoning. Yet, there's a kinship between so many #MeToo accounts and the original grimmer fairy tales that came before the 20th century.[32]

The tales, however, become too real. Bluebeard has become less a fictional "Other" in a distant land, safely tucked away in a book, but a "confirmation that curiosity, suspicion, and gut feelings were hinting at violent truth: Something is wrong in this house."[33]

In less gendered and more metaphorically imperial terms, Bill Willingham's 2002–15 series, *Fables*, Bluebeard reemerged as a central character of the fairy-tales-meet-real-life story line. Returning to his French roots, *Fables'* Bluebeard pushed away the Orientalized version so omnipresent in the fin de siècle; however, the artistic choice to depict him as a bald man with a neatly manicured beard and a gold hoop earring suggests at least a passing gesture toward the Orient. This nearly piratical imagery is reminiscent of *jinn* (genie), a lurker on the fringes of mainstream society, "even Perrault's villain betokened an outsider, a libertine, a ruffian."[34] Thus, Bluebeard embodies an element of society acknowledged, but not considered wholly respectable, "as fundamentally foreign while . . . the more appealing fairy tale husbands [are] familiar, even local."[35] What makes the Bluebeard story, inside the *Fables'* universe, particularly interesting for our purposes is that in the end, well, that is to say in Bluebeard's end, he is torn apart and eaten by Shere Khan, the tiger and archetypal villain of Rudyard Kipling's

The Jungle Book. Khan begins to consume Bluebeard before he is pulled away from the corpse. If we interpret Shere Khan as a different vision of the Orient, although not necessarily one far removed from the despotic formulation offered elsewhere at the turn of the twentieth century, then his devouring the French nobleman-turned-Oriental-style-tyrant provides a fascinating lens through which to view Western imperialisms' narrative about how "Eastern" states rule themselves. The Western despot made Oriental meets his demise at the hands of the foreboding native, Eastern threat. In the context of the fin de siècle the rising tide of nationalist and anti-imperialist sentiment underlay frantic fears of empires being toppled, in Western media. Shere Khan can be read, therefore, as the embodiment of the native nationalists, having learned from their imperial governors how to wield Western-style power and using that same power to overthrow those same empires.

Empowerment and education

The empowerment that is gained by positive representations of Muslims, like Kamala Khan or Bilal Asselah, should not be undervalued. In a 2018 interview for *Pod Save America*, Rashida Tlaib, an unopposed candidate to Michigan's 13th Congressional District, the first (Muslim) Palestinian-American, woman in Congress, reflected on the power one comic had in helping her understand ways in which Islam is perceived in the United States and the way it potentially shaped her son's understanding as well. Tlaib described the cartoon, which ran in *USA Today*, as depicting a skeleton wearing a Nazi uniform and speaking the words "Allahu Akbar" (God is great).[36] The cartoon unnerved Tlaib, who feared Americans would see Muslims as Nazis, and that this one cartoon spoke for the sentiment of millions. The cartoon, likely the one drawn by Cameron Cardow of the *Ottawa Citizen*, ran in *USA Today* as its daily editorial cartoon on February 2, 2015.[37] Tlaib, vocalizing the fears she faced in that one moment, pertaining to that one cartoon, speaks volumes in the narrative history of comics. More than the glib, or childish, offhand thoughts of artists looking for a little extra income, comics, cartoons, and all sequential art have the power to dominate and guide discussion. The intertwined and subtle use of imagery and words are evocative and powerful. We have been taught how to view the world through the lessons of the comic sheets.

Between the turn of the twentieth century and the present the comics industry has undergone wild fluctuations in its cultural significance. Since the turn of the twenty-first century, the United States has seen a resurgence in enthusiasm for comics, with attempts to press forward the notion that the medium is a legitimate form of not only art but also literature and history, as well as a tremendous conduit for education. Along with this resurgence there was an uptick in (re)claiming the medium by marginalized voices. Since 2000, Marvel has introduced more diverse character lines, like the reboot of *Ms. Marvel* or as is Ta-Nehisi Coates's and Brian Stelfreeze's relaunch of *Black Panther*.[38] Much more work may still be done in this field, particularly in terms of the historical significance and place of comics and cartoons. The archive is deep and largely untapped. Other voices can be retrieved from the backgrounds of fin de siècle, not only in the United States but also around the world. The new directions comics are going today have their feet in earlier eras. Finding those diverse identities in the past only enrichens their modern interpretations.

Notes

Chapter 1

1 "The Kaiser's Swing around the Oriental Circle," *New York Journal and Advertiser*, November 6, 1898, accessed October 26, 2018, https://www.loc.gov/item/sn830 30180/1898-11-06/ed-1/

2 Examples from before the First World War include articles like "Best Immigrants Come from East," *Heppner Gazette*, September 13, 1906, http://chroniclingam erica.loc.gov/lccn/sn94049698/1906-09-13/ed-1/seq-3/. The article cited a California irrigation official as saying, "The immigration today was not a patriotic immigration, but a parasitic immigration." Such sentiment did not die away with the First World War, however, in 1920. Frederick A. Wallis, "Regulate Immigrant Flood, Urges Commissioner Wallis; A System of Restraint and Selection Is Advocated," *New York Tribune*, December 12, 1920, http://chroniclingamerica.loc. gov/lccn/sn83030214/1920-12-12/ed-1/seq-69/. Wallis says of Central European immigrants whom he recently saw at Ellis Island: "They would never make constructive citizens. They were of a class that can be nothing more than parasites."

3 For example, see William Jennings Bryan, "Lecture on Missions," *Evening Star*, 1913, http://chroniclingamerica.loc.gov/lccn/sn83045462/1913-09-28/ed-1/seq-53/

4 The most quintessential example of such wars is the British battle against the Mahdist forces in the Sudan, the Battle of Khartoum.

5 For further information on the periodization of comics history, see Shirrel Rhoades, *A Complete History of American Comic Books* (New York: Peter Lang, 2008), 5–6.

6 Scott McCloud, *Understanding Comics: The Invisible Art* (New York: Harper Paperbacks, 1994), 9.

7 Ibid., 20.

8 Ibid., 20–21.

9 Sarah Rhett, *Marginalia*, Paragraph editorial remarks ed. (Google Docs, 2016).

10 McCloud, 13. The Bayeux Tapestry, which dates from about the 1470s, is the enormous embroidery work depicting the Norman conquest of England and includes the Battle of Hastings alongside about forty-nine other scenes of the war. The Mexican Codex to which McCloud is referring is one of many codices (pictorial manuscripts) from the region around present-day Mexico City. These codices,

which date from shortly after the arrival of Spanish conquistadors, give a great deal of information about sociocultural and geographic aspects of Aztec and other local tribes' lives.

11 Marc Singer, "'Black Skins' and White Masks: Comic Books and the Secret of Race," *African American Review* 36, no. 1 (Spring 2002): 107.

12 Henry James, "Du Maurier and London Society," *The Century*, May 1883, 51.

13 Fredic Wertham, *Seduction of the Innocent* (New York: Rinehart and Company, 1954).

14 David Hajdu, *The Ten-Cent Plague: The Great Comic-Book Scare and How It Changed America* (New York: Picador, 2008), 291.

15 Ibid.

16 "Another Protest against the Comic Supplement," *The Literary Digest* 33, no. 7 (August 18, 1906): 210.

17 "Must the Comic Supplement Go," *The Literary Digest* 37, no. 19 (November 7, 1908): 669.

18 Ibid.

19 Where this idea comes from remains under question. Some have attributed it Mark Twain, others to Ambrose Bierce, and still others to modern comedians like Paul Rodriguez and Jon Stewart. Strong evidence suggests that the idea began evolving in the late 1800s as the notion is certainly present in a number of publications and speeches of the time. One potential early example of the notion comes from G. Mercer Adam, *Rose-Belford's Canadian Monthly and National Review*, ed. Rose-Belford Publishing Co, vol. III (Toronto, 1879), 119. The quote reads, "For whatever evil war brings in its train, it has value in teaching us geography."

20 "The Evolution of the Comic Picture and the Comic Artist," *The San Francisco Call*, November 12, 1905, http://chroniclingamerica.loc.gov/lccn/sn85066387/1905-11-12/ed-1/seq-4/. Another such article, but one that focuses more on the American-ness of cartoons, and with a much clearer sense of the adult audience, is "The Evolution and Influence of the Newspaper Cartoon," *The Evening Times*, April 16, 1902.

21 L. M. Glackens, "Hoist, the Friend of the Comic People," *Puck*, October 31, 1906. Some of the comics this depiction included, like the Yellow Kid and Happy Hooligan both of whom we will see more of later, were superstars of the day. Just as ubiquitous as Garfield or Snoopy today Yellow Kid and Happy Hooligan were everywhere in American popular culture at the turn of the twentieth century.

22 *The Hawaiian Star*, August 2, 1899.

23 The *Gettysburg Star and Sentinel*, on May 19, 1909, ran a short discussion of an upcoming issue of Hairbreadth Harry linking the current series to President Theodor Roosevelt's travels in Africa.

24 "Suffrage and the Humorous Magazines," *Maryland Suffrage News*, June 13, 1914, http://chroniclingamerica.loc.gov/lccn/sn89060379/1914-06-13/ed-1/seq-7/

25 Lou Rogers, "Tearing Off the Bonds," *Judge*, October 19, 1912.

26 "She Changed Comics: Lou Rogers, Advocate for Women's Rights," *Comic Book Legal Defense Fund*, March 17, 2017, 2016, accessed November 30, 2017, 2017, http://cbldf.org/2017/03/she-changed-comics-lou-rogers-advocate-for-womens-rights/

27 "Suffrage and the Humorous Magazines."

28 "The Power of Cartoons," *The Colored American*, January 18, 1902.

29 Ibid.

30 "Psychiatrist Asks Crime Comics Ban," *The New York Times*, December 14, 1950.

31 F. Opper, "Caricature Country and Its Inhabitants," *The Independent*, 1901.

32 M. Keith Booker, ed. *Encyclopedia of Comic Books and Graphic Novels* (Santa Barbara, CA: Greenwood, 2010), 495.

33 Donald D. Markstein, "Happy Hooligan," *Don Markstein's Toonopedia*, 2000, accessed 2017, http://www.toonopedia.com/hooligan.htm

34 Allan Holtz, "Obscurity of the Day: Jerry Macjunk," *Stripper's Guide*, June 2, 2006, accessed 2017, http://strippersguide.blogspot.com.es/2006/06/obscurity-of-day-jerry-macjunk.html

35 Kjell Knudde, "F.M. Howarth," last modified March 2, 2018, accessed October 29, 2018, https://www.lambiek.net/artists/h/howarth_fm.htm

36 Bernard A. Drew, *Black Stereotypes in Popular Series Fiction, 1851-1955: Jim Crow Era Authors and Their Characters* (Jefferson, NC: McFarland, 2015), 265.

37 According to the *N.W. Ayer and Sons American Newspaper Annual and Directory*, in 1916, *Puck's* publishers reported a circulation of 53,000 for the weekly. *Life* had a circulation of 130,000; *Harper's Weekly* was at 39,956. See *N.W. Ayer & Son's American Newspaper Annual and Directory* (Philadelphia, PA: N. W. Ayer & Son, 1916). In 1918 *Judge* had a circulation of 131,973. See *N. W. Ayer & Son's American Newspaper Annual and Directory* (Philadelphia, PA: N. W. Ayer & Son, 1918), 677. *Cartoons Magazine* was published between 1912 and 1921 as such. In 1921 it was acquired by *Wayside Tales Magazine* and was produced as *Wayside Tales and Cartoons Magazine*, both published by H. H. Windsor, the same publisher of *Popular Mechanics*. The Ayers indexes, while including *Cartoons* in its listings, do not have circulation numbers.

38 Newspapers of the day often included pages devoted to cartoons from around the world. One such example comes from "The Charge of the Pen Brigade," *The Ogden Standard*, December 5, 1914, http://chroniclingamerica.loc.gov/lccn/sn85058396/1914-12-05/ed-1/seq-15/. The article examines "how the conflict in Europe is viewed by Artists in Germany and by Cartoonists backing the Armies of the Allies." *Cartoons Magazine*, too, is a rich example of the global comic and cartoon world. Every issue incorporates cartoons, and analysis thereof, from all over the world.

39 For further information on non-British Punches, see Hans Harder and Barbara Mittler, eds., *Asian Punches: A Transcultural Affair* (Heidelberg: Springer Science & Business Media, 2013).

40 Sarah F. Howell, "Inventing the American Mosque: Early Muslims and Their Institutions in Detroit, 1910-1980" (Ph.D. diss., The University of Michigan, 2009), 23.

41 Susan Nance, *How the Arabian Nights Inspired the American Dream, 1790–1935* (Chapel Hill, NC: The University of North Carolina Press, 2009), 12.

42 Ibid.

43 Sarah Howell, *Old Islam in Detroit: Rediscovering the Muslim American Past* (Oxford: Oxford University Press, 2014), 23.

44 Ibid., 24–25.

45 Nance, 5.

46 Edward W. Said, *Orientalism* (New York: Vintage Books, 1979), 4.

47 Marshall G. S. Hodgson's *Islamicate* may be a useful alternative to "Oriental" more often than not. It succinctly brings together connected and yet supposedly disparate ideas, as it refers to something as Islamic, though not necessarily wholly religious. For example, we may speak of "Islamic architecture," but that style may be neither religious nor necessarily practiced by Muslims. Islamicate, then, allows us to talk about the cultural and political world around the religious world of Islam, without claiming that all who participated in that world were either Muslims or religious. Similarly, the term "umma" is useful, referring as it does to the global community of Muslims, incorporating the variations of sect. It is comparable to the term "Christendom," in its utility in incorporating Eastern Orthodox, Roman Catholic, and so on under one term, but whereas Christendom tends to denote a historic presence in the past, "umma" is very much a living term and can fall too easily to the purposes of conflation. For our purposes umma helps bring the Filipino Moro into the same sentence with the Libyan Senussi, just as periodicals from the 1880s to the 1920s are littered with stories that do just that, but we must be careful to not argue, however, that the umma speaks with one voice, as that leads us back to the pitfalls of "Oriental." For further information on Hodgson and the term "Islamicate," see Marshall G. S. Hodgson, *The Venture of Islam: Conscience and History in a World Civilization*, vol. 1: The Classical Age of Islam, 3 vols. (Chicago, IL: University of Chicago Press, 1977).

48 "Hindu, Thought to Be an Anarchist, Is Jailed," *The San Francisco Call*, October 29, 1910, http://chroniclingamerica.loc.gov/lccn/sn85066387/1910-10-29/ed-1/seq-5/. Other articles from the same time, like one in the *Deseret Evening News*, do not refer to Rahim as a Hindu but rather as an "East Indian Agitator."

49 See, for example, "The Moslem Menace," *The Seattle Republican*, April 20, 1906, http://chroniclingamerica.loc.gov/lccn/sn84025811/1906-04-20/ed-1/seq-3/

50 Of this particular point more will be said in Chapter 5.

51 Edward E. Curtis, *Muslims in America: A Short History* (Oxford: Oxford University Press, 2009), 49.

52 Stacy D. Fahrenthold, *Between the Ottomans and the Entente: The First World War in the Syrian and Lebanese Diaspora, 1908–1925* (Oxford: Oxford University Press, 2019), 22–23. The term "mahjar" Fahrenthold uses refers to the "lands of emigration" the physical spaces Arabs in diaspora inhabit.

53 Curtis, 49.

54 Ibid., 53.

55 The history of the use of "Moslem" versus "Muslim" is interesting. Some scholars have contended that Moslem "in Arabic means 'one who is evil and unjust' when the word is pronounced, as it is in English, *Mozlem* with a *z*" (see: http://historyn ewsnetwork.org/article/524). Conversely, *Garner's Modern English Usage* notes that both Moslem and Muslim are seen in English works from the fifteenth century on, and appear to be the same word spelled differently. Moslem fell out of common World English usage in the 1940s; in Britain and the United States it became Muslim closer the 1960s. Moslem continues to today to be closely linked to the phrase "Black Moslem," that is, members of the Nation of Islam (see Bryan Garner, *Garner's Modern English Usage* (Oxford: Oxford University Press, 2016)).

56 This idea that Moro is a corruption of Moor is discussed almost any time "Moro" comes up. Two examples, of the many, include War Department, *The Report of the Philippine Commission (1900-1915)* (Washington, DC: Government Printing Office, 1915) and John A. Larkin, *Sugar and the Origins of Modern Philippine Society* (Berkeley: University of California Press, 1993), http://www.netlibrary.com/urlapi. asp?action=summary&v=1&bookid=10049

57 G. M. Lamsa, *Life in the Harem* (Washington, DC: s.n., 1921).

58 "Are Moslem Harems Possible in the U.S.?" *The Herald*, December 12, 1897, https://chroniclingamerica.loc.gov/lccn/sn85042461/1897-12-12/ed-1/seq-29/

59 Lucy (Lucile) Duff-Gordon, "Negligees and Bathing Suits," *Richmond Times-Dispatch*, June 17, 1917, accessed December 8, 2016, http://chroniclingamerica.loc. gov/lccn/sn83045389/1917-06-17/ed-1/seq-46/

60 Valerie Steele, *Fashion and Eroticism: Ideals of Feminine Beauty from the Victorian Era to the Jazz Age* (New York: Oxford University Press, 1985), 232.

61 "Diplomacy of Oscar Straus," *Corvallis Daily Gazette*, May 17, 1909, http://chronicl ingamerica.loc.gov/lccn/2014260100/1909-05-17/ed-1/seq-3/. This article ran in a variety of papers including Rock Island, IL; Marshalltown, IA; and New Ulm, MN; as well as in a briefer, revised version in Salt Lake City, UT.

62 See Stacy Fahrenthold, "What We Can Learn from America's Other Muslim Ban (Back in 1918)," *Tropics of Meta*, February 8, 2017, accessed 2017, https://tropics ofmeta.wordpress.com/author/stacydfahrenthold/

63 The number of articles following the events in the Sudan is incredibly high; just two examples are as follows: Herbert V. G. Morrell, "How General Kitchener Prepared Himself for His Great Work in the Soudan," *San Francisco Call*, October 16, 1898, http://chroniclingamerica.loc.gov/lccn/sn85066387/1898-10-16/ed-1/seq-19/; "General Gordon's Mission," *The Hawaiian Gazette*, April 8, 1885, http://chroniclingamerica.loc.gov/lccn/sn83025121/1885-04-08/ed-1/seq-5/

64 One article from the *Omaha Daily Bee*, in talking about "Prominent Fort Dodge Society Girls," contended that the Boxers were Muslims, led to rebellion by the "riotous and unruly" nature of their faith. "Star-Eyed Egyptian," *Omaha Daily Bee*, October 21, 1900, http://chroniclingamerica.loc.gov/lccn/sn99021999/1900-10-21/ed-1/seq-15/

65 Senussi has been spelled Sanusi(a) at various times in history as well. Jonathan Royce, "Story of a Vast Mohammedan Conspiracy," *Omaha Daily Bee*, April 19, 1903, http://chroniclingamerica.loc.gov/lccn/sn99021999/1903-04-19/ed-1/seq-23/

66 Susan Kollin, *Captivating Westerns: The Middle East in the American West* (Lincoln, NE: University of Nebraska Press, 2015), 3.

Chapter 2

1 "Table: Muslim Population by Country," *Pew Research Center: Religion & Public Life*, accessed October 25, 2016, http://www.pewforum.org/2011/01/27/table-muslim-population-by-country/

2 Besheer Mohamed, "A New Estimate of the U.S. Muslim Population," *Pew Research Center: Religion & Public Life*, accessed October 25, 2016. http://www.pewresearch.org/fact-tank/2016/01/06/a-new-estimate-of-the-u-s-muslim-population/

3 Anne Farris Rosen, "Appendix 3: A Brief History of Religion and the U.S. Census," *Pew Research Center's Forum on Religion & Public Life*, 2008, accessed October 25, 2016, http://www.pewforum.org/files/2008/02/report-religious-landscape-study-appendix3.pdf

4 Ibid.

5 Ibid.

6 Bureau of the Census Commerce Department, *Religious Bodies: 1916*, Vol. Part I: Summary and General Tables (Washington DC: Government Printing Office, 1919), 11.

7 See Allyson Chiu, "Stop Calling the Mormon Church 'Mormon,' Says Church Leader. 'Lds' Is out, Too," *The Washington Post*, August 17, 2018, accessed August 20, 2018, https://www.washingtonpost.com/news/morning-mix/wp/2018/08/17/stop-calling-the-mormon-church-mormon-says-church-leader-lds-is-out-too/?utm_term=.d5b35ce5cc44

8 "Style Guide—the Name of the Church," *The Church of Jesus Christ of Latter-day Saints: Newsroom*, 2018, accessed August 20, 2018, https://www.mormonnewsroom.org/style-guide

9 Bureau of the Census Commerce Department, *Religious Bodies: 1936*, Vol. Part I: Summary and Detailed Tables (Washington DC: Government Printing Office, 1941), 7.

10 "A. A. O. N. M. S.," *Detroit Free Press*, April 16, 1882, https://www.newspapers.com/image/117675319

11 "Shriners to Enjoy Home-Coming Week: Moslem Temple Plans to Entertain 5000 Guests Here," *Detroit Free Press*, May 29, 1921, https://www.newspapers.com/image/119041983

12 See, for example, "Moslems Celebrate Feast of Id-Ul-Filtr," *Detroit Free Press*, June 8, 1921, https://www.newspapers.com/image/119047683

13 For further detail, see Philip Deslippe, "The Hindu in Hoodoo: Fake Yogis, Pseudo-Swamis, and the Manufacture of African American Folk Magic," *Amerasia Journal* 40, no. 1 (2014).

14 See Michael Lipka, "A Closer Look at Jehovah's Witnesses Living in the U.S.," *Pew Research Center: Religion & Public Life*, accessed May 24, 2018. http://www.pewresearch.org/fact-tank/2016/04/26/a-closer-look-at-jehovahs-witnesses-living-in-the-u-s/

15 See Tony Carnes, "The Period of New York Muslim Experimentation, 1893-1939: Retrospective on Mosque City Ny, Part 3," *A Journey through NYC religions*, accessed May 24, 2018. http://www.nycreligion.info/period-york-muslim-experimentation-18931939/#

16 Bureau of the Census—Commerce Department, *Religious Bodies: 1936*, Vol. 2, pt. Part 2: Denominations, K To Z - Statistics, History, Doctrine, Organization, And Work (Washington DC: Government Printing Office, 1941), 1273.

17 Curtis, 48.

18 Howell, 51.

19 "School and Church," *The Cape Girardeau Democrat*, September 21, 1895, http://chroniclingamerica.loc.gov/lccn/sn89066818/1895-09-21/ed-1/seq-7/

20 Louise Seymour Houghton, "Syrians in the United States II: Business Activities," *The Survey: Social, Charitable, Civic: A Journal of Constructive Philanthropy* 26 (August 5, 1911): 660, https://babel.hathitrust.org/cgi/pt?id=pst.000014234194

21 "Islam in America," *Wood County Reporter*, December 24, 1896, http://chroniclingamerica.loc.gov/lccn/sn85033078/1896-12-24/ed-1/seq-2/

22 "Mahometans in Philadelphia," *Huntsville Weekly Democrat*, November 20, 1907, https://www.newspapers.com/image/348654856/

23 "Mohammedans Now Have a Place of Worship Here," *The Sun*, February 25, 1912, https://chroniclingamerica.loc.gov/lccn/sn83030272/1912-02-25/ed-1/seq-57/

24 "From Many Lands," *The Farmington Times*, May 7, 1915, http://chroniclingamerica .loc.gov/lccn/sn89066996/1915-05-07/ed-1/seq-2/

25 "Mohammedans to Celebrate Feast," *Detroit Free Press*, September 28, 1916, https://www.newspapers.com/image/118679400/

26 "Census Shows 8000 Moslems Living in This Land," *San Francisco Chronicle*, October 24, 1920, https://www.newspapers.com/image/27534474/

27 Kambiz GhaneaBassiri, *A History of Islam in America: From the New World to the New World Order* (Cambridge: Cambridge University Press, 2010), 168.

28 "Mohammedans Build Mosque in Detroit," *Evening Star*, September 3, 1921, https://chroniclingamerica.loc.gov/lccn/sn83045462/1921-09-03/ed-1/seq-6/

29 GhaneaBassiri, 136.

30 Richard Hughes Seager, ed. *The Dawn of Religious Pluralism: Voices from the World's Parliament of Religions, 1893* (La Salle, IL: Open Court, 1993), 247.

31 Ibid.

32 Frederick Burr Opper, "Puck's Suggestion to the Congress of Religions," *Puck*, September 13, 1893.

33 "Muezzin May Call," *The Wheeling Daily Intelligencer*, June 6, 1893, https://chroniclingamerica.loc.gov/lccn/sn84026844/1893-06-06/ed-1/seq-6/

34 Ibid.

35 Seager, 271.

36 "Are Moslem Harems Possible in the U.S.?"

37 William A. Rogers, *The Arab Turkish Colony in New York City*, c. 1872, Wash drawing, accessed November 22, 2016, Retrieved from the Library of Congress, https://www.loc.gov/item/2010717854/. The scene may very well be depicting New York's "Little Syria," which as Stacy Fahrenthold notes is only six miles from where Trump Tower stands today. See https://tropicsofmeta.wordpress.com/2017/02/08/ what-we-can-learn-from-americas-other-muslim-ban-back-in-1918/#_ftnref4

38 A New York Detective, "The Bradys and the Black Giant; Or, the Secrets of 'Little Syria,'" *Secret Service Old and Young Brady, Detectives*, January 24, 1908, 6.

39 Ibid.

40 Ibid., 7.

41 Ibid., 6.

42 Garnet Warren, "Miniature Foreign Lands in New York City: Little Syria," Los Angeles *Herald*, April 11, 1909, https://chroniclingamerica.loc.gov/lccn/sn850 42462/1909-04-11/ed-1/seq-65/

43 Işil Acehan, "'Made in Massachusetts': Converting Hides and Skins into Leather and Turkish Immigrants into Industrial Laborers (1860s–1920s)" (Dissertation, Bilkent University, 2010), 55, accessed November 28, 2016, http://www.thesis.bilkent.edu. tr/0006939.pdf

44 State Department, *Memorandum Regarding the Inadvisability of a Declaration of War by the United States against Turkey and Bulgaria at the Present Time*, ed. Robert Lansing, Vol. 1 (Washington DC: Government Printing Office, 1917). Emphasis added.

45 William P. Dillingham and Immigration Commission, *Reports of the Immigration Commission: Abstracts of Reports of the Immigration Commission* (Washington DC: Government Printing Office, 1911), 17, https://archive.org/details/reportsofimm igra01unitrich

46 Ibid., 19.

47 Ibid. This is the exact same discussion that was being had, at roughly the same time, in Great Britain, and factored into the eventual creation of the Balfour Declaration (1917).

48 Ibid., 19–20.

49 James Sleeth, "Biography of Joel Dorman Steele," accessed October 28, 2018. http://ccld.lib.ny.us/joel-dorman-steele/

50 Joel Dorman Steele and Esther Baker Steele, *A Brief History of Ancient, Mediaeval, and Modern Peoples, with Some Account of Their Monuments, Institutions, Arts, Manners, and Customs* (Cincinnati, OH: The Eclectic Press, 1883), 10.

51 Ibid.

52 "Are Turks White Men," *The Plymouth Tribune*, September 30, 1909, https://chroniclingamerica.loc.gov/lccn/sn87056244/1909-09-30/ed-1/seq-4/

53 "What Is a White Man before Law," *Paducah Evening Sun*, November 11, 1909, https://chroniclingamerica.loc.gov/lccn/sn85052114/1909-11-11/ed-1/seq-6/

54 Ibid.

55 Sarah M. A. Gualtieri, *Between Arab and White: Race and Ethnicity in the Early Syrian American Diaspora* (Berkeley, CA: University of California Press, 2009), 69.

56 Ibid., 73.

57 Ibid., 74.

58 "Citizenship," *Herald*, September 24, 1909, accessed February 28, 2017, http://chr oniclingamerica.loc.gov/lccn/sn85042462/1909-09-24/ed-1/seq-4/

59 Marian L. Smith, "Race, Nationality, and Reality: Ins Administration of Racial Provisions in U.S. Immigration and Nationality Law since 1898, Part 2," *Prologue*, Summer, 2002.

60 Ibid.

61 William P. Dillingham, *Dictionary of Races or Peoples* (Washington DC: Government Printing Office, 1911), 3.

62 Dillingham and Immigration Commission, 217.

63 Ibid., 259.

64 Ibid., 282. Emphasis added.

65 It is worth noting that, even before the increased attention given to Islam in the
    1890s, according to A. N. Muhammad and Muslim American Veterans Association,
    Muslim Veterans of American Wars: Revolutionary War, War of 1812, Civil War,
    World War I & II (Washington DC: FreeMan Publications, 2007), there were as
    many as 292 Muslim (or Islamic-sounding) last names in the troop listings for
    the Civil War. The majority of those listed fought for the Union, only ten for the
    Confederate Army, and the highest ranking Muslim officer in the Union Army was
    Captain Moses Osman. What is more, Osman appears to have been fully immersed
    in the "American Way of Life," as he ran on the Democratic ticket for County
    Treasurer in 1865, in Ottawa, IL. See *The Ottawa Free Trader*, November 4, 1865,
    http://chroniclingamerica.loc.gov/lccn/sn84038582/1865-11-04/ed-1/seq-2/
66 *The Report of the Philippine Commission (1900–1915)*, 326.

Chapter 3

1   Leonard Raven-Hill, *Multum Ex Parvo*, 1910, political cartoon, Bradbury, Agnew &
    Co., Ld., illus. in *Punch*, 138: 417, accessed March 2, 2017, https://archive.org/detai
    ls/punchvol138a139lemouoft
2   Theodore Roosevelt, "Expansion of the White Races" (paper presented at the
    address at the celebration of the African Diamond Jubilee of the Methodist
    Episcopal Church, Washington, DC, 1909), January 18, 1909, http://www.theodore-
    roosevelt.com/images/research/speeches/trwhiteraces.pdf
3   Louis Dalrymple, "School Begins," *Puck*, January 25, 1899.
4   Ibid.
5   John S. Pughe, "Visitors' Day," *Puck*, April 12, 1905.
6   W. A. Rogers, "Uncle Sam's New Class in the Art of Self-Government," *Harper's*
    Weekly, 1898.
7   Udo J. Keppler, "It's 'up to' Them," *Puck*, November 20, 1901.
8   Karine V. Walther, *Sacred Interests: The United States and the Islamic World,*
    1821–1921 (Chapel Hill: University of North Carolina Press, 2015), 212.
9   Charles "Bart" L. Bartholomew, "Something Lacking," *The Minneapolis Journal's*
    Cartoons of the Spanish-American War (1899): 100.
10 F. Victor Gillam, "The White Man's Burden (Apologies to Kipling)," *Life*, March 16, 1899.
11 Grant Hamilton, "The Filipino's First Bath," *Judge*, June 10, 1899.
12 For more information on Pears soap its imperial and racial history, see Anandi
    Ramamuthy, *Imperial Persuaders: Images of Africa and Asia in British Advertising*
    (Manchester: Manchester University Press, 2003).
13 James F. Rusling, "Interview with President Mckinley," *The Christian Advocate* 78,
    no. 4 (1903): 160.

14 Walther, 191.

15 John P. Finely, "The Mohammedan Problem in the Philippines," *The Journal of Race Development* 5, no. 4 (April 1915). The work Finely appears to have "lifted liberally" if not outright plagiarized passages from, was Anna Northend Benjamin, "Our Mohammedan Wards in Sulu," *The Outlook* (1899). Benjamin's work was one of many pieces she compiled as one of only two female correspondents to cover the Spanish-American War. In "Mohammedan Wards in Sulu," Benjamin discussed the history of the Moros, likening them to the "Norsemen" as "they sallied forth from their villages on the coast to plunder and pillage in much the same way, if under a warmer sun" (675). Similarly, Finley describes the peoples of Mindanao and Jolo as "brave sea-rovers, the 'Norsemen' of the East. They pushed their 'praos' into all the waters of the archipelago and made incursions on the settlements" (354). This comparison of the Moros to the Norse is not unimaginable, but nor was it common.

16 Walther, 199.

17 "Republican Party Platform of 1856," *The American Presidency Project*, June 18, 1856, accessed 2018, http://www.presidency.ucsb.edu/ws/?pid=29619

18 Sarah Barringer Gordon, "'The Liberty of Self-Degradation': Polygamy, Woman Suffrage, and Consent in Nineteenth-Century America," *The Journal of American History* 83, no. 3 (December 1996): 820.

19 This list highlights the phrasing used in newspapers and journals in the era to describe the Muslims of the Philippines, then under American jurisdiction.

20 "Faces a New Problem," *Barbour County Index*, July 10, 1901, http://chroniclingamerica.loc.gov/lccn/sn82015080/1901-07-10/ed-1/seq-1/

21 Theodore W. Noyes, *Oriental America and Its Problems* (Washington, DC: Press of Judd and Detweiler, 1903), 47.

22 Henry O. Dwight, "Uncle Sam's Legacy of Slaves," *The Forum* May (1900): 297.

23 Ibid.

24 "No Ambuscades for Democracy," *Journal and Advertiser*, December 17, 1899, https://www.loc.gov/resource/sn83030180/1899-12-17/ed-1/?sp=18

25 "Pen Points," *Los Angeles Times*, March 11, 1906, accessed February 26, 2019, https://www.newspapers.com/image/380209753

26 This phrase is often attributed to Phillip Sheridan, although he claimed to have no memory of saying it. Theodor Roosevelt is also supposed to have made a similar claim: "'I don't go so far as to think that the only good Indians are the dead Indians, but I believe nine out of every 10 are,' Roosevelt said during a January 1886 speech in New York. 'And I shouldn't like to inquire too closely into the case of the tenth.'" Alysa Landry, "Theodore Roosevelt: 'The Only Good Indians Are the Dead Indians,'" *Indian Country Today Media Network*, June 28, 2016, accessed 2018, https://indiancountrymedianetwork.com/history/events/theodore-roosevelt-the-only-good-indians-are-the-dead-indians/

27 John T. McCutcheon, "Abandoning the Philippines," *Chicago Tribune,* 1913, https://www.newspapers.com/image/355228959

28 Michael Salman, *The Embarrassment of Slavery: Controversies over Bondage and Nationalism in the American Colonial Philippines* (Berkeley: University of California Press, 2001), 1.

29 "Real Live Mohammedan Sultan with a Harem Now Belongs to Us!" *New York Journal and Advertiser*, December 4, 1898, https://www.loc.gov/resource/sn8303 0180/1898-12-04/ed-1/?sp=20

30 "Pirates and Water Dwellers of the South Seas," *The San Francisco Call*, May 20, 1900, http://chroniclingamerica.loc.gov/lccn/sn85066387/1900-05-20/ed-1/seq-9/

31 "The United States Sultan," *The Topeka State Journal*, September 4, 1899, accessed May 4, 2018, http://chroniclingamerica.loc.gov/lccn/sn82016014/1899-09-04/ed-1/seq-2/

32 "The Sulu Treaty," *San Francisco Call*, August 22, 1899, http://chroniclingamerica.loc.gov/lccn/sn85066387/1899-08-22/ed-1/seq-6/

33 Noyes, 54.

34 Edward Atkinson, *The Anti-Imperialist*, I, no. 5 (September 15, 1899): 2.

35 Ibid., 7.

36 Noyes, 54–55.

37 "Polygamy Reduced in the Philippines," *Grand Forks Herald*, June 23, 1920, Evening Edition, http://chroniclingamerica.loc.gov/lccn/sn85042414/1920-06-23/ed-1/seq-3/

38 See, for example, S. D. Ehrhart, "If They'll Only Be Good," *Puck*, January 31, 1900; Keppler, "It's 'up to' Them."

39 Gordon, 816.

40 Joseph Ferdinand Keppler et al., "A Desperate Attempt to Solve the Mormon Question, *Puck*," *Puck*, February 13, 1884. Opper was a particularly well-known cartoonist during the era; he was the author/illustrator of the *Happy Hooligan* series as well, of which more will be said in Chapter 4.

41 Rolf Armstrong, "The Mascot," *Puck*, February 20, 1915; Keppler et al. "A Desperate Attempt to Solve the Mormon Question, *Puck*."

42 On the usage of the term "Mormon" please see discussion in Chapter 2.. The term "Mormon" is one in common usage today as it was in the nineteenth century, but as will become noticeable in some of the quote used herein, not all people who non-Mormons would call Mormons would chose that term for themselves. It is not uncommon for practitioners of the faith to refer to themselves as Latter-Day Saints. For the purposes of this work the term Mormon will be used by the author for ease of reading/writing.

43 "'Mormonism,' Not Mohammedanism," *Deseret Evening News*, September 21, 1900, http://chroniclingamerica.loc.gov/lccn/sn83045555/1900-09-21/ed-1/seq-4/

44 Bruce Kinney, *Mormonism: The Islam of America* (New York: Fleming H. Revell Company, 1912), 5.

45 Walther, 64. Also see "Recognition of Crete," *Congressional Globe* Session 40–43 (January 7, 1869).

46 Victor Rousseau, *Mr. Axel's Shady Past, The Tracer of Egos* (Hope, ND: The Hope Pioneer, 1917).

47 Ibid.

48 Ibid.

49 Deirdre M. Moloney, "Muslims, Mormons and U.S. Deportation and Exclusion Policies: The 1910 Polygamy Controversy and the Shaping of Contemporary Attitudes," in *The Social, Political and Historical Contours of Deportation*, ed. B. Anderson, M. Gibney, and E. Paoletti (New York City: Springer, 2013), 13.

50 Arthur Conan Doyle, *Study in Scarlet* (1887).

51 Samuel D. Ehrhart, "Out in Salt Lake City," *Puck*, April 20, 1904; Udo J. Keppler, "The Real Objection to Smoot," *Puck*, April 27, 1904.

52 Winsor McCay, "Ain't You Glad You're Not Mormon," *Omaha Daily Bee*, June 1, 1912, http://chroniclingamerica.loc.gov/lccn/sn99021999/1912-06-01/ed-1/seq-17/. Also: https://www.newspapers.com/image/85039629/; Winsor McCay, "Ain't You Glad You're Not Mormon," *Omaha Daily Bee*, May 24, 1912, http://chroniclingamerica.loc.gov/lccn/sn99021999/1912-05-24/ed-1/seq-9/. Also see Allan Holtz, "Obscurity of the Day: Aren't You Glad You're Not a Mormon," *Stripper's Guide*, November 16, 2009, accessed October 29, 2018, http://strippersguide.blogspot.com/2009/11/obscurity-of-day-arent-you-glad-youre.html

53 Kristine Haglund, "What the 'Mormon Moment' Actually Accomplished," *Slate*, accessed December 13, 2016, http://www.slate.com/articles/life/faithbased/2014/12/mormon_moment_is_over_but_it_changed_mormon_culture_for_good.html. Also see "Public Expresses Mixed Views of Islam, Mormonism," *Pew Research Center: Religion & Public Life*, last modified September 25, accessed October 29, 2018, http://www.pewforum.org/2007/09/25/public-expresses-mixed-views-of-islam-mormonism-2/

54 "See New Danger in Alien Problem," *The Washington Herald*, February 3, 1914, http://chroniclingamerica.loc.gov/lccn/sn83045433/1914-02-03/ed-1/seq-1/

55 Moloney, "Muslims, Mormons and U.S. Deportation and Exclusion Policies."

56 *Appendix to the Congressional Globe: Containing Speeches, Important State Papers, Laws, Etc. of the Third Session, Thirty-Fourth Congress*, ed. John C. Rives (Washington DC: Office of John C. Rives, 1857), 288. Also see Moloney, "Muslims, Mormons and U.S. Deportation and Exclusion Policies," 14.

57 Rives, 288.

58 "Imperialist Discords," *The San Francisco Call*, February 11, 1899, http://chroniclingamerica.loc.gov/lccn/sn85066387/1899-02-11/ed-1/seq-6/

59 "Turks Can't Come Here," *The Sun*, November 19, 1897, http://chroniclingamerica.loc.gov/lccn/sn83030272/1897-11-19/ed-1/seq-1/. Articles or snippets of articles related to the case ran across the country within the next few days.

60 Ibid.

61 Ibid.

62 "Printed in Arabic," *Harrisburg Telegraph*, April 29, 1892, https://www.newspape
    rs.com/image/44551627/

63 Rufus R. Wilson, "Men from All Lands," *Boston Post*, August 12, 1894, https://ww
    w.newspapers.com/image/74631070

64 "Turks Can't Come Here."

65 T. V. Powderly, "Immigration's Menace to the National Health," *The North American
    Review* 175, no. 548 (July 1902).

66 Ibid.

67 "Polygamy Amendment to Immigration Bill," *Ogden Standard*, January 1, 1915,
    http://chroniclingamerica.loc.gov/lccn/sn85058396/1915-01-01/ed-1/seq-4/

68 *Immigration Act* (1917).

69 Moloney, "Muslims, Mormons and U.S. Deportation and Exclusion Policies," 13.

70 Ibid., 14.

71 Ibid.

72 Ibid.

73 Ibid., 15.

74 "Native Moros Abide by Koran's Rule of Four Wives to Man," *The Greenwood
    Commonwealth*, December 9, 1924, https://www.newspapers.com/image/237588066/

75 "Why Not Herron?" *Harvey's Weekly*, 1919.

76 Ibid.

77 Ibid.

78 "Menace to Caucasian Race," *Free Trader Journal*, November 16, 1918, http://chr
    oniclingamerica.loc.gov/lccn/sn92053240/1918-11-16/ed-1/seq-5/

79 Ibid.

Chapter 4

1 Dane Kennedy, *The Highly Civilized Man: Richard Burton and the Victorian World*
   (Cambridge, MA: Harvard University Press, 2005), 63.

2 It has been remarked upon a number times that the relationship between Harry and
   Rudolph(o) is much like, and was probably a precursor to, the characters Dudley
   Do Right and Snidely Whiplash.

3 C. W. Kahles, "Hairbreadth Harry: The Tale of Bel-in-Dah and Blue Whiskers," *The
   Washington Herald*, October 29, 1922, Sunday Edition.

4 He actually says, "Mrs. Bluebeard" the narrator of the comic calls him "Blue
   Whiskers," a phrasing that is reflective of the general relaxed narrative style of
   Hairbreadth Harry comics in general.

5 Kennedy, 235.

6 Ibid.

7 Some have argued that at least one model for the Wonder Woman persona was Margret Sanger. Jill Lepore, *The Secret History of Wonder Woman* (New York: Vintage Books, 2015), 187.

8 Ibid., 242.

9 Lars Eckstein, "Monk Lewis's Timour the Tartar, Grand Romantic Orientalism and Imperial Melancholy," in *Text or Context: Reflections on Literary and Cultural Criticism*, ed. Rüdiger Kunow and Stephan Mussil (Würzburg: Königshausen und Neumann, 2013), 124. It is possible, too, that Abomelique is a play on the name Abimelech, the king who nearly takes Sarah as a wife in Genesis 20: 1–18. However, Abimelech does not display the reprehensible traits of Abomelique, thus the only real connection between the two is a "foreign" quality. Abimelech was not of Abraham's faith; Abomelique was an "Oriental."

10 Casie Hermansson, *Bluebeard: A Reader's Guide to the English Translation* (Jackson, MS: University of Mississippi Press, 2009), 66.

11 Additionally, in 1923 a silent film "Bluebeard's Eighth Wife," based on the 1921 play *La Huitème de Barbe-Bleue* was released and marketing associated with the film helped inflate the number of times the term appeared in publications.

12 Walter McDougall, "The True Story of Bluebeard's Forbidden Room: Another Fable Exposed," *Chicago Record-Herald*, May 31, 1903.

13 Walter C. Kledaisch, "Miss Bluebeard, 1904," *The Tacoma Times*, January 1, 1904, http://chroniclingamerica.loc.gov/lccn/sn88085187/1904-01-01/ed-1/seq-3/

14 John Sheldon, "Unearthing the Crimes of Modern Bluebeards," *The Washington Times*, June 6, 1920, http://chroniclingamerica.loc.gov/lccn/sn84026749/1920-06-06/ed-1/seq-28/

15 This search was done in early September 2017.

16 Bernard Partridge, "The End of the Thousand-and-One Nights," *Cartoon Magazine*, 1917, 185.

17 *La Silhouette: politique, satirique et financière* was a French satirical periodical which ran from 1880 to 1914. *The Bookman* was an American publication which from 1895 to 1933.

18 Frederic Taber Cooper and Arthur Bartlett Mauricce, "The History of the Nineteenth Century in Caricature," *The Bookman* (September 1903): 47. The cartoon can be seen on page 44.

19 Summary description of the card on the LOC archive website: http://www.loc.gov/pictures/item/2011645458/

20 *Bluebeard of New Orleans, c.* 1862, photographic print on carte de visite mount, New Orleans, LA, accessed February 22, 2017, https://www.loc.gov/resource/ds.00287/

21 Udo J. Keppler, "A Tip to Fatima Ted," *Puck*, August 15, 1906.

22 William D. Moore, *Masonic Temples: Freemasonry, Ritual Architecture, and Masculine Archetypes* (Knoxville: The University of Tennessee Press, 2006), 94.

23 *A Short History of Shriners Hospitals for Children and Shriners of North America* (Tampa, FL), 6–7.

24 Nance, 81.

25 Kollin, 32.

26 Nance, 81.

27 Moore, xiv.

28 Ibid., 115.

29 "The Carnival of the Mystic Shrine," *Kawkab America,* أمريكا كوكب, January 27, https ://lebanesestudies.omeka.chass.ncsu.edu/items/show/11611

30 First produced between 1910 and 1914, the series was later syndicated through World Color Printing and from thence to the Ogden *Standard*.

31 Walter Hoban, "Jerry Macjunk Learns Something of Harems," *The Ogden Standard*, April 27, 1918, City Edition, http://chroniclingamerica.loc.gov/lccn/sn85058396/ 1918-04-27/ed-1/seq-6/

32 Ibid.

33 Rana Kabbani, *Europe's Myths of Orient* (London: Macmillan, 1986), 67.

34 Bud Fisher, "Mutt Finds the Scenery Very Annoying," *El Paso Herald*, February 20, 1913, accessed August 29, 2017, http://chroniclingamerica.loc.gov/lccn/sn8808 4272/1913-02-20/ed-1/seq-10/

35 Cyrus Edson, "When and How to Bathe: Ex-President of the New York Board of Health," *The Ladies' Home Journal*, 13, no. 7 (June 1896): 19.

36 John Elfreth Watkins, "Joy of Bathing," *The Salt Lake Tribune*, May 17, 1908, Sunday Morning, http://chroniclingamerica.loc.gov/lccn/sn83045396/1908-05-17/ed-1/seq-17/

37 *Belle of Nelson Old Fashion Hand Made Sour Mash Whiskey, Library of Congress* (Philadelphia, PA: Wells & Hope Co., 1882). In all honesty the advertisement is essentially a plagiarized version of Gérôme's work. The scene is exactly the same except that the colors of the two rooms are different, the original being bluer in tone, the advertisement more golden. The skin tone of the servant is significantly lighter (more bronze) than in the original, which means the facial features are easier to distinguish. Like the servant and the scantily clad harem women the facial features are noticeably different, less crisp and thoughtful than Gérôme's, the servants taking on a bit more of caricature-like quality.

38 Irving Berlin, *Harem Life* (New York: Irving Berlin Inc., 1919).

39 Kabbani, 71.

40 Berlin.

41 *An International Flirtation*, 1912, Cover, Life Publishing Company, Life, http://www .magazineart.org/main.php/v/humor/life/Life1912-05-09.jpg.html

42 Irving Berlin, *I'm the Guy Who Guards the Harem* (New York: Irving Berlin, Inc., 1919).

43 See G. K. Spivak, "Can the Subaltern Speak?" in *Marxism and the Interpretation of Culture*, ed. C. Nelson and L. Grossberg (Urbana: University of Illinois Press, 1988).

44 Helen Ring Robinson, "Making the World Safe for Monogamy," *Pictorial Review* 104 (November 1918): 5.

45 Ibid., 36.

46 Some examples include Clive Marshall, "Women Martyrs to Prussian Savagery," *The Daily Ardmoreite*, March 13, 1918, http://chroniclingamerica.loc.gov/lccn/sn8504 2303/1918-03-13/ed-1/seq-6/; "Polygamy to Purify Morals," *Goodwin's Weekly: A Thinking Paper for Thinking People*, June 29, 1918, http://chroniclingamerica .loc.gov/lccn/2010218519/1918-06-29/ed-1/seq-7/; "Germany's Race Problem," *Harrisburg Telegraph*, January 16, 1918, http://chroniclingamerica.loc.gov/lccn/s n85038411/1918-01-16/ed-1/seq-6/

47 "No Prospect of Polygamy," *The Oklahoma City Times*, April 10, 1918, Late Street Edition, http://chroniclingamerica.loc.gov/lccn/sn86064187/1918-04-10/ed-1/seq-20/

48 Howell, 15.

49 "Famous Artist's Cartoon in Favor of the Harem Skirt," *The Tacoma Times*, April 11, 1911, http://chroniclingamerica.loc.gov/lccn/sn88085187/1911-04-11/ ed-1/seq-5/

50 "Harem Skirt Wearers Face Jail Sentence," *Evening Star*, March 30, 1911, http://chr oniclingamerica.loc.gov/lccn/sn83045462/1911-03-30/ed-1/seq-8/

51 "Famous Artist's Cartoon in Favor of the Harem Skirt."

52 "The Hip Sash Modish Feature of Summer Frocks," *The Lake County Times*, February 28, 1913, Evening Edition, http://chroniclingamerica.loc.gov/lccn/sn8605 8242/1913-02-28/ed-1/seq-11/

53 Nance, 4.

54 "The Skirt Question," *The Seattle Star*, April 18, 1911, http://chroniclingamerica.loc. gov/lccn/sn87093407/1911-04-18/ed-1/seq-4/

55 Gayle V. Fischer, *Pantaloons and Power: A Nineteenth-Century Dress Reform in the United States* (Kent, OH: The Kent State University Press, 2001), 85; Steele, 232.

56 Steele, 232.

57 Duff-Gordon.

58 Oxford English Dictionary, *"Chatelaine, N."* (Oxford University Press).

59 Tansy McNab, "Fairy Tales for Grown-Ups," *New York Tribune*, May 22, 1921, http://chroniclingamerica.loc.gov/lccn/sn83030214/1921-05-22/ed-1/seq-62/. Illustration by Sophia T. Balcom.

60 Steele, 232.

61 Kennedy, 77. Also see Kabbani, 48.

62 Marguerite Mooers Marshall, "Calls Suffrage Workers Yellow Peril of America," *The Evening World*, December 1, 1911, Night Edition, http://chroniclingamerica.loc. gov/lccn/sn83030193/1911-12-01/ed-1/seq-20/

63 For example, see "Harem Skirt and Woman Suffrage," *The Washington Herald*, February 28, 1911, http://chroniclingamerica.loc.gov/lccn/sn83045433/1911-02-28 /ed-1/seq-12/; "Harem Skirt Urged for All Suffragists," *The Washington Herald*, February 27, 1911, http://chroniclingamerica.loc.gov/lccn/sn83045433/1911-02-27/ ed-1/seq-2/

64 Ivan Narodny, "The Vanishing Harem," *Evening Star*, December 22, 1912, http://chr oniclingamerica.loc.gov/lccn/sn83045462/1912-12-22/ed-1/seq-43/

65 Ibid. Emphasis added.

66 There are a lot of good works on the history of coffee, an easily accessible one is Tom Standage, *A History of the World in 6 Glasses* (New York: Walker & Co.: Distributed to the trade by Holtzbrinck Publishers, 2005).

67 Mrs. A. J. Baird, "Wearer Should Be Given Ninety Days," *San Francisco Call*, April 23, 1911, http://chroniclingamerica.loc.gov/lccn/sn85066387/1911-04-23/ed-1/ seq-11/

68 Mrs. Henry M. Moreno, "Down with Dress Reform!" *San Francisco Call*, April 23, 1911, http://chroniclingamerica.loc.gov/lccn/sn85066387/1911-04-23/ed-1/seq-11/

69 Esther Purvis, "Who Will Be the Emancipator of Woman?" *San Francisco Call*, April 23, 1911, http://chroniclingamerica.loc.gov/lccn/sn85066387/1911-04-23/ ed-1/seq-11/

70 Rosalind Toynbee, "The Turkish Women of to-Day," *The Forum* (September 1, 1928): 416.

Chapter 5

1 Frederick Burr Opper, "Happy Hooligan's Honeymoon," *El Paso Herald*, April 7, 1917, http://chroniclingamerica.loc.gov/lccn/sn88084272/1917-04-07/ed-1/seq-32/

2 C. W. Kahles, "Hairbreadth Harry: It Looks as Though Rodolph's Fine Clothes Will Have to Be Ironed out Again," *The Washington Herald*, April 01, 1917, http://chr oniclingamerica.loc.gov/lccn/sn83045433/1917-04-01/ed-1/seq-31/

3 C. W. Kahles, "Hairbreadth Harry: The Omipotent Oom Gets Two Costumers," *The Washington Herald*, April 15, 1917, http://chroniclingamerica.loc.gov/lccn/sn8304 5433/1917-04-15/ed-1/seq-29/

4 "The Unspeakable Turk," *The Citizen*, October 26, 1916, http://chroniclingamerica .loc.gov/lccn/sn85052076/1916-10-26/ed-1/seq-1/

5 Ibid.

6 Ibid.

7 Edson.

8 Tamara Jones and Michael O'Sullivan, "Supreme Court Frieze Brings Objection," *Washington Post*, March 8, 1997, https://www.washingtonpost.com/wp-srv/nationa l/longterm/supcourt/stories/sculpture.htm?noredirect=on

9 Edward Gibbon, *History of the Decline and Fall of the Roman Empire*, vol. V (1788). See Chapter L, Part I; "Mahomet with the sword in one hand and the Koran in the other, erected his throne on the ruins of Christianity and of Rome."

10 Moulavi Cheragh Ali, *A Critical Exposition of the Popular "Jihád"* (Calcutta: Thacker, Spink and Co., 1885), i.

11 See, for example, *The Lumberjack*, February 20, 1913, http://chroniclingamerica.loc. gov/lccn/sn88064459/1913-02-20/ed-1/seq-1/

12 See Chapter 1 and James.

13 Bud Fisher, "Jeff's Bump of Caution Is Highly Developed," *El Paso Herald*, February 6, 1913, accessed December 15, 2016, http://chroniclingamerica.loc.gov/lccn/s n88084272/1913-02-06/ed-1/seq-10/. As was discussed in the previous chapter.

14 See Anthony Slide, ed. *Ravished Armenia and the Story of Aurora Mardiganian* (Jackson, MS: University of Mississippi Press, 2014).

15 Walther, 283.

16 Ibid.

17 Aurora Mardiganian, "In the House of Hadji-Ghafour" (Washington DC: The Washington Times, 1918).

18 George Hand Wright, *And All Those Dead of Belgium and All That Mighty Procession of the Slain in Armenia—How If All These Hosts Still Live?* 1917, Illustration in: "Stars in the Dust Heap" by Booth Tarkington, *Metropolitan Magazine*, 46:19, New York, accessed December 15, 2016, http://www.loc.gov/pictures/collection/cai/it em/2010718524/

19 See Fae Brauer, "'Moral Girls' and 'Filles Fatales': The Fetishisation of Innocence," *Australian and New Zealand Journal of Art* 10, no. 1 (2011): 122–43.

20 "The Sick Man of Europe," *Aberdeen Herald*, November 12, 1915, http://chronicl ingamerica.loc.gov/lccn/sn87093220/1915-11-12/ed-1/seq-1/

21 Walther, 282.

22 "Like a Story in the Fairy Books," *The Washington Times*, January 5, 1919, http://chr oniclingamerica.loc.gov/lccn/sn84026749/1919-01-05/ed-1/seq-22/

23 Thomas H. Wilson, *Sold to the Sultan, or, the Strange Adventures of Two Yankee Middies* (New York: Frank Tousey, 1914), 3.

24 "Awful Traffic Disclosed," *The Plymouth Tribune*, October 26, 1905, http://chronicl ingamerica.loc.gov/lccn/sn87056244/1905-10-26/ed-1/seq-1/

25 Edgar Rice Burroughs, *The Eternal Lover* (The Breckenridge News, 1915).

26 Mrinalini Sinha, *Colonial Masculinity: The 'Manly Englishman' and the 'Effeminate Bengali' in the Late Nineteenth Century* (New Delhi: Raj Press, 1995), 11.

27 Ibid., 46–47.
28 Frederick M. Denny, *An Introduction to Islam*, Third ed. (New York: Prentice Hall, 2005), 321. Also see Marshall G. S. Hodgson, *The Venture of Islam: Conscience and History in a World Civilization*, vol. 3: The Gunpowder Empires and Modern Times, 3 vols. (Chicago: University of Chicago Press, 1974), 237.
29 See, for example, "The Late Mahdi's War Plans," *Salt Lake Evening Democrat*, August 3, 1885, http://chroniclingamerica.loc.gov/lccn/sn85058117/1885-08-03/ed-1/seq-1/
30 "The Real Moslem Peril," *The Literary Digest*, October 5, 1907, 473.
31 Ibid.
32 See, for example, Jack Remington, "Christmas in Zone of Heartaches and Tears Described by Remington," *Daily Herald* December 21, 1915, http://chroniclingamerica.loc.gov/lccn/sn89074405/1915-12-21/ed-1/seq-2/
33 "Foreign Telegraphic Summary," *The Daily Gazette*, September 4, 1879, http://chroniclingamerica.loc.gov/lccn/sn82014805/1879-09-04/ed-1/seq-4/
34 "Latest by Mail," *Press and Daily Dakotaian*, August 4, 1881, http://chroniclingamerica.loc.gov/lccn/sn91099608/1881-08-04/ed-1/seq-1/
35 See "A Mohammedan Conspiracy in Java," *St. Paul Daily Globe*, April 15, 1894, https://chroniclingamerica.loc.gov/lccn/sn90059522/1894-04-15/ed-1/seq-19/; Royce, *The Evening Times*, July 6, 1897, https://chroniclingamerica.loc.gov/lccn/sn84024441/1897-07-06/ed-1/seq-4/; "Somaliland," *New York Tribune*, November 2, 1902, http://chroniclingamerica.loc.gov/lccn/sn83030214/1902-11-02/ed-1/seq-41/; "The Congo Basin: The Mohammedan Races of the Equatorial Belt in Arms," *The Republic*, May 23, 1885, accessed September 17, 2018, https://www.newspapers.com/image/128069309
36 "The Congo Basin: The Mohammedan Races of the Equatorial Belt in Arms."
37 Walther, 284.
38 "New Fears of Holy War," *The Literary Digest*, December 15, 1917, 28.
39 John Buchan, *Greenmantle* (Boston: Houghton Mifflin Company, 1916), 17–18.
40 Ibid.
41 I wish I had more room here to discuss the history of Wellington House, but as it was purely a British operation I will leave it for future work. However, as the products of propaganda offices like Wellington were often materials similar to those this work is reflecting on, I think it is important to note something about those who produced the materials. According to records, the staff of Wellington House comprised 203, of whom 47 were men; thus, nearly 84 percent of the people producing "books, pamphlets and illustrated periodicals" as well as collecting pictures and preparing and distributing "Lantern Slide Lectures, Picture Postcards, maps, diagrams, posters, gramophone records etc. and Films," were women. We know women were deeply embedded in the production of comics and cartoons,

but like in this instance of propaganda production, their voices are often unheard. Activities of Wellington House During the Great War 1914–18," Department of Information: INF 4/1B, London.

42 Public Records Office (PRO), War Propaganda, May–August 1917, Foreign Office: FO 228/2732, London.

43 Ibid.

44 Clarence Herbert New, *The Unseen Hand: Stories of Diplomatic Adventure* (New York: W. R. Caldwell & Co., 1918), 82.

45 Buchan, 35.

46 Ibid., 234.

47 Ibid., 241.

48 Clarence Herbert New, "Further Adventures of a Diplomatic Free Lance: No. Xi— the Mohammedan Conspiracy," *Blue Book Magazine*, February 1912, 802.

49 John O'Donnell, "Sees Mohammedan Threat of New World War," *The Seattle Star*, April 7, 1922, http://chroniclingamerica.loc.gov/lccn/sn87093407/1922-04-07/ed-1/ seq-13/

50 Lothrop Stoddard, *The Rising Tide of Color against White World-Supremacy* (New York: Scribner, 1920), 66.

51 "'Mohammedan Peril Threatens New World War,' Eastern-Expert Says," *South Bend News-Times*, April 14, 1922, http://chroniclingamerica.loc.gov/lccn/sn87055779/ 1922-04-14/ed-1/seq-36/

52 "Muslim War in the Main Is Shadowy Danger," *The Bourbon News*, November 3, 1914, http://chroniclingamerica.loc.gov/lccn/sn86069873/1914-11-03/ed-1/seq-3/

53 "How One Man Might Get Us in Two Wars," *The Evening World* 1917, accessed August 31, 2018, http://chroniclingamerica.loc.gov/lccn/sn83030193/1917-08-06/ ed-1/seq-10/. This assertion is certainly a queer one, as no such "tables" ever appear to have existed. Nonetheless this sentence appears in papers across the United States at the time, even finding its way to New Zealand: "Talk of 'Holy War," *Oamaru Mail*, November 12, 1914, https://paperspast.natlib.govt.nz/newspapers/OAM19 141112.2.8

54 "Muslim War in the Main Is Shadowy Danger."

55 Adachi Kinnosuke, "Can the Kaiser Explode the Mahometan Bomb?" *New York Tribune*, March 31, 1918, http://chroniclingamerica.loc.gov/lccn/sn83030214/1918- 03-31/ed-1/seq-27/

56 Bernard O'Reilly, "The African Slave Trade, a Review," *The Sun*, April 27, 1890, http: //chroniclingamerica.loc.gov/lccn/sn83030272/1890-04-27/ed-1/seq-15/

57 "The Shadow of the Turk on the Cross of Christianity," *The New York Journal and Advertiser*, April 25, 1897, https://www.loc.gov/item/sn83030180/1897-04-25/ed-1/

58 "Saturday Evening Post Advertisement," *Richmond Times-Dispatch* 1922, http://chr oniclingamerica.loc.gov/lccn/sn83045389/1922-11-02/ed-1/seq-5/

59 "Turks a Yellow Peril," *New York Tribune*, May 10, 1909, http://chroniclingamerica
   .loc.gov/lccn/sn83030214/1909-05-10/ed-1/seq-5/

60 "Dr. James L. Vance Address to the General Assembly Meeting on Foreign
   Missions," *The Presbyterian of the South: [combining the] Southwestern Presbyterian,
   Central Presbyterian, Southern Presbyterian*, June 4, 1913, http://chroniclingamerica
   .loc.gov/lccn/10021978/1913-06-04/ed-1/seq-3/

61 Bryan.

Chapter 6

1 W. L. Wells, "Old Opie Dilldock's Stories, 31 January 1909," *Chicago Tribune*, https://
   www.newspapers.com/image/354919163/

2 The *War Puzzles* are not signed, but various issues of *The Fourth Estate*, "a
   newspaper for the makers of newspapers and investors in advertising" mention
   Tanner in relation various International Syndicate puzzle series, including one titled
   War Puzzles. Additionally see "A Maker of Puzzle Pictures," in *The Inland Printer*
   (Maclean-Hunter Publishing Corporation, 1902), 74–75.

3 "War Puzzles: Sheik-Ul-Islam," *Honolulu Star-Bulletin*, December 15, 1917, https://
   www.newspapers.com/image/290466336/

4 Thomas E. Curtis, "The Humorous Artists of America—III," *The Strand Magazine*,
   May 1902, 551.

5 Jared Gardner, *Projections: Comics and the History of Twenty-First Century
   Storytelling* (Stanford, CA: Stanford University Press, 2012), 7.

6 Dean Bergen, "Lucy, That Old Mallard Hen," *Outdoor Recreation: The Magazine that
   Brings the Outdoors In*, January 1919, 8.

7 W. L. Wells, "Old Opie Dilldock's Stories, 25 April 1909," *Chicago Tribune*, accessed
   October 29, 2018, https://www.newspapers.com/image/355171468/

8 "The Evacuation of Sambo," *The Topeka State Journal*, August 26, 1911, http://chr
   oniclingamerica.loc.gov/lccn/sn82016014/1911-08-26/ed-1/seq-16/

9 Bud Fisher, "Mutt and Jeff—Yes, Indeed, These Mohammedan Troops Are Very
   Fierce. Oh, My, Yes.," *The Seattle Star*, January 17, 1916, http://chroniclingamerica
   .loc.gov/lccn/sn87093407/1916-01-17/ed-1/seq-7/

10 Detective, 7.

11 Howell, 12.

12 F. M. Howarth, "How They Got Rid of the Rajah Abul Khan—the Story of a
   Bloodless Revolution," *Puck*, 1896.

13 Ibid.

14 Kollin, 21.

15 Department of Agriculture, *Report of the Chief of the Bureau of Animal Industry*, by Charles C. Carroll (Washington DC: U.S. Government Printing Office, 1904), 391.

16 Ibid.

17 Ibid., 392.

18 Kenneth Weisbrode, "The Short Life of the Camel Corps," *New York Times*, December 27, 2012, https://opinionator.blogs.nytimes.com/2012/12/27/the-short-life-of-the-camel-corps/

19 Mukhtar Ali Isani, "The Vogue of Omar Khayyám in America," *Comparative Literature Studies* 14, no. 3 (September 1977): 256.

20 Ibid.

21 "The Omar Khayyam Cult up to Date," *New York Tribune*, March 13, 1904, http://chroniclingamerica.loc.gov/lccn/sn83030214/1904-03-13/ed-1/seq-43/. Bernard Partridge revisited this same scene for *Punch* in 1938, but instead of a camel standing behind the Khayyam figure it is John Bull and the sounds coming out of the gramophone are of anti-British propaganda. See Bernard Partridge, "Roma Khayyam or the Arab and His Set," *Punch*, 1938.

22 "A Plain Country Woman," *The Ladies' Home Journal*, April 1916.

23 "Discoveries: By Our Observers and Experimenters," *Good Housekeeping*, March 1904.

24 Lucile Duff-Gordon, "The New 'Harem Veils,'" *Omaha Daily Bee*, March 9, 1913, http://chroniclingamerica.loc.gov/lccn/sn99021999/1913-03-09/ed-1/seq-20/

25 Ibid.

26 Ibid.

27 Paul West, "The Widow Wise," *The Washington Herald*, October 8, 1911, http://chroniclingamerica.loc.gov/lccn/sn83045433/1911-10-08/ed-1/seq-27/. Illustrations by W. H. Loomis.

28 Bud Fisher, "Jeff Is Some Escort," *El Paso Herald*, March 6, 1913, http://chroniclingamerica.loc.gov/lccn/sn88084272/1913-03-06/ed-1/seq-10/

Chapter 7

1 Singer, 107.

2 "Psychiatrist Asks Crime Comics Ban."

3 Michel Faber, "Habibi by Craig Thompson," *The Guardian*, September 16, 2011, accessed October 15, 2018, https://www.theguardian.com/books/2011/sep/16/habibi-craig-thompson-review

4 Christiane Gruber, "Between Logos (Kalima) and Light (Nūr): Representations of the Prophet Muhammad Is Islamic Paintings," *Muqarnas: An Annual on the Visual Culture of the Islamic World* XXVI (2009): 229.

5 Ibid., 234.

6 Ibid., 231.

7 Ibid.

8 "High Lights of History, Chapter 84: The Mohammedan Conquests," *Evening Star*, June 17, 1928, http://chroniclingamerica.loc.gov/lccn/sn83045462/1928-06-17/ed-1 /seq-110/

9 "High Lights of History, Chapter 83: Mohammed, Phrophet [Sic] of Islam," *Evening Star*, June 10, 1928, http://chroniclingamerica.loc.gov/lccn/sn83045462/1928-6-10/ ed-1/seq-104/

10 "Camel Driver Rose to Fame," *Evening Star*, April 15, 1932, http://chroniclingam erica.loc.gov/lccn/sn83045462/1932-04-15/ed-1/seq-44/

11 Gruber, 229.

12 Ibid.

13 Ibid., 230.

14 Ibid.

15 Ibid.

16 LLC Endeavor Films, *Independent Lens*, Public Broadcasting Station vols., *Wham! Bam! Islam!* (2011).

17 Carol Hill, "A Saudi Fatwa Shuns the First Comic Book to Feature Muslim Superheroes," March 29, 2014, accessed October 14, 2018, https://www.pri.org/ stories/2014-03-28/saudi-fatwa-shuns-first-comic-book-feature-muslim-superh eroes. A fatwa is simply a ruling on a point of Islamic law. For those not well versed in Islamic legal history, the first example to come to mind is likely to be Salman Rushdie and the fatwa issued against his book *The Satanic Verses* by the Ayatollah Khomeini. This instance is not a good example of what a fatwa is in a more prosaic sense. Fatwas are typically bureaucratic and mundane rulings, which on occasion have been propelled to international significance by the judicious use of media and inflammatory rhetoric, as in the Rushdie example. They do not reach across the Islamic world, because, as we have discussed in various other ways, there is not uniform central code or culture to Islam, nor even to Islamic law.

18 Gruber, 254.

19 Ibid., 231.

20 Faber.

21 A. David Lewis, "Kismet Seventy Years Later: Recognizing the First Genuine Muslim Superhero," *ISLAMiCommentary*, 2014, accessed October 14, 2018, https:// hcommons.org/deposits/item/hc:13597/

22 Ibid.

23 "Dust," Marvel, accessed October 14, 2018. https://www.marvel.com/characters/ dust

24 George Pierpoint, "'Sexualised' Niqab Hero Gets Makeover after Costume Criticism," last modified August 29, accessed October 14, 2018, https://www.bbc .com/news/blogs-trending-45331730

25 Ibid.

26 David Hine, *Batman Annual #12* (DC Comics, 2010).

27 *Wonder Women! The Untold Story of American Superheroines*, directed by Kristy Guevara-Flanagan, 2012, http://wonderwomendoc.com/

28 Nick Spencer, "15 August 2017, 7:29 P.M.," accessed August 19, 2017, https://twitter .com/nickspencer/status/897601180347641856; Rosie Marx, "13 August 2017, 3:58 P.M.," accessed August 19, 2017, https://twitter.com/RosieMarx/status/89682339 9204433920. As of October 27, 2018, Spencer's Twitter account has been locked, only confirmed followers have access to his feed.

29 Andy Khouri, "Racists Totally Freak out over Muslim 'Batman of Paris,'" *ComicsAlliance*, December 28, 2010, 2010, accessed 2011, http://www.comicsall iance.com/2010/12/28/racists-batman-muslim-paris/#ixzz1L34iM5Z5. The Council for Conservative Citizens is a white supremacist organization that the Southern Poverty Law Center has called "the modern reincarnation of the old White Citizens Councils." https://www.splcenter.org/fighting-hate/extremist-files/group/council-conservative-citizens

30 For more information on *Punch* around the world see Harder and Mittler.

31 Interestingly, in Kurt Vonnegut reimagined the Bluebeard tale in his 1987 novel, *Bluebeard, the Autobiography of Rabo Karabekian (1916–1988)* in which the eponymous character was Armenian-American. While Vonnegut's work lacks the violence in the original story, role of women in Karabekian's life are central to the narrative.

32 Kelly Faircloth, "Something Is Wrong in This House: How Bluebeard Became the Definitive Fairy Tale of Our Era," *Jezebel*, October 17, 2018, accessed 2018, https:// pictorial.jezebel.com/something-is-wrong-in-this-house-how-bluebeard-became-1 829596691?utm_medium=sharefromsite&utm_source=jezebel_copy&utm_ca mpaign=top

33 Ibid.

34 Ibid.

35 Ibid.

36 "Pod Save America," The White Nationalist Variety Hour, August 14, 2018, accessed October 14, 2018, https://crooked.com/podcast/the-white-nationalist-variety-hour/

37 Jim Naureckas, "Muslims Are Nazis, USA Today Jokes," *FAIR: Fairness & Accuracy in Reporting*, February 3, 2015, accessed October 14, 2018, https://fair.org/ home/muslims-are-nazis-usa-today-jokes/. Also see *USA Today*'s response and

Naureckas's counterresponse at Jim Naureckas, "Muslims Are Nazis, 'USA Today' Jokes," *Mondoweiss*, February 9, 2015, accessed 2018, https://mondoweiss.net/20 15/02/muslims-today-jokes/

38 Yanan Wang, "Ta-Nehisi Coates, 'Black Panther' and Superhero Diversity: A Major Public Intellectual Turns to Comic Books," *Washington Post – Blogs*, September 23, 2015, accessed February 27, 2017. DC's attempts at adding a more diverse series of story lines has largely fallen short and sparked much ridicule on internet fan and comic analysis sites. (Kristian Wilson, "DC's 'Rebirth' Line of Comic Books Fails at Diversity," *The Bustle*, February 25, 2016, accessed February 27, 2017, https://ww w.bustle.com/articles/143697-dcs-rebirth-line-of-comic-books-fails-at-diversity

Bibliography

"A. A. O. N. M. S." *Detroit Free Press.* April 16, 1882, https://www.newspapers.com/image/117675319

Acehan, Işil. "'Made in Massachusetts:' Converting Hides and Skins into Leather and Turkish Immigrants into Industrial Laborers (1860s–1920s)." Dissertation, Bilkent University, 2010. Accessed November 28, 2016, http://www.thesis.bilkent.edu.tr/0006939.pdf

"Activities of Wellington House During the Great War 1914–18." Department of Information: INF 4/1B. National Archives/Public Records Office, London. 1917.

Adam, G. Mercer, ed. *Rose-Belford's Canadian Monthly and National Review*, ed. Rose-Belford Publishing Co., Vol. III. Toronto, 1879.

Ali, Moulavi Cheragh. *A Critical Exposition of the Popular "Jihád."* Calcutta: Thacker, Spink and Co., 1885.

"Another Protest against the Comic Supplement." The Literary Digest 33, no. 7 (August 18, 1906).

Appendix to the Congressional Globe: Containing Speeches, Important State Papers, Laws, Etc. Of the Third Session, Thirty-Fourth Congress, by John C. Rives, 1857.

"Are Moslem Harems Possible in the U.S.?" *The Herald.* December 12, 1897, https://chroniclingamerica.loc.gov/lccn/sn85042461/1897-12-12/ed-1/seq-29/

"Are Turks White Men." *The Plymouth Tribune.* September 30, 1909, https://chroniclingamerica.loc.gov/lccn/sn87056244/1909-09-30/ed-1/seq-4/

Armstrong, Rolf. "The Mascot." *Puck.* February 20, 1915.

Atkinson, Edward. *The Anti-Imperialist I*, no. 5 (September 15, 1899).

"Awful Traffic Disclosed." *The Plymouth Tribune.* October 26, 1905, http://chroniclingamerica.loc.gov/lccn/sn87056244/1905-10-26/ed-1/seq-1/

Baird, Mrs. A. J. "Wearer Should Be Given Ninety Days." *San Francisco Call.* April 23, 1911, http://chroniclingamerica.loc.gov/lccn/sn85066387/1911-04-23/ed-1/seq-11/

Bartholomew, Charles. "Bart" L. "Something Lacking." *The Minneapolis Journal's Cartoons of the Spanish-American War*, 1899.

Belle of Nelson Old Fashion Hand Made Sour Mash Whiskey. Library of Congress. Philadelphia, PA: Wells & Hope Co., 1882.

Benjamin, Anna Northend. "Our Mohammedan Wards in Sulu." *The Outlook* (1899): 675–79.

Bergen, Dean Lucy, "That Old Mallard Hen." *Outdoor Recreation: The Magazine that Brings the Outdoors In*, January 1919.

Berlin, Irving. *Harem Life.* New York: Irving Berlin Inc., 1919.

Berlin, Irving. *I'm the Guy Who Guards the Harem*. New York: Irving Berlin, Inc., 1919.

"Best Immigrants Come from East." *Heppner Gazette*. September 13, 1906, http://chroniclingamerica.loc.gov/lccn/sn94049698/1906-09-13/ed-1/seq-3/

Booker, M. Keith, ed. *Encyclopedia of Comic Books and Graphic Novels*. Santa Barbara, CA: Greenwood, 2010.

Brauer, Fae. "'Moral Girls' and 'Filles Fatales': The Fetishisation of Innocence." *Australian and New Zealand Journal of Art* 10, no. 1 (2011): 122–43.

Bryan, William Jennings. "Lecture on Missions." *Evening Star* 1913, http://chroniclingamerica.loc.gov/lccn/sn83045462/1913-09-28/ed-1/seq-53/

Buchan, John. *Greenmantle*. Boston: Houghton Mifflin Company, 1916.

Bureau of the Census Commerce Department. *Religious Bodies: 1916*. Part I: Summary and General Tables, 1919.

Bureau of the Census – Commerce Department. *Religious Bodies: 1936*. Part I: Summary and Detailed Tables, 1941.

Bureau of the Census – Commerce Department. *Religious Bodies: 1936*. Vol. 2. Part 2: Denominations, K to Z - Statistics, History, Doctrine, Organization, and Work, 1941.

Burroughs, Edgar Rice. *The Eternal Lover*. The Breckenridge News, 1915.

"Camel Driver Rose to Fame." *Evening Star*. April 15, 1932, http://chroniclingamerica.loc.gov/lccn/sn83045462/1932-04-15/ed-1/seq-44/

Carnes, Tony. "The Period of New York Muslim Experimentation, 1893–1939: Retrospective on Mosque City NY, Part 3." A Journey through NYC religions. Last modified 2015. Accessed May 24, 2018, http://www.nycreligion.info/period-york-muslim-experimentation-18931939/#

"The Carnival of the Mystic Shrine." *Kawkab America*, كوكب أمريكا. January 27, https://lebanesestudies.omeka.chass.ncsu.edu/items/show/11611

"Census Shows 8000 Moslems Living in This Land." *San Francisco Chronicle*. October 24, 1920, https://www.newspapers.com/image/27534474/

"The Charge of the Pen Brigade." *The Ogden Standard*. December 5, 1914, http://chroniclingamerica.loc.gov/lccn/sn85058396/1914-12-05/ed-1/seq-15/

Chiu, Allyson. "Stop Calling the Mormon Church 'Mormon,' Says Church Leader. 'Lds' Is out, Too." *The Washington Post*. August 17, 2018. Accessed August 20, 2018, https://www.washingtonpost.com/news/morning-mix/wp/2018/08/17/stop-calling-the-mormon-church-mormon-says-church-leader-lds-is-out-too/?utm_term=.d5b35ce5cc44

"Citizenship." *Herald*. September 24, 1909. Accessed February 28, 2017, http://chroniclingamerica.loc.gov/lccn/sn85042462/1909-09-24/ed-1/seq-4/

"The Congo Basin: The Mohammedan Races of the Equatorial Belt in Arms." *The Republic*. May 23, 1885. Accessed September 17, 2018, https://www.newspapers.com/image/128069309

Cooper, Frederic Taber and Arthur Bartlett Mauricce. "The History of the Nineteenth Century in Caricature." *The Bookman* (September 1903): 36–68.

Curtis, Edward E. *Muslims in America: A Short History*. Oxford: Oxford University Press, 2009.

Curtis, Thomas E. "The Humorous Artists of America – III." *The Strand Magazine*, May 1902.

Dalrymple, Louis. "School Begins." *Puck*. January 25, 1899.

Denny, Frederick M. *An Introduction to Islam*. 3rd ed. New York: Prentice Hall, 2005.

Department of Agriculture. *Report of the Chief of the Bureau of Animal Industry*, by Charles C. Carroll, 1904.

Deslippe, Philip. "The Hindu in Hoodoo: Fake Yogis, Pseudo-Swamis, and the Manufacture of African American Folk Magic." *Amerasia Journal* 40, no. 1 (2014): 34–56.

Dillingham, William P. *Dictionary of Races or Peoples*. Washington DC: Government Printing Office, 1911.

Dillingham, William P. and Immigration Commission. *Reports of the Immigration Commission: Abstracts of Reports of the Immigration Commission*. Washington DC: Government Printing Office, 1911.

"Diplomacy of Oscar Straus." *Corvallis Daily Gazette*. May 17, 1909, http://chroniclingamerica.loc.gov/lccn/2014260100/1909-05-17/ed-1/seq-3/

"Discoveries: By Our Observers and Experimenters." *Good Housekeeping*, March 1904.

Doyle, Arthur Conan. *Study in Scarlet*, 1887.

"Dr. James L. Vance Address to the General Assembly Meeting on Foreign Missions." *The Presbyterian of the South: [Combining the] Southwestern Presbyterian, Central Presbyterian, Southern Presbyterian*. June 4, 1913, http://chroniclingamerica.loc.gov/lccn/10021978/1913-06-04/ed-1/seq-3/

Drew, Bernard A. *Black Stereotypes in Popular Series Fiction, 1851–1955: Jim Crow Era Authors and Their Characters*. Jefferson, NC: McFarland, 2015.

Duff-Gordon, Lucile. "The New 'Harem Veils." *Omaha Daily Bee*. March 9, 1913, http://chroniclingamerica.loc.gov/lccn/sn99021999/1913-03-09/ed-1/seq-20/

Duff-Gordon, Lucy (Lucile). "Negligees and Bathing Suits." *Richmond Times-Dispatch*. June 17, 1917. Accessed December 8, 2016, http://chroniclingamerica.loc.gov/lccn/sn83045389/1917-06-17/ed-1/seq-46/

"Dust." *Marvel*. Accessed October 14, 2018, https://www.marvel.com/characters/dust

Dwight, Henry O. "Uncle Sam's Legacy of Slaves." *The Forum* May (1900): 283–97.

Eckstein, Lars. "Monk Lewis's Timour the Tartar, Grand Romantic Orientalism and Imperial Melancholy." In *Text or Context: Reflections on Literary and Cultural Criticism*, ed. Rüdiger Kunow and Stephan Mussil, 113–28. Würzburg: Königshausen und Neumann, 2013.

Edson, Cyrus. "When and How to Bathe: Ex-President of the New York Board of Health." *The Ladies' Home Journal* 13, no. 7 (June 1896).

Ehrhart, Samuel D. "If They'll Only Be Good." *Puck*. January 31, 1900.

Ehrhart, Samuel D. "Out in Salt Lake City." *Puck*. April 20, 1904.

Endeavor Films, LLC. *Independent Lens*. Public Broadcasting Station vols. Wham! Bam! Islam! ed. Isaac Solotaroff, 2011.

"The Evacuation of Sambo." *The Topeka State Journal*. August 26, 1911, http://chroniclingamerica.loc.gov/lccn/sn82016014/1911-08-26/ed-1/seq-16/

The Evening Times. July 6, 1897, https://chroniclingamerica.loc.gov/lccn/
    sn84024441/1897-07-06/ed-1/seq-4/

"The Evolution and Influence of the Newspaper Cartoon." *The Evening Times.* April 16,
    1902.

"The Evolution of the Comic Picture and the Comic Artist." *The San Francisco Call.*
    November 12, 1905, http://chroniclingamerica.loc.gov/lccn/sn85066387/1905-11-
    12/ed-1/seq-4/

Faber, Michel. "Habibi by Craig Thompson." *The Guardian.* September 16, 2011.
    Accessed October 15, 2018, https://www.theguardian.com/books/2011/sep/16/
    habibi-craig-thompson-review

"Faces a New Problem." *Barbour County Index.* July 10, 1901, http://chroniclingamerica.
    loc.gov/lccn/sn82015080/1901-07-10/ed-1/seq-1/

Fahrenthold, Stacy. "What We Can Learn from America's Other Muslim Ban (Back
    in 1918)." *Tropics of Meta*, February 8, 2017. Accessed 2017, https://tropicsofmeta.
    wordpress.com/author/stacydfahrenthold/

Fahrenthold, Stacy D. *Between the Ottomans and the Entente: The First World War in
    The Syrian and Lebanese Diaspora, 1908–1925.* Oxford: Oxford University Press,
    2019.

Faircloth, Kelly. "Something Is Wrong in This House: How Bluebeard Became the
    Definitive Fairy Tale of Our Era." *Jezebel.* October 17, 2018. Accessed 2018, https://
    pictorial.jezebel.com/something-is-wrong-in-this-house-how-bluebeard-became-
    1829596691?utm_medium=sharefromsite&utm_source=jezebel_copy&utm_
    campaign=top

"Famous Artist's Cartoon in Favor of the Harem Skirt." The *Tacoma Times.* April 11,
    1911, http://chroniclingamerica.loc.gov/lccn/sn88085187/1911-04-11/ed-1/seq-5/

Finely, John P. "The Mohammedan Problem in the Philippines." *The Journal of Race
    Development* 5, no. 4 (April 1915): 353–63.

Fischer, Gayle V. *Pantaloons and Power: A Nineteenth-Century Dress Reform in the
    United States.* Kent, OH: The Kent State University Press, 2001.

Fisher, Bud. "Jeff's Bump of Caution Is Highly Developed." *El Paso Herald.* February
    6, 1913. Accessed December 15, 2016, http://chroniclingamerica.loc.gov/lccn/
    sn88084272/1913-02-06/ed-1/seq-10/

Fisher, Bud. "Mutt Finds the Scenery Very Annoying." *El Paso Herald.* February
    20, 1913. Accessed August 29, 2017, http://chroniclingamerica.loc.gov/lccn/
    sn88084272/1913-02-20/ed-1/seq-10/

Fisher, Bud. "Jeff Is Some Escort." *El Paso Herald.* March 6, 1913, http://
    chroniclingamerica.loc.gov/lccn/sn88084272/1913-03-06/ed-1/seq-10/

Fisher, Bud. "Mutt and Jeff - Yes, Indeed, These Mohammedan Troops Are Very Fierce.
    Oh, My, Yes." *The Seattle Star.* January 17, 1916, http://chroniclingamerica.loc.gov/
    lccn/sn87093407/1916-01-17/ed-1/seq-7/

"Foreign Telegraphic Summary." *The Daily Gazette.* September 4, 1879, http://
    chroniclingamerica.loc.gov/lccn/sn82014805/1879-09-04/ed-1/seq-4/

"From Many Lands." *The Farmington Times.* May 7, 1915, http://chroniclingamerica.loc.gov/lccn/sn89066996/1915-05-07/ed-1/seq-2/

Gardner, Jared. *Projections: Comics and the History of Twenty-First Century Storytelling.* Stanford, CA: Stanford University Press, 2012.

Garner, Bryan. *Garner's Modern English Usage.* Oxford: Oxford University Press, 2016.

GhaneaBassiri, Kambiz. *A History of Islam in America: From the New World to the New World Order.* Cambridge: Cambridge University Press, 2010.

"General Gordon's Mission." *The Hawaiian Gazette.* April 8, 1885, http://chroniclingamerica.loc.gov/lccn/sn83025121/1885-04-08/ed-1/seq-5/

"Germany's Race Problem." *Harrisburg Telegraph.* January 16, 1918, http://chroniclingamerica.loc.gov/lccn/sn85038411/1918-01-16/ed-1/seq-6/

Gibbon, Edward. *History of the Decline and Fall of the Roman Empire.* Vol. V, 1788.

Gillam, F. Victor. "The White Man's Burden (Apologies to Kipling)." *Life.* March 16, 1899.

Glackens, L. M. "Hoist, the Friend of the Comic People." *Puck.* October 31, 1906.

Gordon, Sarah Barringer. "'The Liberty of Self-Degradation': Polygamy, Woman Suffrage, and Consent in Nineteenth-Century America." *The Journal of American History* 83, no. 3 (December 1996): 815–47.

Gruber, Christiane. "Between Logos (Kalima) and Light (Nūr): Representations of the Prophet Muhammad Is Islamic Paintings." *Muqarnas: An Annual on the Visual Culture of the Islamic World* XXVI (2009): 229–62.

Gualtieri, Sarah M. A. *Between Arab and White: Race and Ethnicity in the Early Syrian American Diaspora.* Berkeley, CA: University of California Press, 2009.

Haglund, Kristine. "What the 'Mormon Moment' Actually Accomplished." *Slate.* Last modified 2014. Accessed December 13, 2016, http://www.slate.com/articles/life/faithbased/2014/12/mormon_moment_is_over_but_it_changed_mormon_culture_for_good.html

Hajdu, David. *The Ten-Cent Plague: The Great Comic-Book Scare and How It Changed America.* New York: Picador, 2008.

Hamilton, Grant. "The Filipino's First Bath." *Judge.* June 10, 1899.

Harder, Hans and Barbara Mittler, eds. *Asian Punches: A Transcultural Affair.* Heidelberg: Springer Science & Business Media, 2013.

"Harem Skirt and Woman Suffrage." *The Washington Herald.* February 28, 1911, http://chroniclingamerica.loc.gov/lccn/sn83045433/1911-02-28/ed-1/seq-12/

"Harem Skirt Urged for All Suffragists." *The Washington Herald.* February 27, 1911, http://chroniclingamerica.loc.gov/lccn/sn83045433/1911-02-27/ed-1/seq-2/

"Harem Skirt Wearers Face Jail Sentence." *Evening Star.* March 30, 1911, http://chroniclingamerica.loc.gov/lccn/sn83045462/1911-03-30/ed-1/seq-8/

The Hawaiian Star. August 2, 1899.

Hermansson, Casie. *Bluebeard: A Reader's Guide to the English Translation.* Jackson, MS: University of Mississippi Press, 2009.

"High Lights of History, Chapter 83: Mohammed, Phrophet [Sic] of Islam." *Evening Star*. June 10, 1928, http://chroniclingamerica.loc.gov/lccn/sn83045462/1928-06-10/ed-1/seq-104/

"High Lights of History, Chapter 84: The Mohammedan Conquests." *Evening Star*. June 17, 1928, http://chroniclingamerica.loc.gov/lccn/sn83045462/1928-06-17/ed-1/seq-110/

Hill, Carol. "A Saudi Fatwa Shuns the First Comic Book to Feature Muslim Superheroes." March 29, 2014. Accessed October 14, 2018, https://www.pri.org/stories/2014-03-28/saudi-fatwa-shuns-first-comic-book-feature-muslim-superheroes

"Hindu, Thought to Be an Anarchist, Is Jailed." *The San Francisco* Call. October 29, 1910, http://chroniclingamerica.loc.gov/lccn/sn85066387/1910-10-29/ed-1/seq-5/

Hine, David. *Batman Annual #12*. DC Comics, 2010.

"The Hip Sash Modish Feature of Summer Frocks." *The Lake County Times*. February 28, 1913, http://chroniclingamerica.loc.gov/lccn/sn86058242/1913-02-28/ed-1/seq-11/

Hoban, Walter. "Jerry Macjunk Learns Something of Harems." *The Ogden Standard*. April 27, 1918, http://chroniclingamerica.loc.gov/lccn/sn85058396/1918-04-27/ed-1/seq-6/

Hodgson, Marshall G. S. *The Venture of Islam: Conscience and History in a World Civilization*. Vol. 3: The Gunpowder Empires and Modern Times, 3 vols. Chicago: University of Chicago Press, 1974.

Hodgson, Marshall G. S. *The Venture of Islam: Conscience and History in a World Civilization*. Vol. 1: The Classical Age of Islam, 3 vols. Chicago: University of Chicago Press, 1977.

Holtz, Allan. "Obscurity of the Day: Jerry Macjunk." *Stripper's Guide*, June 2, 2006. Accessed 2017, http://strippersguide.blogspot.com.es/2006/06/obscurity-of-day-jerry-macjunk.html

Holtz, Allan. "Obscurity of the Day: Aren't You Glad You're Not a Mormon." *Stripper's Guide*. November 16, 2009. Accessed October 29, 2018, http://strippersguide.blogspot.com/2009/11/obscurity-of-day-arent-you-glad-youre.html

Houghton, Louise Seymour. "Syrians in the United States II: Business Activities." *The Survey: Social, Charitable, Civic: A Journal of Constructive Philanthropy* 26 (August 5, 1911): 647–65, https://babel.hathitrust.org/cgi/pt?id=pst.000014234194

"How One Man Might Get Us in Two Wars." *The Evening World* 1917. Accessed August 31, 2018, http://chroniclingamerica.loc.gov/lccn/sn83030193/1917-08-06/ed-1/seq-10/

Howarth, F. M. "How They Got Rid of the Rajah Abul Khan – the Story of a Bloodless Revolution." *Puck*, 1896.

Howell, Sarah. *Old Islam in Detroit: Rediscovering the Muslim American Past*. Oxford: Oxford University Press, 2014.

Howell, Sarah F. "Inventing the American Mosque: Early Muslims and Their Institutions in Detroit, 1910–1980." Ph.D. diss., The University of Michigan, 2009.

"Imperialist Discords." *The San Francisco Call*. February 11, 1899, http://chroniclingamerica.loc.gov/lccn/sn85066387/1899-02-11/ed-1/seq-6/

Isani, Mukhtar Ali. "The Vogue of Omar Khayyám in America." *Comparative Literature Studies* 14, no. 3 (September 1977): 256–73.

"Islam in America." *Wood County Reporter*. December 24, 1896, http://chroniclingamerica.loc.gov/lccn/sn85033078/1896-12-24/ed-1/seq-2/

James, Henry. "Du Maurier and London Society." *The Century*. May 1883.

Jones, Tamara and Michael O'Sullivan. "Supreme Court Frieze Brings Objection." *Washington Post*. March 8, 1997, https://www.washingtonpost.com/wp-srv/national/longterm/supcourt/stories/sculpture.htm?noredirect=on

Kabbani, Rana. *Europe's Myths of Orient*. London: Macmillian, 1986.

Kahles, C. W. "Hairbreadth Harry: It Looks as Though Rodolph's Fine Clothes Will Have to Be Ironed out Again." *The Washington Herald*. April 01, 1917, http://chroniclingamerica.loc.gov/lccn/sn83045433/1917-04-01/ed-1/seq-31/

Kahles, C. W. "Hairbreadth Harry: The Omnipotent Oom Gets Two Costumers." *The Washington Herald*. April 15, 1917, http://chroniclingamerica.loc.gov/lccn/sn83045433/1917-04-15/ed-1/seq-29/

Kahles, C. W. "Hairbreadth Harry: The Tale of Bel-in-Dah and Blue Whiskers." *The Washington Herald*. October 29, 1922.

"The Kaiser's Swing around the Oriental Circle." *New York Journal and Advertiser*. November 6, 1898. Accessed October 26, 2018, https://www.loc.gov/item/sn83030180/1898-11-06/ed-1/

Kennedy, Dane. *The Highly Civilized Man: Richard Burton and the Victorian World*. Cambridge, MA: Harvard University Press, 2005.

Keppler, Joseph Ferdinand, Frederick Burr Opper, Bernhard Gillam, and F.(Friedrich) Graetz. "A Desperate Attempt to Solve the Mormon Question, *Puck*." *Puck*. February 13, 1884.

Keppler, Udo J. "It's 'up to' Them." *Puck*. November 20, 1901.

Keppler, Udo J. "The Real Objection to Smoot." *Puck*. April 27, 1904.

Keppler, Udo J. "A Tip to Fatima Ted." *Puck*. August 15, 1906.

Khouri, Andy. "Racists Totally Freak Out over Muslim 'Batman of Paris.'" *ComicsAlliance*. December 28, 2010. Accessed 2011, http://www.comicsalliance.com/2010/12/28/racists-batman-muslim-paris/#ixzz1L34iM5Z5

Kinney, Bruce. *Mormonism: The Islam of America*. New York: Fleming H. Revell Company, 1912.

Kinnosuke, Adachi. "Can the Kaiser Explode the Mahometan Bomb?" *New York Tribune*. March 31, 1918, http://chroniclingamerica.loc.gov/lccn/sn83030214/1918-03-31/ed-1/seq-27/

Kledaisch, Walter C. "Miss Bluebeard, 1904." *The Tacoma Times*. January 1, 1904, http://chroniclingamerica.loc.gov/lccn/sn88085187/1904-01-01/ed-1/seq-3/

Knudde, Kjell. "F.M. Howarth." Last modified March 2, 2018, 2018. Accessed October 29, 2018, https://www.lambiek.net/artists/h/howarth_fm.htm

Kollin, Susan. *Captivating Westerns: The Middle East in the American West*. Lincoln, NE: University of Nebraska Press, 2015.

Lamsa, G. M. *Life in the Harem*. Washington DC: s.n., 1921.

Landry, Alysa. "Theodore Roosevelt: 'The Only Good Indians Are the Dead Indians.'" *Indian Country Today Media Network*. June 28, 2016. Accessed 2018, https://indiancountrymedianetwork.com/history/events/theodore-roosevelt-the-only-good-indians-are-the-dead-indians/

Larkin, John A. *Sugar and the Origins of Modern Philippine Society*. Berkeley: University of California Press, 1993, http://www.netlibrary.com/urlapi.asp?action=summary&v=1&bookid=10049loc.gov/lccn/sn91099608/1881-08-04/ed-1/seq-1/

"The Late Mahdi's War Plans." *Salt Lake Evening Democrat*. August 3, 1885, http://chroniclingamerica.loc.gov/lccn/sn85058117/1885-08-03/ed-1/seq-1/

"Latest by Mail." *Press and Daily Dakotaian*. August 4, 1881, http://chroniclingamerica.

Lepore, Jill. *The Secret History of Wonder Woman*. New York: Vintage Books, 2015.

Lewis, A. David. "Kismet Seventy Years Later: Recognizing the First Genuine Muslim Superhero." *ISLAMiCommentary*, 2014. Accessed October 14, 2018, https://hcommons.org/deposits/item/hc:13597/

"Like a Story in the Fairy Books." *The Washington Times*. January 5, 1919, http://chroniclingamerica.loc.gov/lccn/sn84026749/1919-01-05/ed-1/seq-22/

Lipka, Michael. "A Closer Look at Jehovah's Witnesses Living in the U.S." *Pew Research Center: Religion & Public Life*. Last modified 2016. Accessed May 24, 2018, http://www.pewresearch.org/fact-tank/2016/04/26/a-closer-look-at-jehovahs-witnesses- living-in-the-u-s/

The Lumberjack. February 20, 1913, http://chroniclingamerica.loc.gov/lccn/sn88064459/1913-02-20/ed-1/seq-1/

"Mahometans in Philadelphia." *Huntsville Weekly Democrat*. November 20, 1907, https://www.newspapers.com/image/348654856/

"A Maker of Puzzle Pictures." In *The Inland Printer*, vol. 28. Maclean-Hunter Publishing Corporation, 1902.

Mardiganian, Aurora. *In the House of Hadji-Ghafour*, 24–25. Washington DC: The Washington Times, 1918.

Markstein, Donald D. "Happy Hooligan." *Don Markstein's Toonopedia*, 2000. Accessed 2017, http://www.toonopedia.com/hooligan.htm

Marshall, Clive. "Women Martyrs to Prussian Savagery." *The Daily Ardmoreite*. March 13, 1918, http://chroniclingamerica.loc.gov/lccn/sn85042303/1918-03-13/ed-1/seq-6/

Marshall, Marguerite Mooers. "Calls Suffrage Workers Yellow Peril of America." *The Evening World*. December 1, 1911, http://chroniclingamerica.loc.gov/lccn/sn83030193/1911-12-01/ed-1/seq-20/

Marx, Rosie. "13 August 2017, 3:58 P.M." Last modified 2017. Accessed August 19, 2017, https://twitter.com/RosieMarx/status/896823399204433920

McCay, Winsor. "Ain't You Glad You're Not Mormon, 24 May 1912." *Omaha Daily Bee*, http://chroniclingamerica.loc.gov/lccn/sn99021999/1912-05-24/ed-1/seq-9/

McCay, Winsor. "Ain't You Glad You're Not Mormon, 1 June 1912." *Omaha Daily Bee*, http://chroniclingamerica.loc.gov/lccn/sn99021999/1912-06-01/ed-1/seq-17/. Also: https://www.newspapers.com/image/85039629/

McCloud, Scott. *Understanding Comics: The Invisible Art*. New York: Harper Paperbacks, 1994.

McCutcheon, John T. "Abandoning the Philippines." *Chicago Tribune*, 1913, https://www.newspapers.com/image/355228959

McDougall, Walter. "The True Story of Bluebeard's Forbidden Room: Another Fable Exposed." *Chicago Record-Herald*. May 31, 1903.

McNab, Tansy. "Fairy Tales for Grown-Ups." *New York Tribune*. May 22, 1921, http://chroniclingamerica.loc.gov/lccn/sn83030214/1921-05-22/ed-1/seq-62/

"Menace to Caucasian Race." *Free Trader Journal*. November 16, 1918, http://chroniclingamerica.loc.gov/lccn/sn92053240/1918-11-16/ed-1/seq-5/

Mohamed, Besheer. "A New Estimate of the U.S. Muslim Population." *Pew Research Center: Religion & Public Life*. Last modified 2016. Accessed October 25, 2016, http://www.pewresearch.org/fact-tank/2016/01/06/a-new-estimate-of-the-u-s-muslim-population/

"'Mohammedan Peril Threatens New World War,' Eastern-Expert Says." *South Bend News-Times*. April 14, 1922, http://chroniclingamerica.loc.gov/lccn/sn87055779/1922-04-14/ed-1/seq-36/

"A Mohammedan Conspiracy in Java." *St. Paul Daily Globe*. April 15, 1894, https://chroniclingamerica.loc.gov/lccn/sn90059522/1894-04-15/ed-1/seq-19/

"Mohammedans Build Mosque in Detroit." *Evening Star*. September 03, 1921, https://chroniclingamerica.loc.gov/lccn/sn83045462/1921-09-03/ed-1/seq-6/

"Mohammedans Now Have a Place of Worship Here." *The Sun*. February 25, 1912, https://chroniclingamerica.loc.gov/lccn/sn83030272/1912-02-25/ed-1/seq-57/

"Mohammedans to Celebrate Feast." *Detroit Free Press*. September 28, 1916, https://www.newspapers.com/image/118679400/

Moloney, Deirdre M. "Muslims, Mormons and the U.S. Deportation and Exclusion Policies: The 1910 Polygamy Controversy and the Shaping of Contemporary Attitudes." In *The Social, Political and Historical Contours of Deportation*, ed. Bridget Anderson, Matthew Gibney, and Emanuela Paoletti, 9–24. New York: Springer, 2013.

Moore, William D. *Masonic Temples: Freemasonry, Ritual Architecture, and Masculine Archetypes*. Knoxville: The University of Tennessee Press, 2006.

Moreno, Mrs. Henry M. "Down with Dress Reform!" *San Francisco Call*. April 23, 1911, http://chroniclingamerica.loc.gov/lccn/sn85066387/1911-04-23/ed-1/seq-11/

"'Mormonism,' Not Mohammedanism." *Deseret Evening News*. September 21, 1900, http://chroniclingamerica.loc.gov/lccn/sn83045555/1900-09-21/ed-1/seq-4/

Morrell, Herbert V. G. "How General Kitchener Prepared Himself for His Great Work in the Soudan." *San Francisco Call.* October 16, 1898, http://chroniclingamerica.loc. gov/lccn/sn85066387/1898-10-16/ed-1/seq-19/

"Moslems Celebrate Feast of Id-Ul-Filtr." *Detroit Free Press.* June 8, 1921, https://www. newspapers.com/image/119047683

"The Moslem Menace." *The Seattle Republican.* April 20, 1906, http:// chroniclingamerica.loc.gov/lccn/sn84025811/1906-04-20/ed-1/seq-3/

Muhammad, A. N. and Muslim American Veterans Association. *Muslim Veterans of American Wars: Revolutionary War, War of 1812, Civil War, World War I & II.* Washington DC: FreeMan Publications, 2007.

"Muezzin May Call." *The Wheeling Daily Intelligencer.* June 06, 1893, https:// chroniclingamerica.loc.gov/lccn/sn84026844/1893-06-06/ed-1/seq-6/

"Muslim War in the Main Is Shadowy Danger." *The Bourbon News.* November 3, 1914, http://chroniclingamerica.loc.gov/lccn/sn86069873/1914-11-03/ed-1/seq-3/

"Must the Comic Supplement Go." The Literary Digest 37, no. 19 (November 7, 1908): 669–70.

N. W. Ayer & Son's American Newspaper Annual and Directory. Philadelphia: N. W. Ayer & Son, 1916.

N. W. Ayer & Son's American Newspaper Annual and Directory. Philadelphia: N. W. Ayer & Son, 1918.

Nance, Susan. *How the Arabian Nights Inspired the American Dream, 1790–1935.* Chapel Hill, NC: The University of North Carolina Press, 2009.

Narodny, Ivan. "The Vanishing Harem." *Evening Star.* December 22, 1912, http:// chroniclingamerica.loc.gov/lccn/sn83045462/1912-12-22/ed-1/seq-43/

"Native Moros Abide by Koran's Rule of Four Wives to Man." *The Greenwood Commonwealth.* December 9, 1924, https://www.newspapers.com/image/237588066/

Naureckas, Jim. "Muslims Are Nazis, USA Today Jokes." *FAIR: Fairness & Accuracy in Reporting.* February 3, 2015. Accessed October 14, 2018, https://fair.org/home/ muslims-are-nazis-usa-today-jokes/

Naureckas, Jim. "Muslims Are Nazis, 'USA Today' Jokes." *Mondoweiss.* February 9, 2015. Accessed 2018, https://mondoweiss.net/2015/02/muslims-today-jokes/

New, Clarence Herbert. "Further Adventures of a Diplomatic Free Lance: No. Xi - the Mohammedan Conspiracy." Blue Book Magazine. February 1912.

New, Clarence Herbert. *The Unseen Hand: Stories of Diplomatic Adventure.* New York: W. R. Caldwell & Co., 1918.

"New Fears of Holy War." The Literary Digest. December 15, 1917.

A New-York Detective. "The Bradys and the Black Giant; or, the Secrets of 'Little Syria.'" *Secret Service Old and Young Brady, Detectives.* January 24, 1908.

"No Ambuscades for Democracy." *Journal and Advertiser.* December 17, 1899, https:// www.loc.gov/resource/sn83030180/1899-12-17/ed-1/?sp=18

"No Prospect of Polygamy." The Oklahoma City Times. April 10, 1918, http:// chroniclingamerica.loc.gov/lccn/sn86064187/1918-04-10/ed-1/seq-20/

Noyes, Theodore W. *Oriental America and Its Problems*. Washington DC: Press of Judd and Detweiler, 1903.

O'Donnell, John. "Sees Mohammedan Threat of New World War." *The Seattle Star*. April 7, 1922, http://chroniclingamerica.loc.gov/lccn/sn87093407/1922-04-07/ed-1/seq-13/

"The Omar Khayyam Cult up to Date." *New York Tribune*. March 13, 1904, http://chroniclingamerica.loc.gov/lccn/sn83030214/1904-03-13/ed-1/seq-43/

Opper, F. "Caricature Country and Its Inhabitants." *The Independent*, 1901. https://books.google.com/books?id=0zMxAQAAMAAJ&dq=

Opper, Frederick Burr. "Puck's Suggestion to the Congress of Religions." *Puck*. September 13, 1893.

Opper, Frederick Burr. "Happy Hooligan's Honeymoon." *El Paso Herald*. April 7, 1917, http://chroniclingamerica.loc.gov/lccn/sn88084272/1917-04-07/ed-1/seq-32/

O'Reilly, Bernard. "The African Slave Trade, a Review." *The Sun*. April 27, 1890, http://chroniclingamerica.loc.gov/lccn/sn83030272/1890-04-27/ed-1/seq-15/

The Ottawa Free Trader. November 4, 1865, http://chroniclingamerica.loc.gov/lccn/sn84038582/1865-11-04/ed-1/seq-2/

Oxford English Dictionary. "*Chatelaine, N.*" Oxford University Press.

Partridge, Bernard. "The End of the Thousand-and-One Nights." *Cartoon Magazine*, 1917.

Partridge, Bernard. "Roma Khayyam or the Arab and His Set." *Punch*, 1938.

Pierpoint, George. "'Sexualised' Niqab Hero Gets Makeover after Costume Criticism." Last modified August 29, 2018. Accessed October 14, 2018, https://www.bbc.com/news/blogs-trending-45331730

"Pen Points." *Los Angeles Times*. March 11, 1906. Accessed February 26, 2019, https://www.newspapers.com/image/380209753

"Pirates and Water Dwellers of the South Seas." *The San Francisco Call*. May 20, 1900, http://chroniclingamerica.loc.gov/lccn/sn85066387/1900-05-20/ed-1/seq-9/

"A Plain Country Woman." *The Ladies' Home Journal*. April 1916.

"Pod Save America." *The White Nationalist Variety Hour*. August 14, 2018. Accessed October 14, 2018, https://crooked.com/podcast/the-white-nationalist-variety-hour/

"Polygamy Amendment to Immigration Bill." *Ogden Standard*. January 1, 1915, http://chroniclingamerica.loc.gov/lccn/sn85058396/1915-01-01/ed-1/seq-4/

"Polygamy Reduced in the Philippines." *Grand Forks Herald*. June 23, 1920, http://chroniclingamerica.loc.gov/lccn/sn85042414/1920-06-23/ed-1/seq-3/

"Polygamy to Purify Morals." *Goodwin's Weekly: A Thinking Paper for Thinking People*. June 29, 1918, http://chroniclingamerica.loc.gov/lccn/2010218519/1918-06-29/ed-1/seq-7/

Powderly, T. V. "Immigration's Menace to the National Health." *The North American Review* 175, no. 548 (July 1902): 53–60.

"The Power of Cartoons." *The Colored American*. January 18, 1902.

"Printed in Arabic." *Harrisburg Telegraph*. April 29, 1892, https://www.newspapers.com/image/44551627/

"Psychiatrist Asks Crime Comics Ban." *New York Times*. December 14, 1950.

"Public Expresses Mixed Views of Islam, Mormonism." *Pew Research Center: Religion & Public Life*. Last modified September 25, 2007. Accessed October 29, 2018, http://www.pewforum.org/2007/09/25/public-expresses-mixed-views-of-islam-mormonism-2/

Public Records Office (PRO). *War Propaganda, May–August*. Foreign Office: FO 228/2732. The National Archives, London.

Pughe, John S. "Visitors' Day." *Puck*. April 12, 1905.

Purvis, Esther. "Who Will Be the Emancipator of Woman?" *San Francisco Call*. April 23, 1911, http://chroniclingamerica.loc.gov/lccn/sn85066387/1911-04-23/ed-1/seq-11/

Ramamuthy, Anandi. *Imperial Persuaders: Images of Africa and Asia in British Advertising*. Manchester: Manchester University Press, 2003.

"Real Live Mohammedan Sultan with a Harem Now Belongs to Us!" *New York Journal and Advertiser*. December 4, 1898, https://www.loc.gov/resource/sn83030180/1898-12-04/ed-1/?sp=20

"The Real Moslem Peril." *The Literary Digest* 35, no. 14 (October 5, 1907): 473.

"Recognition of Crete." *Congressional Globe*, Session 40–3. January 7, 1869, 244–45.

Remington, Jack. "Christmas in Zone of Heartaches and Tears Described by Remington." *Daily Herald*. December 21, 1915, http://chroniclingamerica.loc.gov/lccn/sn89074405/1915-12-21/ed-1/seq-2/

"Republican Party Platform of 1856." *The American Presidency Project*. June 18, 1856. Accessed 2018, http://www.presidency.ucsb.edu/ws/?pid=29619

Rhett, Sarah. *Marginalia*. Paragraph editorial remarks ed., ed. Maryanne Rhett. Google Docs, 2016.

Rhoades, Shirrel. *A Complete History of American Comic Books*. New York: Peter Lang, 2008.

Robinson, Helen Ring. "Making the World Safe for Monogamy." *Pictorial Review* 104 (November 1918): 5, 36.

Rogers, Lou. "Tearing Off the Bonds." *Judge*. October 19, 1912.

Rogers, W. A. "Uncle Sam's New Class in the Art of Self-Government." *Harper's Weekly*, 1898.

Roosevelt, Theodore, "Expansion of the White Races." Address at the celebration of the African Diamond Jubilee of the Methodist Episcopal Church, Washington DC, January 18, 1909, http://www.theodore-roosevelt.com/images/research/speeches/trwhiteraces.pdf

Rosen, Anne Farris. "Appendix 3: A Brief History of Religion and the U.S. Census." *Pew Research Center's Forum on Religion & Public Life*, 2008.

Rousseau, Victor. *Mr. Axel's Shady Past*. The Tracer of Egos. Hope, ND: The Hope Pioneer, 1917.

Royce, Jonathan. "Story of a Vast Mohammedan Conspiracy." *Omaha Daily Bee*. April 19, 1903, http://chroniclingamerica.loc.gov/lccn/sn99021999/1903-04-19/ed-1/seq-23/

Rusling, James F. "Interview with President Mckinley." *The Christian Advocate* 78, no. 4 (1903): 160.

Said, Edward W. *Orientalism*. New York: Vintage Books, 1979.

Salman, Michael. *The Embarrassment of Slavery: Controversies over Bondage and Nationalism in the American Colonial Philippines*. Berkeley: University of California Press, 2001.

"Saturday Evening Post Advertisement." *Richmond Times-Dispatch*, 1922, http://chroniclingamerica.loc.gov/lccn/sn83045389/1922-11-02/ed-1/seq-5/

"School and Church." *The Cape Girardeau Democrat*. September 21, 1895, http://chroniclingamerica.loc.gov/lccn/sn89066818/1895-09-21/ed-1/seq-7/

Seager, Richard Hughes, ed. *The Dawn of Religious Pluralism: Voices from the World's Parliament of Religions, 1893*. La Salle, IL: Open Court, 1993.

"See New Danger in Alien Problem." *The Washington Herald*. February 3, 1914, http://chroniclingamerica.loc.gov/lccn/sn83045433/1914-02-03/ed-1/seq-1/

"The Shadow of the Turk on the Cross of Christianity." *The New York Journal and Advertiser*. April 25, 1897, https://www.loc.gov/item/sn83030180/1897-04-25/ed-1/

"She Changed Comics: Lou Rogers, Advocate for Women's Rights." *Comic Book Legal Defense Fund*. March 17, 2017. Accessed November 30, 2017, http://cbldf.org/2017/03/she-changed-comics-lou-rogers-advocate-for-womens-rights/

Sheldon, John. "Unearthing the Crimes of Modern Bluebeards." *The Washington Times*. June 6, 1920, http://chroniclingamerica.loc.gov/lccn/sn84026749/1920-06-06/ed-1/seq-28/

A Short History of Shriners Hospitals for Children and Shriners of North America, ed. Shriners International. Tampa, FL.

"Shriners to Enjoy Home-Coming Week: Moslem Temple Plans to Entertain 5000 Guests Here." *Detroit Free Press*. May 29, 1921, https://www.newspapers.com/image/119041983

"The Sick Man of Europe." *Aberdeen Herald*. November 12, 1915, http://chroniclingamerica.loc.gov/lccn/sn87093220/1915-11-12/ed-1/seq-1/

Singer, Marc. "'Black Skins' and White Masks: Comic Books and the Secret of Race." *African American Review* 36, no. 1 (Spring 2002): 107–19.

Sinha, Mrinalini. *Colonial Masculinity: The 'Manly Englishman' and the 'Effeminate Bengali' in the Late Nineteenth Century*. New Delhi: Raj Press, 1995.

"The Skirt Question." *The Seattle Star*. April 18, 1911, http://chroniclingamerica.loc.gov/lccn/sn87093407/1911-04-18/ed-1/seq-4/

Sleeth, James. "Biography of Joel Dorman Steele." Last modified 2018. Accessed October 28, 2018, http://ccld.lib.ny.us/joel-dorman-steele/

Slide, Anthony, ed. *Ravished Armenia and the Story of Aurora Mardiganian*. Jackson, MS: University of Mississippi Press, 2014.

Smith, Marian L. "Race, Nationality, and Reality: Ins Administration of Racial Provisions in U.S. Immigration and Nationality Law since 1898, Part 2." *Prologue*, Summer 2002.

"Somaliland." *New York Tribune.* November 2, 1902, http://chroniclingamerica.loc.gov/lccn/sn83030214/1902-11-02/ed-1/seq-41/

Spencer, Nick. "15 August 2017, 7:29 P.M." Last modified 2017. Accessed August 19, 2017, https://twitter.com/nickspencer/status/897601180347641856

Spivak, G. K. "Can the Subaltern Speak?" In *Marxism and the Interpretation of Culture*, ed. C. Nelson and L. Grossberg. Urbana, IL: University of Illinois Press, 1988.

Standage, Tom. *A History of the World in 6 Glasses.* New York: Walker & Co.: Distributed to the trade by Holtzbrinck Publishers, 2005.

"Star-Eyed Egyptian." *Omaha Daily Bee.* October 21, 1900, http://chroniclingamerica.loc.gov/lccn/sn99021999/1900-10-21/ed-1/seq-15/

State Department. *Memorandum Regarding the Inadvisability of a Declaration of War by the United States against Turkey and Bulgaria at the Present Time*, by Robert Lansing. Vol. 1, 1917.

Steele, Joel Dorman and Esther Baker Steele. *A Brief History of Ancient, Mediaeval, and Modern Peoples, with Some Account of Their Monuments, Institutions, Arts, Manners, and Customs.* Cincinnati, OH: The Eclectic Press, 1883.

Steele, Valerie. *Fashion and Eroticism: Ideals of Feminine Beauty from the Victorian Era to the Jazz Age.* New York: Oxford University Press, 1985.

Stoddard, Lothrop. *The Rising Tide of Color against White World-Supremacy.* New York: Scribner, 1920.

"Style Guide - the Name of the Church." *The Church of Jesus Christ of Latter-day Saints: Newsroom.* Last modified 2018. Accessed August 20, 2018, https://www.mormonnewsroom.org/style-guide

"Suffrage and the Humorous Magazines." *Maryland Suffrage News.* June 13, 1914, http://chroniclingamerica.loc.gov/lccn/sn89060379/1914-06-13/ed-1/seq-7/

"The Sulu Treaty." *San Francisco Call.* August 22, 1899, http://chroniclingamerica.loc.gov/lccn/sn85066387/1899-08-22/ed-1/seq-6/

"Table: Muslim Population by Country." *Pew Research Center: Religion & Public Life.* Last modified 2011. Accessed October 25, 2016, http://www.pewforum.org/2011/01/27/table-muslim-population-by-country/

"Talk of 'Holy War.'" *Oamaru Mail.* November 12, 1914, https://paperspast.natlib.govt.nz/newspapers/OAM19141112.2.8

Toynbee, Rosalind. "The Turkish Women of to-Day." *The Forum* (September 1, 1928): 412–20.

"Turks a Yellow Peril." *New York Tribune.* May 10, 1909, http://chroniclingamerica.loc.gov/lccn/sn83030214/1909-05-10/ed-1/seq-5/

"Turks Can't Come Here." *The Sun.* November 19, 1897, http://chroniclingamerica.loc.gov/lccn/sn83030272/1897-11-19/ed-1/seq-1/

"The United States Sultan." *The Topeka State Journal*. September 4, 1899. Accessed May 4, 2018, http://chroniclingamerica.loc.gov/lccn/sn82016014/1899-09-04/ed-1/seq-2/

"The Unspeakable Turk." *The Citizen*. October 26, 1916, http://chroniclingamerica.loc.gov/lccn/sn85052076/1916-10-26/ed-1/seq-1/

US Congress. House. Immigration Act. H. Res. 10384. 64th Cong. February 15, 1917. http://library.uwb.edu/static/USimmigration/39%20stat%20874.pdf

Wallis, Frederick A. "Regulate Immigrant Flood, Urges Commissioner Wallis; a System of Restraint and Selection Is Advocated." *New York Tribune*. December 12, 1920, http://chroniclingamerica.loc.gov/lccn/sn83030214/1920-12-12/ed-1/seq-69/

Walther, Karine V. *Sacred Interests: The United States and the Islamic World, 1821–1921*. Chapel Hill, NC: University of North Carolina Press, 2015.

Wang, Yanan. "Ta-Nehisi Coates, 'Black Panther' and Superhero Diversity: A Major Public Intellectual Turns to Comic Books." *Washington Post – Blogs*. September 23, 2015. Accessed February 27, 2017, https://www.washingtonpost.com/news/morning- mix/wp/2015/09/23/ta-nehisi-coates-black-panther-and-superhero-diversity/?utm_ term=.bbce3989ecfb

War Department. *The Report of the Philippine Commission* (1900–1915), 1915.

"War Puzzles: Sheik-Ul-Islam." *Honolulu Star-Bulletin*. December 15, 1917, https://www.newspapers.com/image/290466336/

Warren, Garnet. "Miniature Foreign Lands in New York City: Little Syria." Los Angeles *Herald*. April 11, 1909, https://chroniclingamerica.loc.gov/lccn/sn85042462/1909-04-11/ed-1/seq-65/

Watkins, John Elfreth. "Joy of Bathing." *The Salt Lake Tribune*. May 17, 1908, http://chroniclingamerica.loc.gov/lccn/sn83045396/1908-05-17/ed-1/seq-17/

Weisbrode, Kenneth. "The Short Life of the Camel Corps." *New York Times*. December 27, 2012, https://opinionator.blogs.nytimes.com/2012/12/27/the-short- life-of-the-camel-corps/

Wells, W. L. "Old Opie Dilldock's Stories, 25 April 1909." *Chicago Tribune*. Accessed October 29, 2018, https://www.newspapers.com/image/355171468/

Wells, W. L. "Old Opie Dilldock's Stories, 31 January 1909." *Chicago Tribune*, https://www.newspapers.com/image/354919163/

Wertham, Fredric. *Seduction of the Innocent*. New York: Rinehart and Company, 1954.

West, Paul. "The Widow Wise." *The Washington Herald*. October 8, 1911, http://chroniclingamerica.loc.gov/lccn/sn83045433/1911-10-08/ed-1/seq-27/

"What Is a White Man before Law." *Paducah Evening Sun*. November 11, 1909, https://chroniclingamerica.loc.gov/lccn/sn85052114/1909-11-11/ed-1/seq-6/

"Why Not Herron?" *Harvey's Weekly*, no. 24 (1919). Accessed August 31, 2018. https://hdl.handle.net/2027/uiug.30112108101632?urlappend=%3Bseq=404

Wilson, Kristian. "DC's 'Rebirth' Line of Comic Books Fails at Diversity." *The Bustle*. February 25, 2016. Accessed February 27, 2017, https://www.bustle.com/articles/143697-dcs-rebirth-line-of-comic-books-fails-at-diversity

Wilson, Rufus R. "Men from All Lands." *Boston Post*. August 12, 1894, https://www.newspapers.com/image/74631070

Wilson, Thomas H. *Sold to the Sultan, or, the Strange Adventures of Two Yankee Middies*. New York: Frank Tousey, 1914.

Wonder Women! The Untold Story of American Superheroines. Directed by Guevara-Flanagan, Kristy, 2012.

Index